AN EVALUATION OF FINANCIAL PERFORMANCE OF THE SAPTAGIRI GRAMEENA BANK.

I0468490

By

Dr. PADMAVATHI AGARWAL

UGC – Post Doctoral Fellow,

Sri Venkateswara University,

Tirupati

Prof. B. BHAGAVAN REDDY

Principal & Dean, Faculty of Commerce and Management,

Sri Venkateswara University,

Tirupati

ABOUT AUTHORS

Dr. PADMAVATHI AGARWAL did postgraduation and Ph.D courses in Sri Venkateswara University, Tirupati during 2004 and 2010 respectively. She has published thirteen research based articles in reputed journals and attended several conferences/seminars/workshops. Presently she is a UGC Post Doctoral Fellow.

Prof. B. BHAGAVAN REDDY is presently Principal & Dean, Faculty of Commerce and Management in Sri Venkateswara University, Tirupati. He is with 37 years of post-graduate teaching experience and successfully guided 31 Ph. D., and 15 M. Phil. students. He has published 113 articles in reputed journals and authored 10 books. There are 3 major research projects to his credit. He is the members of various bodies like UGC, AICTE, UPSC, APSC etc .

ABOUT THE BOOK

The book presents the financial performance of Saptagiri Grameena bank after merger during 2006. The study is presented in 7 chapters. The first chapter deals with an overview of RRB's in India. The second chapter contains review of literature and research design and methodology. The third and fourth chapters provide profile of the bank and mobilisation of deposits and credit operations sequentially. The financial performance is analysed in the fifth chapter while non - performing assets are evaluated in the sixth chapter. The last chapter presents summary of findings, suggestions, conclusion and hints for further research in future.

ACKNOWLEDGEMENTS

I deem it a great privilege to express my profound respect and deep sense of gratitude to my research supervisor **Prof. B. Bhagavan Reddy,** Principal, S.V.U. College of Commerce, Management and Computer Science & Dean, Faculty of Commerce and Management, Sri Venkateswara University, Tirupati for his constant encouragement and able guidance throughout the period of research. The meticulous care with which he scrutinized the earlier drafts and offered constructive suggestions helped me in preparing this thesis successfully.

I take this opportunity to express my gratitude to **Prof. P. Mohan Reddy,** Chairman, Board of studies in Commerce, S.V. University, Tirupati and **Prof. K. Jaya chandra,** Head of the department of Commerce, S.V. University, Tirupati for their constant encouragement and help. My respectful thanks to **Prof. S. Vijayulu Reddy** and **Prof. B. Sakuntala,** Department of Commerce for their extreme cooperation and encouragement althrough my research study. My sincere thanks are due to the faculty members of the Department of Commerce, S.V.University, Tirupati for their kind cooperation.

My sincere thanks are due to **Sri B. Suri babu,** Chairman, **Sri N. Mastan Khan** and **Sri K. Sai babu,** Directors, nominees of central government, **Smt K. Anuradha** Asst. General Manager, nominee of RBI, **Sri S. Subba Rao** Asst. General Manager, nominee of NABARD, **Sri R.Manimaran,** General Manager, nominee of Sponsor bank and **Sri S.Subba Rao,** Deputy General Manager, nominee of Sponsor bank, **Sri L.Prem Chandra Reddy,** IAS, Principal Secretary, and **Sri Siddharth Jain** IAS, Collector and District Magistrate, for extending their full cooperation while providing the required data as and when I approached them. I am extremely grateful to the Bank Managers and Staff at Chittoor for granting me permission to use official records and reports.

I would like to express with profound respect, my deep sense of gratitude to my beloved parents late **Sri A. Varaprasad, B.Com, B.L.,** and **Smt. A.V. Sathiya Kumari** for their love, affection and blessings throughout my career. I am also grateful to my father-in-law late **Sri K. Bala Kondaiah** Rtd. AEE., and mother-in-law **Smt. M. Nirmala B.Sc., B.Ed.,** Rtd. Govt. School Headmistress for their repeated encouragement to complete the work. I take this opportunity to express my heartfelt thanks to my husband **Mr. K. Mahesh, M.Tech, (Structures)** for his keen interest, constant encouragement and support in completion of this academic endeavour. I am extremely thankful to my son **K. Vishwak Agarwal,** for his

5

love and support. His pride and encouragement instilled energy for me in all my endeavours. I am also greatful to my brothers **Dr. Sudarsan Agarwal, MBBS, M.S, M.Ch., (Neurosurgery), Mr. Vinod Agarwal, B.Arch., M.Tech., (Planning)** and sister-in-law **Dr. K. Santhoshi Devi MBBS** for their constant encouragement in my effort.

Last but not least, I earnestly acknowledge my sincere thanks to all the authors and researches whose contributions are quoted in this study.

Dr. PADMAVATHI AGARWAL

CONTENTS

LIST OF TABLES

List of Figures

CHAPTER – I

AN OVERVIEW OF RRB'S IN INDIA

A modest attempt is made in this chapter to examine the need for regional rural banks (RRBs) and review their progress in the country in the light of the objectives for which they were established. It would be quite appropriate to touch upon the overall performance of RRBs in India before conducting a detailed enquiry into the financial performance of the Saptagiri Grameena Bank (SGB).

1. Genesis of RRBs in India:

Consistent with the objectives of the successive Five Year Plans in the realm of rural poverty alleviation, a number of programmes were formulated and implemented for improving the living conditions of the rural poor. All the rural development programmes considered credit one of the strategic inputs for their successful implementation. The supply of rural credit lags much behind the demand for credit. Further, non - institutional credit has not proved beneficial to farmers as it hardly provides any incentive to effect improvement in agriculture. Furthermore, credit by private agencies is mostly unproductive. Hence, the development of institutional credit is a basic condition for rural poverty eradication. The objective of institutional credit is to break the vicious circle of poverty and debt. In other words, it is the conversion of static credit into dynamic credit.[1] to suit the requirements of various rural development programmes, a variety of rural credit agencies were established in the country. These have achieved varying degrees of success.

Cooperatives were nurtured as primary institutions to relieve rural people from the vicious circle of non - institutional debt. The only agency that conceptually satisfies all the criteria of a good system of rural credit is the cooperative credit society.[2] These institutions have grown in size with slight structural changes over their long standing. The organisation was revamped several times. The functions of these institutions were extended to cover all activities of villagers. They have established firm roots in the rural India. Nearly, all the villages were covered by cooperatives.[3] The share of institutional agencies in the total borrowings of rural households has remarkably increased against a substantial decline in the proportion of non - institutions. The proportion of cooperatives in the total borrowings of rural households raised significantly. Despite growth, cooperative credit was marked by regional disparities, imbalances and mounting overdues.[4] Further, organisational structure and conventional land based norms of security have inhibited their progress. Small and marginal farmers and agricultural labour did not receive their due share in the cooperative credit.[5] The cooperative credit is often considered inelastic, dilatory and inadequate largely owing to inefficiency, high - handedness and selfishness of the managing committees. As a result, it turned out 'closed shops' of the affluent sections by paying only 'lip service' to the poor and socially oppressed communities. The cooperatives were unable to meet the entire credit needs of the rural public and thereby led to a large unfilled gap.[6]

The government took several measures for rural debt relief. But these were not of much help in context of scarcity of credit. Historically commercial bank branches were confined to urban areas and bank credit was made available to a few leaders of commerce and industry. The lopsided role played by banking institutions has received special attention of government. Multi - agency approach was viewed as a better alternative. Therefore, commercial banks were inducted into the field of rural credit. With much increased rural branch network, commercial banks could not bridge the gap in rural credit.

In the light of these, the government thought of evolving an alternate source of credit for rural development by establishing rural banks as new institutions. As a result of it, Government of India, appointed a Working Group during 1975 with Sri M. Narasimham, as Chairman, to examine indepth the setting up of new rural banks as subsidiaries of public sector banks to cater to the needs of rural clientele[7.] The Working Group proceeded with its enquiry reckoning the multi - agency approach as a solution to problems of institutional credit in the rural sector. After a thorough evaluation of the issue, the Working Group recommended the setting up of state sponsored, regionally based and rural oriented commercial banks called RRBs[8].

Consequent on the acceptance of the recommendations, on 26th September, 1975, the government promulgated an Ordinance for the setting up of RRBs. The Ordinance was later replaced by an enactment of RRBs Act during February, 1976. Thus, RRBs came into being on the evolutionary scene of rural credit to form the third component of multi - agency credit system. The establishment of RRBs is a landmark in the history of Indian banking. Thus the responsibility of rural credit has fallen on the shoulders of cooperatives, commercial banks and RRBs. Each one of them is presumed to function as part of a system with close coordination while planning credit provisions. Further, they are together visualised as instruments for rooting out the non - institutional agents from the scene of rural credit over a period of time in a phased manner.

2. Features:

RRBs are required to confine their activities mainly to the weaker sections of the rural society. The target group comprises small and marginal farmers, agricultural labourers, rural artisans, small entrepreneurs and persons of small means in trade, commerce, industry or other productive activities within the area of operation of the bank.[9] Nonetheless; they accept all types of deposits and render other banking services consistent with the needs of the area. The main objective of RRB is to provide credit and service in the rural areas so that the economy can be accelerated on the path of development. Its object is to provide at one place the special type of credit, banking facilities and other related services needed by agriculturists and others. RRBs strive to develop the rural economy with special emphasis on weakest of the weak. One of the important objectives of RRBs is to wipe out rural indebtedness and bridge the credit gap in the rural areas. RRBs are sponsored by scheduled commercial banks, usually, public sector commercial banks. RRBs Act, 1976 clearly states that RRBs would be set up with a view to develop the rural economy by providing credit for the purpose of development of agriculture, trade, commerce, industry and other productive activities in rural areas, credit and other facilities, particularly to

17

small and marginal farmers, agricultural labourers, artisans and small entrepreneurs and for matters connected therewith and incidental thereto. The other objectives of RRBs are to generate employment opportunities in rural areas and to bring down the cost of purveying credit in rural areas.

Financing outside the target group is exceptional and incidental. Generally, operational area of each RRB is confined to a compact area of one to five revenue districts with homogeneity in agro - climatic conditions and rural clientele, indicating and identifying commonality of problems. RRBs open branches in the unbanked and underbanked centres. Usually, RRBs are sponsored by scheduled public sector commercial banks. They are set up with the initiative of sponsoring bank in consultation with the concerned state government, central government and under license from RBI.

The sponsoring bank was required to provide managerial and financial assistance for the first five years and thereafter, on the basis of mutually agreed terms. The authorised capital of each RRB is set at Rs. 5 crores. The issued and paid - up capital is a minimum of Rs. 25 lakhs and could be a maximum of one crore at the first instance. The capital would be subscribed by government of India, state government and sponsor bank in the proportion of 50 : 15 : 35 respectively. Management vests with the Board of Directors headed by Chairman. The Board of Directors, besides the Chairman, consist of eight members, nominated two each by Central Government, sponsor bank, state government and one each by the RBI and the National Bank for Agriculture and Rural Development (NABARD). The Central government may raise the total number of Directors up to an aggregate of fifteen. The Chairman of RRB shall be appointed by the sponsor bank in consultation with the NABARD where he is an officer of the sponsor bank. He can be appointed with the prior approval of the central government where he is not an officer of the sponsor bank. The Chairman is a full - time professional executive. Generally, supervision and control of RRBs vest with the NABARD. The NABARD is empowered to inspect the books of accounts.

Every RRB shall carry on and transact the business of a bank as defined in clause (b) of section 5 of the Banking Regulation Act, 1949, and may engage in one or more forms of business specified in sub - section (i) of section 6 of that Act. Without prejudice to the generality of provisions of sub - section (i), every RRB may, in particular, undertake business like granting of loans and advances to small and marginal farmers and agricultural labourers whether individually or in groups and to cooperatives for agricultural purposes or agricultural operations or for other purposes connected therewith and to artisans, small entrepreneurs and persons of small means engaged in trade, commerce or industry and other productive activities within the operational area of RRB.[10] They can also provide loans for consumption purposes within the specified limits.

RRB was normally expected to recruit its own staff, but in the initial years, the sponsor bank provides the necessary staff, particularly at the senior levels. The staffs are paid on par with those working in commercial banks. The subscribed and paid–up capital is the cost free fund available to the bank. Reserves constitute internally generated funds by way of accumulated profits, depreciation and other statutory reserves. As per the Banking Regulation Act, each RRB should transfer 25 per cent of annual net profit to reserve fund, in addition to the provision to be made for bad and doubtful debts. Refinance is available to RRBs from the institutions like the NABARD, sponsor bank and the Industrial Development Bank of India

(IDBI). RRBs were allowed to maintain a lower level of cash reserve ratio of 3 per cent and statutory liquidity ratio of 25 per cent of their demand and time liabilities. With a view to improve deposits, they were allowed to pay half per cent more interest on deposits as compared to other banks in the country. They were eligible to avail themselves of refinance from the NABARD to the extent of 90 per cent of their schematic lending and 50 per cent of non - schematic lending at a concessional rate. The sponsor bank provides refinance up to 20 per cent of non - schematic lending at a concessional rate.

3. Organisational structure:

The Chairman is the Chief Executive of the bank. The policy execution is vested with the chairman while the Board of Directors formulates the policy. The general manager looks after the day to day affairs of the bank. In the head office, senior managers look after planning, accounts, loans, human resources, administration, audit, inspection etc. Area manager works at the area office. There are managers at the level of branches. They are assisted by a field officer, clerical and sub - staff.

4. Progress:

The trend in the progress of RRBs in the country in terms of their geographical coverage, branch network, deposit mobilisation, credit disbursement, recovery, overdues, profit and loss and non - performing assets (NPA) are briefly described in the following pages.

4.1. Branch network:

The branch network in terms of yearly growth, coverage of states / union territories/ districts and sponsor bank – wise are discussed.

4.1.1. Yearly growth:

Immediately after the promulgation of Ordinance, first five RRBs were established in four states at Moradabad and Gorakhpur in Uttar Pradesh (U.P), Bhiwani in Haryana, Jaipur in Rajasthan and Malda in West Bengal (W.B.) on 2nd October, 1975. Later on, one more bank was opened in the same year. At the end of December, 1976, there were 40 RRBs covering 84 districts through a network of 489 branches (see **Table 1.1**). By the end of December 1986, the number of banks stood at 194 spread over 351 districts with 12,838 branches. In the next decade, only 2 banks were started. The

Table 1.1: Progress of RRBs in India since Inception till 2014

Year	No. of RRBs established	Total No. of RRBs	Total No. of branches	No. of districts covered
1975	6	6	11	12
1976	34	40	489	84
1986	154	194	12,838	351
1996	2	196	14,497	427
2005	-	196	14,484	523
2006	-	133	14,494	525
2007	-	96	14,520	534
2008	-	91	14,761	534
2009	-	86	15,181	616
2010	-	82	15,480	618
2011	-	82	16,001	620
2012	-	82	16,914	635
2013	-	64	17,856	635
2014	-	57	19,082	642

Source: Relevant issues of Statistics on RRBs, NABARD, Bombay.

number of RRBs stood at 196 at the end of 1996. The number of branches spread over 427 districts was 14,497. It remained as such till 2005. The number of banks was reduced to 133 in 2006 due to reorganisation. The number of branches and districts covered increased. Though there is a rise in absolute figures, there are marked fluctuations in the decadal growth of RRBs. For example, the highest numbers of banks (154) were opened during the decade 1976 - 86. The number of banks was reduced to 57 in 2014. It may be noted that there is no expansion in the number of RRBs between 1996 and 2014. It can be further observed that the progress in the setting up of RRBs slowed down. This, indeed, was due to the reason that there was some uncertainty about the future of RRBs. In fact, the working Group[11] set up in 1977 to review the working of RRBs observed that the expansion was unnecessarily hurried. However, the committee put an end to the uncertainty on the basis of review of performance of RRBs and concluded that RRBs have demonstrated their ability to serve the intended purpose that RRBs should become an integral part of the rural structure.

The branch expansion of RRBs has been phenomenal. Rapid growth in the number of branches was the result of continued emphasis on the extension of network. This is so because the RBI gave preference to RRBs for opening more branch offices in rural areas. It is pertinent to add that the branch expansion of RRBs considerably exceeded that of commercial banks. Such a high pace of branch expansion has sizably contributed to the extension of institutional finance to the rural hinterland in the country, especially backward regions. As many as 642 districts were covered with a branch network of 19,082 in the nation. More than 90 per cent of branches are found in rural centres.

The main objective of branch licensing policy is to provide banking facilities in deficient rural areas, especially where identifiable spatial gaps exist. The expansion will be allowed taking into account the need, spatial gaps and financial viability of proposed branches. Hilly tracks, sparsely populated regions and tribal areas will be given special consideration and expansion in such areas will be allowed on a comparatively liberal basis taking into account existing gaps in the availability of banking facilities. The NABARD should evolve a branch licensing policy in a manner consistent with the objective of fulfiling the rural credit gap in backward, hilly and tribal regions.

4.1.2 : State - wise:

The state - wise particulars of RRBs in India during 2013 are furnished in the **Table 1.2.** It can be observed that, among the states, the highest number of RRBs is located in Uttar Pradesh (9). Next to it, Andhra Pradesh (A.P.) ranked second with 5 RRBs and Karnataka ranked third with 4 RRBs. The states with 3 RRBs are Bihar, Chhattisgarh, Gujarat, Madhya Pradesh, Punjab, Rajasthan, and West Bengal. In Assam, Haryana, Jammu & Kashmir, Jharkhand, Kerala, Maharashtra, Odisha and Tamilnadu there are 2 RRBs. There is only one RRB in each of 9 states such as Arunachal Pradesh, Himachal Pradesh, Manipur, Meghalaya, Mizoram, Nagaland, Puducherry, Tripura and Uttarakhand. With regard to number of branches, the highest are found in U.P (3,518) followed by Bihar (1,718), A.P. (1,630), Karnataka (1,460), Rajasthan (1,157) and Madhya Pradesh (1,132).

In seven states such as Chhatisgarh, Gujarat, West Bengal, Haryana, Kerala, Maharashtra and Odisha branch network is in the order of 500 - 1000. In six states, number of branches is less than 100. In the rest of the states, branch network is between 133 and 442. The trend of RRBs and branch network can be noted in the coverage of districts. For example, U.P. occupied the first place followed by A.P, Karnataka, etc. It may be concluded that there are regional variations in the number of RRBs, branches and districts covered across the states in the nation. This is on account of variations in the geographical area, density of population, predominance of

Table 1.2: State – wise Details of RRBs in India at the end of 2013

| S.no. | Name of the state/ union territory | Number of | | |
		RRBs	Districts covered	Branches
1	Uttar Pradesh	9	81	3,518
2	Andhra Pradesh	5	23	1,630
3	Karnataka	4	30	1,460
4	Bihar	3	38	1,718
5	Chhatisgarh	3	28	555
6	Gujarat	3	26	529
7	Madhya Pradesh	3	50	1,132
8	Punjab	3	24	311
9	Rajastan	3	36	1,157
10	West Bengal	3	18	921
11	Assam	2	27	427
12	Haryana	2	23	507
13	Jammu & Kashmir	2	26	323
14	Jharkhand	2	24	442
15	Kerala	2	15	506
16	Maharashtra	2	33	645
17	Odisha	2	30	901
18	Tamil Nadu	2	31	374
19	Arunachal Pradesh	1	8	27
20	Himachal Pradesh	1	12	188
21	Manipur	1	9	28
22	Meghalaya	1	7	76
23	Mizoram	1	8	71
24	Nagaland	1	5	10
25	Puducherry	1	2	30
26	Tripura	1	8	133
27	Uttarakhand	1	13	237

Source: As in Table 1.1

agriculture, rural - urban intensity, occupational distribution, migration and pace of rural industrialisation among the states are in the country.

4.1.3 Sponsor bank - wise:

A look at the **Table 1.3** shows sponsor bank - wise distribution of RRBs in India during 2013. It can be observed that the State Bank of India has started the highest number of RRBs (15) followed by each of Syndicate Bank, United Bank of India, Central Bank of India and Punjab National Bank (5), Bank of India (4), each of Bank of Baroda, Canara Bank and Indian Bank (3) and each of UCO Bank, Dena Bank and Indian Overseas Bank (2). Ten banks such as each of State Bank of Hyderabad, State Bank of Mysore, State Bank of Bikaner & Jaipur, State Bank of Patiala, Andhra Bank, J&K Bank, Bank of Maharashtra, Punjab & Sind Bank, ICICI Bank Ltd and Allahabad Bank have sponsored one RRB. With regard to branch network, maximum number of branches are established by State Bank of India sponsored RRBs (3,380) followed by Central Bank of India (1,799), Syndicate Bank (1,665), Bank of Baroda (1,526), United Bank of India (1,510) and Punjab National Bank (1,509). Number of branches is less than 100 in RRBs of 3 sponsored banks such as State Bank of Patiala, Punjab and Sind Bank and ICICI Bank Ltd. In the case of Canara Bank, Indian Overseas Bank and Allahabad Bank sponsored RRBs, the number of branches are in the order of 500 – 1000. In the rest of the cases, the number of branches is in the range of 128 – 461. Similar variations exist in the coverage of districts covered across RRBs sponsored by different banks in the country. The highest number of districts were covered by RRBs sponsored by State Bank of India (138) followed Punjab National Bank (69), United Bank of India (61), Central Bank of India (54), Bank of India (54), Bank of Baroda (47), Syndicate Bank (32), Indian Overseas Bank (29) and Canara Bank (23). RRBs sponsored by eight banks like Indian Bank, UCO Bank, Dena Bank,

Table 1.3: Sponsor Bank - wise Distribution of RRBs in India at the Close of 2013

S. No	Name of sponsoring bank	Number of		
		RRBs	Districts covered	Branches
1.	State Bank of India	15	138	3,380
2.	Syndicate Bank	5	32	1,665
3.	United Bank of India	5	61	1,510
4.	Central Bank of India	5	54	1,799
5.	Punjab National Bank	5	69	1,509
6.	Bank of India	4	54	1,252
7.	Bank of Baroda	3	47	1,526
8.	Canara Bank	3	23	963
9.	Indian Bank	3	19	337
10.	UCO Bank	2	13	461
11.	Dena Bank	2	12	305
12.	Indian Overseas Bank	2	29	699
13.	State Bank of Hyderabad	1	5	269
14.	State Bank of Mysore	1	10	334
15.	State Bank of Bikaner & Jaipur	1	12	460
16.	Andhra Bank	1	3	128
17.	State Bank of Patiala	1	5	62
18.	Jammu & Kashmir Bank	1	13	201
19.	Bank of Maharashtra	1	16	351
20.	Punjab & Sind Bank	1	6	31
21.	ICICI Bank Ltd	1	3	59
22.	Allahabad Bank	1	11	555
	Total	64	635	17,856

Source: As in Table 1.1

State Bank of Mysore, State Bank of Bikaner & Jaipur, J & K Bank, Bank of Maharashtra and Allahabad Bank has covered 10 - 20 districts. The Punjab & Sind Bank sponsored RRB has covered six districts. RRBs of each of two sponsored banks such as State Bank of Hyderabad and State Bank of Patiala have covered 5 districts. The Andhra Bank and ICICI Bank Ltd sponsored RRBs have covered three districts. RRBs of remaining of sponsored banks have covered 3 – 6 districts. Five sponsoring banks claimed more than half of the branches. This is on account of the fact that these banks are lead banks in many districts. Thus the number of branches established and the district discovered by RRBs of sponsored banks vary in the country. It may be summed up that the State bank of India has sponsored the highest number of RRBs. These in turn opened the maximum number of branches and covered the districts in the country.

4.2. Deposits and advances:

The mobilisation of deposits, outstanding advances and credit - deposit ratio (CDR) of RRBs in India during 2005– 2014 is furnished in the **Table 1.4.** RRBs have mobilised Rs. 62,143 crores in 2005 as compared to Rs. 2, 39,504 crores in 2014. There is a gradual growth in the amount mobilised during the recent decade. However, there are fluctuations in the yearly progress. Similarly, there is a remarkable progress in the decadal growth of advances outstanding. The credit deployment was Rs. 32,870 crores in 2005 as compared to Rs. 1, 59,660 crores in 2014. There is a progressive increase in outstanding advances during the period. But there are variations in the yearly increment. The CDR was 52.89 per cent in 2005 as compared to 66.66 per cent in 2014. In the meantime, the fluctuations are significant. The CDR was the highest at 66.66 per cent in 2014 while lowest in 2005. It may be concluded that the progress in deposit mobilisation and credit deployment is remarkable in the recent decade as well as earlier years. The CDR is unwelcome. The deposits mobilised by RRBs are transferred to other financial institution including commercial banks. The advances are less than deposits. The CDR never surpassed 100 per cent. With the growth in the number of banks and considerable expansion in the

Table 1.4: Deposits, Advances and Credit – Deposit Ratio of RRBs in India during 2005 – 2014

(Rs. crores)

Year	Deposits	Outstanding advances	Credit – deposit ratio (%)
2005	62,143	32,870	52.89
2006	71,329	39,713	55.68
2007	83,144	48,493	58.32
2008	99,094	58,984	59.52
2009	1,20,190	67,802	56.41
2010	1,45,035	82,819	57.10
2011	1,66,232	98,917	59.51
2012	1,86,336	1,16,385	62.46
2013	2,11,488	1,37,078	64.82
2014	2,39,504	1,59,660	66.66

Source: As in Table 1.1

branch network, there has been a steady increase in the deposits mobilised and outstanding advances. The CDR was unwelcome because rural savings were siphoned off to urban areas.

4.3   Recovery Performance:

The recovery performance of RRBs at the aggregate level during 2005 - 14 is provided in the **Table 1.5.** The amount demanded has gradually gone up from Rs. 17,65,608 lakhs in 2005 to Rs. 29,52,704 lakhs in 2008 without any decline. A similar trend exists in collection. RRBs have collected

Table 1.5: Recovery Performance of RRBs in India during 2005 - 14

(Rs. lakhs)

Year	Demand	Collection	Overdues	% of recovery to demand
2005	17,65,608.	13,71,278.	3,94,330	77.67
2006	19,73,017.	15,75,518.	3,97,499	79.85
2007	24,07,158.	19,20,967	4,86,191.	79.80
2008	29,52,704.	23,76,579	5,76,125.	80.49
2009	NA	NA	NA	77.85
2010	NA	NA	NA	80.09
2011	NA	NA	NA	81.16
2012	NA	NA	NA	81.60
2013	NA	NA	NA	81.20
2014	NA	NA	NA	81.90

Source: As in Table 1.1

NA- Data not Available

Rs.13,71,278 lakhs in 2005 as against Rs. 23,76,579 lakhs in 2008. The overdues were Rs. 3,94,330 lakhs and Rs. 5,76,125 lakhs in the former and latter respectively. The recovery performance was 77.67 per cent in 2005 vis–a–vis 81.90 per cent in 2014. The year to year changes are noticeable. There is a progressive increase in the recovery rate with to and fro changes. It may be summed up that the growth in demand is more than that of collection. As a result, over dues declined and recovery efficiency enhanced during 2005 - 14. The recovery performance is a welcome phenomenon. The causes for favourable recovery are not far to seek. Though the recovery performance was unsatisfactory, it has been better when compared to cooperatives. It is higher in the recent period relative to earlier period.

4.4. Earnings:

The banks work behind the iron curtain of secrecy. It is next to impossible to obtain necessary financial information from banking sector. However, the observation of Manmohan Singh, former Governor of Reserve Bank of India and the former Prime Minister of India, was an eye opener in this regard. He says that there was very large expansion of bank branches since nationalisation as the policy was to move to unbanked rural areas. But most of these rural branches were unprofitable and the loan recoveries were far from satisfactory in rural branches. But the village money lender continued to flourish. We have never heard of inability of money lender to collect his dues[12]. This statement is an indication of intensity of the problem. The bank officials do admit in their informal discussions that almost all the rural branches are under heavy losses. The disquieting feature in the working of RRBs is the unsatisfactory profit and mounting overdues year after year.

4.4.1. Yearly profit/loss:

The Profit / loss of RRBs in India during 2005 - 14 are furnished in the **Table 1.6**. During 2005, 166 RRBs earned a profit of Rs. 90,260 crores vis - a - vis 30 RRBs incurred a loss of Rs. 15,449 crores. In the subsequent year, 2006, 111 RRBs earned a profit of Rs. 80,780 crores, whereas 22 RRBs suffered a loss of Rs. 19,067 crores. The profit has gradually increased year after year whilst loses declined with fluctuations. The Profit was the highest at Rs. 283,300 crores in 2014. The year 2007 reported the maximum loss at Rs. 30,125 crores. The number of profit earned RRBs have increased from 166 in 2005 to 63 in 2013 and 57 in the following year. On the other hand, the number of loss incurred RRBs have declined from 30 to 0 during 2005 – 14. When all the Profit earned and loss incurred RRBs are put together, the profit was Rs. 74,811 crores during 2005. Later, profit recorded ups and downs and reached the highest at Rs. 227,293 crores in 2013. Finally, it

Table 1.6: Profit / Loss of RRBs in India during 2005 – 14

(Rs. crores)

Year	Profit		Loss		Profit / loss
	No. of RRBs	Amount	No. of RRBs	Amount	
2005	166	90,260	30	15,449	74,811
2006	111	80,780	22	19,067	61,713
2007	81	92,260	15	30,125	62,135
2008	82	138,369	8	5,558	132,811
2009	80	182,355	6	3,591	178,764
2010	79	251,483	3	565	250,918
2011	75	178,587	7	7132	171,455
2012	79	188,615	3	2,887	185,728
2013	63	227,500	1	207	227,293
2014	57	283,300	0	0	283,300

Source: As in Table 1.1

ended at Rs. 283,300 crores in 2014. It may be concluded that the number of profit earned RRBs have increased as against loss incurred RRBs. Further, profit has increased during the study period with to and fro changes. The overall trend is welcome for the well being of RRBs in general and the nation in particular. But some of RRBs have incurred a huge loss. RRBs with a life span of 5 – 10 years are expected to cross the gestation period.

Then these banks continued to incur loss without any positive promise for the future. It is really a matter of serious concern which should invite the attention of top level management of RRBs. Unless and until the state governments concerned provide requisite facilities adequately to RRBs to step up their level of operations, they will not be able to achieve the desired profit for a balanced growth.

4.4.2. State and Profit / loss wise:

State and profit / loss wise distribution of RRBs in India at the end of 2013 is furnished in the **Table 1.7**. Among the profit earned RRBs, the highest number of RRBs are found in U.P. (9) followed by Andhra Pradesh (5) and Karnataka (4). There are three RRBs in profit zone in each of seven states such as Bihar, Chhattisgarh, Gujarat, M.P., Punjab, Rajastan, and West Bengal. Similarly, there are two RRBs in each of eight states like Assam, Haryana, Jammu & Kashmir, Jharkhand, Kerala, Maharashtra, Odisha and Tamilnadu. One RRB earned profit in each of 8 states viz., Arunachal Pradesh, Himachal Pradesh, Manipur, Meghalaya, Mizoram, Puducherry, Tripura and Uttarakhand. None of RRBs have earned profits in Nagaland. In other words, all RRBs in these states have earned profit. It may be concluded that, out of 26 states and union territories, most of profit earned RRBs exist in all states except Nagaland. The business of RRBs in all the states is good. In some of the states / union territories, the pace of development is high. Hence, the business of RRBs is satisfactory. The establishment cost is

Table 1.7: State and Profit /loss wise Distribution of RRBs in India during 2013

S.No (1)	Name of the state / union territory (2)	No. of RRBs in		Total (5)
		Profit (3)	Loss (4)	
1	Uttar Pradesh	9	-	9
2	Andhra Pradesh	5	-	5
3	Karnataka	4	-	4
4	Bihar	3	-	3
5	Chhatisgarh	3	-	3
6	Gujarat	3	-	3
7	Madhya Pradesh	3	-	3
8	Punjab	3	-	3
9	Rajastan	3	-	3
10	West Bengal	3	-	3
11	Assam	2	-	2
12	Haryana	2	-	2
13	Jammu & Kashmir	2	-	2
14	Jharkhand	2	-	2
15	Kerala	2	-	2
16	Maharashtra	2	-	2
17	Odisha	2	-	2
18	Tamil Nadu	2	-	2
19	Arunachal Pradesh	1	-	1
20	Himachal Pradesh	1	-	1
21	Manipur	1	-	1
22	Meghalaya	1	-	1
23	Mizoram	1	-	1
24	Nagaland	0	1	1
25	Puducherry	1	-	1
26	Tripura	1	-	1
27	Uttarakhand	1	-	1
	Total	63	1	64

Source: As in Table 1.1

normal. Hence, they are pushed to profit zone. This will continue as such till the economic development reaches a comparable level.

4.4.3. Sponsor - bank and Profit and loss - wise:

Sponsor - bank and Profit / loss wise classification of RRBs at the end of 2013 is shown in the **Table 1.8**. All RRBs sponsored by banks have earned profits leaving State Bank of India at the end of 2013. In the case of RRBs sponsored by State Bank of India, 14 earned profits and one incurred loss. Remaining all RRBs sponsored by Syndicate Bank (5), United Bank of India (5), Central Bank of India (5), Punjab National Bank (5), Bank of India (4), Bank of Baroda (3), Canara Bank (3), Indian Bank (3), UCO Bank (2), Dena Bank (2), Indian Overseas Bank (2), State Bank of Hyderabad (1), State Bank of Mysore (1), State Bank of Bikaner & Jaipur (1), Andhra Bank (1), State Bank of Patiala (1), Jammu & Kashmir Bank (1), Bank of Maharashtra (1), Punjab & Sind Bank (1), ICICI Bank Ltd (1) and Allahabad Bank(1) have earned profits. It may be concluded that all RRBs sponsored by all banks earned profit except State Bank of India. The public sector banks sponsored by RRBs are with heavy profits. It seems that the government culture has percolated into these RRBs and hence earned profit. Their working may be similar and identical to that of public sector undertakings in India. It is held in the literature that several state undertakings were subjected to profit.

34

Table 1.8: Sponsor Bank wise Classification of RRBs India on the basis of Profit / Loss at the end of 2013

S. No	Name of the sponsor bank	No. of RRBs in Profit	No. of RRBs in Loss	Total
1	State Bank of India	14	1	15
2	Syndicate Bank	5	-	5
3	United Bank of India	5	-	5
4	Central Bank of India	5	-	5
5	Punjab National Bank	5	-	5
6	Bank of India	4	-	4
7	Bank of Baroda	3	-	3
8	Canara Bank	3	-	3
9	Indian Bank	3	-	3
10	UCO Bank	2	-	2
11	Dena Bank	2	-	2
12	Indian Overseas Bank	2	-	2
13	State Bank of Hyderabad	1	-	1
14	State Bank of Mysore	1	-	1
15	State Bank of Bikaner & Jaipur	1	-	1
16	Andhra Bank	1	-	1
17	State Bank of Patiala	1	-	1
18	Jammu & Kashmir Bank	1	-	1
19	Bank of Maharashtra	1	-	1
20	Punjab & Sind Bank	1	-	1
21	ICICI Bank Ltd	1	-	1
22	Allahabad Bank	1	-	1
	Total	63	1	64

Source: As in Table 1.1

4.5: Accumulated losses:

The accumulated losses of RRBs during 2005 - 14 are presented in the **Table 1.9.** The number of RRBs with accumulated losses was 11 in 2013 as compared to 83 in 2005. During 2014, these stood at 8. The accumulated loss was Rs. 2,71,501 lakhs in 2005 vis - à - vis Rs. 90,300 lakhs in 2014. In the meantime, there are fluctuations. The accumulated loss was the highest at Rs. 2,75,949 lakhs spread over 39 RRBS in 2007 while the lowest at Rs 90,300 lakhs in 2014. It may be summed up that there is a declining trend in the number of RRBs with accumulated loss and the amount of loss during 2005 – 14. It infers that RRBs did good business and, therefore, number of

Table 1.9: Accumulated Losses of RRBs in India during 2005 - 14

(Rs. lakhs)

Year	No. of RRBs	Amount (Rs.)
2005	83	2,71,501
2006	58	2,63,685
2007	39	2,75,949
2008	36	2,62,422
2009	31	2,29,998
2010	27	1,77,506
2011	23	1,53,239
2012	22	1,33,257
2013	11	1,01,178
2014	8	90,300

Source: As in Table 1.1

RRBs with accumulated loss and the amount of accumulated loss submerged in the period.

It is held in the literature that the accumulated losses in certain RRBs had wiped out the entire share capital. In some other RRBs, losses had eroded even a part of their deposits[13] A number of RRBs were not able to comply with the requirements of statutory liquidity and cash reserve resource ratios prescribed by the RBI. Even if the Kelkar Committee concessions are considered, the number of RRBs incurring losses and accumulated losses would further increase. This is worrying the future of RRBs in the years to come. This has led to the merger of the weak RRBs with the stronger RRBs in the country. Now the picture is somewhat better.

4.6: Non - performing assets:

The NPAs of all RRBs in the country during 2005 – 14 are furnished in the **Table 1.10.** The amount has increased gradually from Rs. 280,434.65

Table 1.10: Non - performing Assets of RRBs in India during 2005 – 14

(Rs. lakhs)

Year	Amount	As a % of outstanding advances
2005	280,434.65	8.53
2006	289,046.53	7.28
2007	317,803.00	6.55
2008	356,634.00	6.05
2009	280,971.00	4.14
2010	308,481.00	3.72
2011	371,200.00	3.75
2012	499,416.00	4.14
2013	790,694.00	6.10
2014	702,504.00	4.40

Source: As in Table 1.1

lakhs in 2005 to Rs. 499,416 lakhs in 2012. Again it rose to reach Rs. 790,694 lakhs in 2013. Finally, it reached to Rs 702,504 lakhs at the end of 2014. Thus there are variations in the NPAs of RRBs during 2005 - 14. The share of NPAs in the total advances outstanding has gradually decreased from 8.53 per cent in 2005 as against 4.40 per cent in 2014. There are variations in the yearly figures. It may be concluded that the NPAs have declined with relative ups and downs during the period. Further, there is a decline in the NPAs as a percentage of outstanding advances with fluctuations during the period.

Despite the existence of RRBs for several years, they have not yet become viable. The factors which contribute to the erosion of profitability of RRBs are many. The factors are endemic to the system structured as it is. Firstly, in terms of the mandate given to them, these banks have to confine their lending to weaker sections in small loans and consequently the interest chargeable to their borrowers has perforce to be low leading to their poor income. This is further compounded by high cost of servicing a large number of small accounts resulting in the process, a low net return on their advances. Secondly, RRBs have opened a number of new branches. A newly opened branch takes time to pave its way, as in the initial years, it does not have much of credit deployment operations. It thus invariably makes a negative contribution to RRBs profitability in the initial years. As returns on their advances being limited, poor financial viability is built in the present arrangement and as the other costs go up, their position will only be aggravated in future.

RRBs are mandated to confine their lending to weaker sections where the interest earned on loans is the lowest in the banking system. Low interest margins and the highest cost of servicing a large number of accounts coupled with low volume of business on account of their restricted clientele are the main factors which make unprofitable working of these banks. Non - availability of competent and trained staff pose serious problems in expanding the business of RRBs. Apart from these causes which are built into the system, haphazard increase in the number of branches, low rate of recycling of funds and mounting overdues account for the inescapable losses in RRBs. Thus the deterioration of profit - making RRBs has posed a serious threat for the very existence of RRBs themselves. This situation has further worsened on account of increase in overhead expenses consequent upon the revision of staff salaries and allowances on par with the staff of commercial banks. A Committee reported that, if RRBs have to reach the break - even point, they have to charge a higher rate of interest than the existing rate. This is obviously not possible at present, as RRBs are to cater to the needs of weaker sections at concessional interest rates, with also no scope for cross - subsidisation, in the absence of loans which could yield higher returns. It is to be noted that RRBs are expected not only to fulfil their socio - economic objectives but also to earn enough profits to sustain their continued operations. This can be done only through a high volume of loan business and a low cost profile. It is to be noted further that the economic viability of RRBs is absolutely necessary for improving the economic well - being of the rural poor. Therefore, there is an urgent need to arrest the trend at the earliest time.

Admittedly, RRBs have achieved considerable degree of success in taking the banking services to the very remote areas which had hitherto remained unbanked and made available institutional credit to the weaker sections in these areas. Their achievement in the coverage of tribal blocks has also been equally significant. Further, in making credit available to the far flung rural areas, they have facilitated the flow of credit from the central money market to these areas through refinance from the NABARD.

References:

1. UNO, <u>Rural Progress through Cooperatives,</u> Washington DC, 1954, pp. 6-7

2. H. Belshaw. (1965) <u>Agricultural Credit in Economically Underdeveloped Countries,</u> ROME, FAO, 232-38.

3. RBI, <u>Report of the Committee to Review Arrangements for Institutional Credit for Agriculture and Rural Development,</u> Bombay, 1981, pp. 117-49.

4. RBI, <u>All India Rural Credit Survey,</u> Bombay, 1954, pp. 117-49 (VOL –II)

5. Government of India, <u>National Commission on Agriculture,</u> New Delhi, 1976, pp.568-70 (abridged report).

6. RBI, <u>Report of the Working Group on Multi - Agency Approach in Agricultural Finance,</u> Bombay, 1978, p.2.

7. Government of India, <u>Report of the Committee on Rural Banks,</u> New Delhi, 1975, (D.O.NO.F.1 - 10/75/AC).

8. <u>Ibid</u> p.9.

9. Government of India, <u>The Gazette of India,</u> New Delhi, 1976, Part II, Section 1, p. 149 (extra ordinary).

10. <u>The Regional Rural Banks Act,</u> 1975, (Ordinance), p.9.

11. RBI<u>, Report of the Review Committee on RRBs,</u> Bombay, 1978.

12. Cited by M.L. Verma. (1988) <u>"Rural Banking in India",</u> Jaipur, Rajendra printers, 191-192.

13. RBI, <u>Report of the Agricultural Credit Review Committee,</u> Bombay, 1990, p.139.

CHAPTER – II
RESEARCH DESIGN AND METHODOLOGY

1. Introduction:

Realising the magnitude of rural poverty, Indian planners and policy – makers have laid special emphasis on rural development, particularly from the Fifth Five Years Plan onwards. All the programmes aimed at rural development considered credit one of the strategic inputs for their successful implementation. To suit to the requirements of several rural development programmes, a multitude of credit agencies were established with varying degrees of success. In India, the history of rural credit starts with cooperatives established in 1904. Though cooperatives have grown in size and operation, their performance has been far from satisfactory. After nationalisation, commercial banks were asked to play a leading role in the socio – economic development of the rural areas. Though commercial banks spread their branch network in the rural areas, they could not wipe out the anamolies and imbalances in the distribution of rural credit in the country.

Considering the deficiencies of cooperatives and commercial banks in meeting the rural credit requirements, particularly of small and marginal farmers and landless labour, a need was felt for setting up a new set of institutions to mop up the deficiencies. Accordingly, the Working Group headed by Shri M. Narasimham recommended the establishment of an institution which combines the local feel and familiarity with rural problems, which the cooperatives possess and the degree of business organisation, ability to mobilise deposits, access to money market and a modernised outlook which the commercial banks have. Consequent on the acceptance of these recommendations, Regional Rural Banks (RRBs) came in to existence to form the third component of multi - agency credit system. Considering the vital role assigned to RRBs to play in the rural development, it became imperative to have a critical evaluation of the working of such institutions. In the light of this, the present study has been undertaken by the researcher.

A well developed banking system is considered the pre - requisite for economic development of a country. In an economy, income is partly spent for consumption purposes and partly saved. Much of the saving is channelled into investment via a variety of financial institutions. Broadly, the financial structure comprises various types of financial institutions. The Indian banking system is constituted by a number of institutions consisting of the Reserve Bank of India (RBI), commercial banks, co - operative banks, RRBs, foreign banks and other specialised ones. Commercial banks constitute the nervous system. This characteristic distinguishes the commercial banks from other financial institutions. Although banks create no new wealth, their lending, investing and related activities facilitate the economic processes of production, distribution and consumption[1].

Public sector banks, being an important group of financial organisations of our economy, act as the back - bone of economic growth and prosperity. These banks are, therefore, treated as the instruments for conversion of static credit into dynamic credit[2]. In terms of role of banks in a planned economy, they may be distinguished from other financial institutions in as much as the former assists the government in the implementation of plans by providing the sinews of development. They primarily perform functions of a technical nature including the fulfilment of credit requirements as per the economic plans of government and control the utilisation of credit according to planned priorities. These roles of banks have assumed an added significance for the development efforts of India through successive Five – Year Plans.

Hence, banks had to be the prime - movers and pace - setters for the achievement of socio - economic objectives of the economy. Moreover, banks were required to play a dynamic role in the economic development and render service in promoting economic growth rather than behaving as orthodox passive spectators[3]. More so, during the post - nationalisation era, besides a massive qualitative change in the operations, banks have been called upon to assume a great variety of new responsibilities in the area of social banking.

Among the banks, RRBs occupied a unique position in the Indian money market by commanding a significant share of banking resources of India. RRBs extended their cooperation to the government in its pursuit of building up an egalitarian society with a rising standard of living by designing their lending policies accordingly. It was observed that during the post - nationalisation era, in spite of the progress made by the banks in general, the profitability of most of RRBs declined due to tough competition among the different bank groups in the banking sector. Thus, in view of

44

removing the serious erosion in the profitability and productivity of RRBs, the Government of India introduced reforms in the banking sector from 1991 and 1998 as per the recommendations of Narasimham Committees I and II sequentially. Hence, broadly, three phases can be considered with regard to movements in the banking system. At the outset, there was a pre - reform banking phase characterised by an unprecedented growth and the pursuit of mass banking. This was followed by an era of reforms which imparted an altogether different dimension to the nuances of banking. Now there is consolidation and convergence in the banking sector.

2. Relevance of the study:

In the process of financial intermediation, banks have come to acquire the nature of multi - product firms. However, their primary function remains the same and these form the most remunerative functions of banks. The performance of these functions pre - suppose that after various costs of such functions are met, a margin of profit is left, and the level of profit should be taken as an index of efficiency of working of the organisation. For that matter, profit as an indicator of working efficiency, is applicable to any business unit. Depending on their size, banks are multi - product firms and they compete with each other for profits. The intra - organisational structure of a bank also treats its constituent units as potential profit centers. This pattern of working has come to be accepted even after nationalisation among banks either as a matter of custom or for reasons of convenience.

With the emergence of the concept of priority sector, social lending etc., which are construed as innovative, profitability in banks as an indicator of efficiency has been pushed aside. Fulfilment of social goals has gained ascendancy over profitability. However, profits work as an incentive for banks to function and retain their individual identities. Therefore, the banking industry must be on sound footing[4]. Moreover, if the banks are to be effective instruments of purveyors of credit towards rational growth with economic justice, they have to be economically strong and their operation, therefore, should continue to be viable. "Economic viability is also essential for the survival of any business activity and the banking industry is no exception to this[5]. Commenting on the objective of profit, the Banking Commission, 1971 observed that, "It is now an accepted principle that these banks are not to run solely or even mainly with the objective of making maximum profits. However, this does not mean that they will not make any profits at all. In particular, there is a substantial investment of public funds in banks and a reasonable return on investment would be expected by the government"[6]. Thus, for continuous growth, it is a must for banks to generate adequate surplus not only to meet current obligations but also to strengthen their reserves to enable them to assume greater responsibility. Since banks perform the main function of financial intermediation, it is, therefore, of utmost importance that the working of this sector is subjected to a close and objective scrutiny for financial viability.

The role of banks has come under scrutiny in the recent past. It is necessary to recognize that banks have played a critical role in the development of Indian economy, particularly in the spread of banking, monetisation of economy, mobilisation of savings and their allocation for plan priorities. For all economies in the early and intermediate stages of development, credit markets face a persistent excess demand, reflecting the existing resource constraints. Moreover, market processes can well exclude the genuine credit needs of weaker sections of the society which do not have the competitive strength to bid for bank credit. Public ownership in Indian banking was intended to address both concerns, i.e., the rationing of credit in the face of excess demand not cleared by market and channeling of bank credit flow to the economically disadvantaged sections of society. A massive expansion of bank branches has ensured equity in the allocation and distribution of bank credit.

At the same time, however, there was erosion in the financial health of banks and deterioration in the quality of customer service. Within the ambit of financial sector reforms, therefore, the focus since the early 1990's has been on the viability, efficiency and competitiveness of banks and financial institutions. Liberalisation and deregulation has come to stay with a greater emphasis on considerations of productivity, asset equality and profitability. There is also an urgent need for Government to divest substantial share holdings to the public, so that these banks can respond effectively to changing market conditions. Under the present circumstances, improvement in the cost structure of banks and work culture are considered important.

There was a growing realisation that the unbridled expansion of banking system entailed a definite and significant cost. Operational efficiency of the system was found low as reflected in high transaction cost vis - à - vis the advanced countries. Allocative efficiency also suffered erosion on account of alleged high level of pre - emptions and mounting up of impaired assets in many segments. More importantly, banks were characterised by unusually high level of business spread and yet, profitability levels were much behind prudent levels coupled with a relatively weak bottom line. Prudential norms and accounting standards were also areas wherein banks lagged behind their overseas counterparts and prudent levels. Hence, Narasimham Committee which signified landmark events in the banking history, made in - depth review of the state of banking and advocated radical measures for addressing the operational and structural deficiencies in the banking system.

It is to the credit of banks that the adjustment process to the reform measures has been smooth and bereft of any major eventuality. Today, most of banks can boast of moving progressively towards international benchmarks in terms of accounting standards, transparency, profitability and compliance with other important international norms. It is also the credit of banks and the regulatory and supervisory climate that the financial system by and large proved immune to the spate of recent contagions. As a result of reforms, attempts are now visible to right size the operations, tone up the functional skills and build up a cushion against possible shocks from within and overseas. The most redeeming feature of reforms relates to its gradual nature as a result of which, banks have been afforded the necessary lead time to tide over possible adversities. There is a flip side as well to the success of banking reforms especially relevant to RRBs[7].

More specifically, in connection with the profitability, last few years have seen many of RRBs posting handsome profits and improving profitability levels. However, sustaining the profit momentum is beset with issues like progressive decline in interest spread, volatile business, and nature of environment, fierce competitive pressures and negative externalities associated with these banks. The ensuing banking sectors will presuppose a shift in focus from size - related issues to concerns of profitability, profit monitoring and efficiency in operations. As a result, restructuring of RRBs took place.

Thus, the financial sector reforms introduced have brought significant improvement in strength, resilience and competitiveness of banks. It is, therefore, relevant to study profitability of RRBs in general and the Saptagiri Grameena Bank (SGB) in particular in the post reform era.

3. Review of literature:

In this section, an attempt is made to review the earlier studies undertaken on RRBs. Right from the time of conceiving the idea of RRBs, until now various committees, commissions, working groups and study groups were constituted by the RBI, the National Bank for Agriculture and Rural Development (NABARD) and the government of India for promotion, reorganisation and restructuring as well as streamlining the functioning of RRBs. These were appointed from time to time for bringing about requisite amendments in the working of these banks as that the scope of their functioning is further enhanced from quantitative and qualitative viewpoints. Apart from these, individual researchers conducted studies concerning these banks. The principal existing research studies within the reach of the researcher are reviewed.

Profitability studies were carried out by bankers, economists and planners over a period of time, especially after the nationalisation of banks. These studies throw light on various approaches to profitability analysis; bring out the importance and relevance of such studies; reveal the trend and tendencies in profitability; and pave the way for further research. The purpose is to critically examine the various profitability studies and bring out their distinctive features. Hence review of literature on the profitability of banks is undertaken here.

Working groups, expert committees and study teams suggested the modifications in the loan application forms, accounting and loaning procedures, documents required and allocation of roles between institutions under multi - agency approach[8]. During 1977, Dantwala Committee reviewed the working of RRBs[9]. Another committee under the Chairmanship of B. Sivaraman as a part of its study assessed RRBs during 1981[10]. At the behest of the NABARD, Agricultural Finance Corporation carried out a comparative study on the performance of two RRBs during 1981.[11] Steering Committee of the RBI had evaluated the financial viability of RRBs in 1981.[12] During 1986, a working group under the Chairmanship of Kelkar organised a study on RRBs touching up on organisational strategies and overdues.[13] The Agricultural Credit Review Committee while reviewing the agriculture credit system in the country, examined the performance of RRBs on all India basis.[14] It merely summed up the assumptions of Narasimham Working Group and findings and expectations of Dantwala Committee and Kelkar Working Group. This Committee recommended the merger of RRBs with their sponsor banks.

Divitia and Ventachalam[15] have said that the banks after 1969 were required to take on certain social as well as economic responsibilities which were ignored by commercial banks in the past. In fulfiling these objectives, profitability was affected in two ways. The cost involved in new tasks was higher; and the return from them was lower in traditional activities. Their view was that, in discharging their duties, banks should not jeopardize profitability. If profits are affected, they can't stay in business to discharge their functions. **Soudamini Nagar**[16] in a study on RRBs in Rajasthan found that these had made creditable progress in deposit mobilisation and credit distribution.

During 1978, **Wadhva**[17] conducted a comprehensive study for two years on the working of two RRBs selected from Haryana and Rajasthan. The major observations made by him were as follows: (i) RRBs inherited complicated procedural formalities from their sponsor banks; (ii) these were not able to meet the targets in disbursement of credit; (iii) limited space for direct lending. (iv) not all branches were set up at the locations where other credit institutions were not operating; (v) deploy more resources than deposits mobilised locally; (vi) RRBs seem to be suffering from a combination of the worse features of commercial banks; and (vii) the state governments did not extend much help while the sponsor banks could shoulder. The author offered a number of suggestions for the reorganisation of RRBs.

Patel and Shete[18] have made a comparative study on the performance and prospects of RRBs located in different parts of the country. In addition, these were compared with cooperatives and commercial banks operating within the jurisdictions of RRBs. **Mohana Rao**[19] in his study on regional rural banks in Andhra Pradesh concluded that, given the coverage, the bank was functioning well in meeting the credit requirements of the target group. **Inu Jain**[20], **Reddy and Suresh Kumar**[21] in their studies came to the conclusions that, weaker sections like small and marginal farmers and agricultural labourers had got the major share of credit from the bank. During 1981, **Panandikar**[22] assessed the top five RRBs in terms of deployment of credit, expenditure, relationship between the NABARD and RRBs and the nexus between commercial banks and RRBs.

Varde and Singh[23] have analysed the overall profitability performance of four RRBs for three years. It is merely an exercise comparing the relative position of an average RRB as between December, 1978 and December, 1980. The study concluded that the profitability performance had improved over the three year period. Further, manpower and other operating costs put together have significantly declined. Manpower and other expenses ratios were higher in RRBs relative to commercial banks. **Varghese**[24] has analysed profits and profitability of groups of banks in India during 1970 - 79 to identify the factors that influence them. Trend in gross profit, net - profit and operating results were analysed. Monetary policy measures such as changes in interest rates, increase in CRR and SLR etc.

were causes for variations in profits. The conclusion was that, among the options available for improving profitability, the best one was better operating and recovery procedures.

Hossain[25] conducted a study on grameena bank in Bangladesh, which was started in 1976 as a pilot experiment and development project for the landless in an area near Chittagong University. The research study focuses attention on the socio-economic conditions of borrowers, use of loan and recovery performance. The findings indicate that the grameena bank has made positive contribution to the alleviation of poverty in the area of its operation. The study by **Abdul Noorbasha and Dakshina Murthy**[26] found that RRBs had shown a tendency to grow and cater to the needs of weaker sections. The study also found that RRBs identify themselves as the perfect matching credit agents of the rural sector, compared to the than that of commercial banks. The study is based on secondary data only. **Lakshmi Narayana**[27] in a study on RRBs in West Bengal found that the recovery of overdue loans together with the normal work of processing new credit proposals and enlisting new borrowers hardly allowed the bank officials any time for guiding them in adopting improved farming techniques and making better use of credit.

Singh and Upadhya[28] conducted a study on the loan recovery aspect of RRBs in Bihar. Crop failure, expenditure on marriage and other social functions in the family were considered important factors of non-payment of loans. Inadequate follow up measures and lack of serious attitude of borrowers towards repayment were also explained as reasons. While, **Jagadeesh Prasad and Sunil Kumar**[29] in a study about RRBs in Bihar found that the loans given to the poor were generally accepted as a dole or relief program, which was pointed out as the main reason for poor repayment. **Prasad**[30] in a study about Sri Visakha Grameena Bank in Andhra

Pradesh revealed that RRBs were catering to the needs of rural society, creating banking consciousness, but also serving as corner stone to the building of rural development. A study by **Nagi Reddy and Rathna Kumar**[31], found that low yield, low market price for produce, repayment of other debts and other domestic expenditure as the main reasons of non-repayment of loans. While, better yield, desire to get future loans, persuasion by bank officials, etc. are the main reasons for prompt repayment. **Balishter**[32] undertook a study to evaluate the performance of the Jamuna Gramin Bank. On the basis of the working results of the bank, it was concluded that, in the event of future expansion of rural banking ,greater importance should be given to the extension and strengthening of the network of RRBs along with the expansion of branches of commercial banks.

Varsha and Singh[33] have conducted studies on various approaches to profit planning. The authors opined that profit planning is important to ensure profitability. Banks are not consciously planning for a desired level of profit because profit is considered as a mere resultant figure and not targeted figure, whatever planning that the banks adopts with regard to number of branches, deposits, credit and manpower. According to them, there are three approaches to profit planning in banks viz., profit and loss account; balance sheet; and product/service. **Deshpande**[34] has emphasised an important aspect so far neglected by the analyst of bank profitability. The loss of interest on cash reserve ratio (CRR) and statutory liquidity ratio (SLR) funds and the penalty paid to the RBI for defaults on maintaining them. The analysts have ignored the effect of CRR and SLR. Of late, many banks were able to keep these reserves at correct level either due to delay in communication and transmission of funds, mismatching of credit expansion versus deposit accretion or non - availability of market funds at the time of need. The accumulated loss of income and penalties though not shown in the balance sheet may work out to enormous amounts which may severally affect the profitability of banks.

Angadi and Devaraj[35] writes to decry the opinion that the deterioration in the profitability in recent days has been chiefly ceased by policy constraints such as CRR and SLR restrictions, administered interest rates, lending norms and priority sector lending. It is contended that the profitability declines since a long time. The study was to find out whether decline in profitability is due to policy constraints called exogenous or factors from within the organisation called endogenous. The conclusion was that profit as a percentage of working funds as well as operating earnings began to decline from the early sixties whereas majority of policy constraints were introduced since the early seventies and have become more rigorous since the mid-seventies. As such, policy constraints were not entirely responsible for decline in profitability. But factors that affect profitability were found outside policy constraints.

Venugopal and Somaskanden[36] have made a study on the trend in profitability in two stages viz., trend in earnings, expenses and gross profit and trend in the appropriation of gross profit. The study reported that the return of gross profit to working funds has declined. Trend in earnings and expenses bears out the decline in profitability though expenses rise faster than income. They concluded that the decline need not be taken as a decline in their performance because these were unique in their conception. **Gupta and Goswami**[37] have said that the aim of a bank like any entrepreneur is to make the most efficient use of resources at its disposal. Profit is the accepted yardstick to measure the most efficient use of resources. The profitability expressed as a share of working fund has declined even though the quantum of profit increased over a period of time. The major causes for decline in profitability are: increase in the pre - emption of funds for statutory obligations; priority sector lending; and enormous increase in establishment expenses.

NABARD[38] published "A study on RRBs viability", which was conducted by Agriculture Finance Corporation in 1986 on behalf of NABARD. The study revealed that viability of RRBs was essentially dependent upon the fund management strategy, margin between resources mobility and their deployment and on the control exercised on current and future costs with advances. The proportion of establishment costs to total cost and expansion of branches were the critical factors, which affected their viability. The study further concluded that RRBs incurred losses due to defects in their systems as such there was need to rectify these and make them viable. The main suggestions of the study include improvement in the infrastructure facilities and opening of branches by commercial banks in such areas where RRBs were already in function. However, the main limitation of the study was that its generalizations were based on the study of only two RRBs, namely, the Mala Prabha Gramin Bank (Karnatka) and The Rayalaseema Gramin Bank (Andhra Pradesh). **Rehman**[39] has assessed the impact of the Grameena Bank on the rural power structure of Bangladesh. The findings of the study indicate that Grammena bank members, being conscious of their status as opposed to the rural elites, have already developed a countervailing force to ensure their participation in the development process.

Another study by **Rehman**[40] highlights the factors which have contributed to the success of Grameena Bank model in Bangladesh, in reaching the poor through an innovative credit program. The design of the program, targeting the rural poor and women as clients, excellent implementation system, decentralized and participative management style and various other innovative polities were cited as factors responsible for its success. An in depth household survey in five project villages and two control villages found that Grameena Bank members had incomes above 43 per cent higher than the non-participants in the adopted project work village. The effect on income was attributed to the increase in income from processing and manufacturing, trading and transport services financed by bank. **Singh**[41] in his paper stated that the profitability of banking system went through several stresses and strain on account of many exogenous and endogenous factors, major of them being continuous increase in SLR, CRR, persistent emphasis on social goals, growing incidence of industrial sickness, rapid branch expansion in banked and unbanked rural areas, unfavorable change in deposit mix and growing incidence of financial disintermediation.

Singh & Kallkundrikar[42] in their study have concluded that RRBs have exclusively financed the weaker sections, showing the image of small man's bank. The study made it clear that since the objectives of RRBs had been the extension of credit to the rural poor and not based on the profit motive. It is not justifiable to argue that the concept of RRBs should be done away with, only because they are proved to be unprofitable. **L.K Naidu**[43] conducted a study on RRBs taking a sample of 48 beneficiaries of rural artisans in Cuddapah district of Andhra Pradesh state under Rayala Seema Gramin Bank. In this study, it was concluded that the beneficiaries were able to find an increase in their income because of bank finance. **Ramakrishanan**[44] in his study revealed that the support from state governments were not forthcoming to the extent it was envisaged and expected by the working group on RRBs. The study also suggested entrusting the control of RRBs to their sponsor banks. In an article, **Sahana**

Ghosh[45] found that the primary objective of taking banking services to un-banked areas had been fulfilled by RRBs.

Rao[46] in an article examines the inherent problems of RRBs. Since there are different agencies like RBI, NABARD, sponsor bank, Government of India, etc., to control RRBs, several decisions are delayed for want of clearance by one after the other agencies concerned. Hence, the study suggests that amalgamation of all the existing RRBs to form a single national rural bank under the single agency. The RBI conducted an important and scientific study in 1988[47] to evaluate the financial viability of RRBs. The study covered 15 RRBs; four branches of each RRB were also taken for in-depth study. RRBs selected were divided into two categories, viz., A and B. RRBs whose business exceeded three crore rupees or those who completed three years of service were brought under the category A and others in category B. The study revealed that the performance of banks in category A, both in terms of deposits and loans was better than the banks in category B. This was obviously because of the fact that the proportion of business rendered by category A banks was higher than that of B.

Parmar, et.al.[48] conducted a study on RRBs in Gujarat state. The study found that about two thirds of total deposits were shared by demand deposits. The branch expansion programme and credit deployment were also commendable. **Naidu and Naidu**[49] in a case study of 48 borrower households of rural artisans financed by Rayalaseema grameena bank showed that regional rural banks were able to play a major role, but that, its credit operations were impaired by the limited knowledge on rural artisan sector. A comprehensive study on RRBs was conducted by **Shete and Karkal**[50]: one of the important findings of the study was that RRBs had not neglected the backward states and regions in spreading the banking services and in serving the rural tribal population. **Dhabal and Bhattacharya**[51] examined the overdue and recovery aspects of RRBs. All these studies made concern about the mounting overdue of RRBs. Some of the important suggestions of these studies to improve recovery were effective supervision by the bank officials, organizing recovery camps, promoting the intention to repay loans and finally, resorting to legal action against select affluent few and willful defaulters, etc.

Moin Quazi[52] in a study found that RRBs have given a massive support to self-employment generation in the rural areas. They also played a major role in the implementation of Integrated Rural Development Programme (IRDP). **Hebber**[53] argues that viability is not a criterion to judge the performance of RRBs. He suggested that RRBs should be merged in the state to form one RRB for each state with its own rural branches. **Garg**[54] in his study analysed the basic determinants of cost, profit and profitability in the banking sector. He made inter - group comparison among SBI and its subsidiaries. Further, the author has studied the impact of monetary policy on the earnings of banks. The author has opined that the profitability of all groups of banks except foreign banks has declined. Again the author pointed out that the decline in profitability is due to faster increase of operating expenses as compared to operating income. **Jain**[55] evaluated the impact of RRBs credit on beneficiaries in terms of income and employment in the state of Rajasthan. It was observed that RRBs function well in the state. The beneficiaries have improved their production, income, employment and capital base.

Anand and Ram[56] have reviewed the theoretical framework of RRBs. There is nothing new in this work. **Bapna**[57] compared the working of four RRBs of Rajasthan with RRBs at the all India level in respect to financial resources, loans and advances, recovery performance and viability. The author discussed these variables peripherally and, therefore, suffers from a detailed analysis. **Kalkundrikar**[58] organised a study on the performance and problems of two RRBs in Karnataka. The issues focused are branch expansion, deposit accretion, credit deployment, recovery and profitability at the macro - level and the contribution of RRBs to the economic development of Karnataka.

Krishnan[59] in a study reveals that, though there have been tremendous developments in the field of branch expansion, deposits and advances by RRBs, the problem of overdue is very serious. **Shete**[60] also commented on the overdue problem of RRBs and suggested that RRBs should consolidate their branches rather than expanding further. **Velayudhan**[61] examined the various aspects of RRBs viz. growth and performance; problems like recovery, mounting losses, viability, management problems, industrial relations, etc. In the light of multi-agency approach to rural credit and as an instrument of income distribution in rural areas, RRBs have an important role to play in rural development. The agricultural credit review committee headed by **A. Kushro**[62] was very critical of the performance of RRBs. The Committee made it clear that, the logic and rationale, which justified the setting-up of RRBs in the mid-seventies, did not any longer exist and it recommended to merge RRBs with commercial banks which had originally sponsored them. A study by **Balishter et.al.**[63] found that there had been a shift in cropping pattern from low-income crops to high-income crops. It also revealed that, there had been perceptible increase in the income and employment of borrowers due to the activities of the bank.

In a study, **Chauhan et.al**[64] found that the demand for loans exceeded the supply. About 35 per cent of total loans were put to unproductive use due to urgent social expenditure needs. It was also revealed that only very little surplus income existed within the sample, ranging 7 - 16 per cent to the average household. **Panda and Lal**[65] in their paper reported that profitability of banks improves through the development of certain internal management techniques. Hence, they concluded that productivity, deployment of funds, quality of advances, information system, organisational set up and branch expansion influence profitability of banks to a great extent. A Working Group[66] under the Chairmanship of Sri. S.M. Kelkar was constituted to review the various aspects of the working of RRBs for the past few years so as to identify appropriate measures for strengthening their organizational structure and improving their overall capabilities. The working group, which submitted the report in June 1992, recommended the continuance of RRBs and greater involvement of sponsor bank in their functioning.

Kallu Rao and Shaji Thomas[67] in a study about Manipur Rural Bank revealed that the growth in the deposit was not satisfactory among the various types of deposits viz, savings bank account. The recovery percentage was unsatisfactory and in all the years. It was below 50 per cent. However, the bank had managed to maintain more than 100 per cent credit deposit ratio throughout the study period. The study strongly felt the need to raise the margin from one and a half per cent to five per cent to give boost to the working funds of RRBs. It is suggested that RRB have to expand their loan business at a compound growth rate of 35 per cent so as to become viable institutions. The study concluded with the observation that RRBs need six years time and a network of 70 branches to become financially viable in their operations. The study also observed that raising new loans requires, filling out redundant forms, screening and monitoring borrowers diligently and pursuing collections intensively, if one was to be in compliance and maintained good asset quality. For a long-time, employees of a bureaucracy had never linked remuneration to performance, there were no incentives for RRB managers and staff to push harder, get motivated, and turn their branches around, if they did not participate to facilitate success in rural financial intermediation. The provision of incentives to staff and clients was significant. **Mishra**[68] made a study on the profitability of banks on the basis of interest and non - interest income and interest expenditure, manpower expenses and other expenses. The author concluded that the profitability of commercial banks declined on account of growing pre - emption of funds in the form of CRR and SLR and acceleration in expenses as compared to income, advances and investment than interest income.

Sadare[69] in his paper entitled Profitability in Banks undertook a study of profitability of three groups of banks for a period of six years. The author has opined that the profitability of banks can be improved with the help of policy - support and increase in effectiveness. **Chandra**[70] observed that though the role of banks was significant in the field of mobilisation of resources and economic growth of the economy, yet they are getting step motherly treatment and discrimination. The author has concluded that in spite of huge working funds, banks were able to show better results owing to high cost of operation. This is because of priority sector advances and increase in the branch network in the rural areas. **Kumar Raj** [71] carried out a study on the topic "Growth and Performance of RRBs in Haryana". It is found that there was an enormous increase in deposits and outstanding advances. The researcher felt the need to increase the share capital to ensure efficient use and distribution channels of finance to beneficiaries. **Toor**[72] is of the opinion that there is a link between the nature of business being handled by banks and their earnings. In his study, he has examined the various aspects of business mix like deposits, advances, expenditure incurred on deposits and income earned on advances. The author viewed that the business mix in banks is of highly varying degree and it certainly has a bearing on their operational efficiency and profitability trend. The author concluded that in the years to come, banks have to alive to the type of business they handle with reference to cost and benefit from such business.

Amandeep[73] in her study examined the trend in profits and profitability of twenty banks with the help of analytical tools like trend analysis, ratio analysis and concentration indices of select parameters. The object of the study was to identify various factors empirically and ascertain their contribution towards profitability in either direction. Through multi - variety analysis, the author reached the conclusion that the efficient management of burden plays a significant role in the determination of profitability of banks. In this study, the author laid emphasis on the control of burden to enhance the profitability of banks. **Panandikar**[74] conducted a study to assess the performance of top five rural banks of India (in terms of deposits) in 1995. This study brought a few things into limelight. (i) RRBs have become very important credit agencies especially in the backward states, where the extent of banking coverage was inadequate; (ii) most of RRBs have confined their credit to weaker sections; and (iii) the cost structure of RRBs was definitely lower than that of commercial banks. Further, the study indicated that the present nexus between RRBs and commercial banks may be continued for further development. It strongly felt that the NABARD should be identified as an apex body for controlling and regulating the activities of RRBs and to imbibe organisational competence among them.

Another interesting empirical study was conducted by **Varde Vasha**[75] to analyse the overall performance including profitability of RRBs. For this purpose, a sample of 40 RRBs was picked-up. This study followed elaborate and complicated process of ascertaining different ratios for the purpose of analysing the profitability of RRBs. It indicated that the profitability performance of RRBs showed increasing trend. This was mainly because of the decline in manpower bill and other operating expenses. The study also compared the manpower and operating ratio of RRBs with those of commercial banks and concluded that it was lower with commercial banks. This was mainly because of higher volume of business handled per employee of commercial bank as compared to its counterpart in RRBs. This study felt that this position could be reversed in future, if RRBs enlarged the volume of business. The study came out with a constructive suggestion that local people should be allowed to participate in equity and no-target group (rich farmers) be lured for the purpose of mobilizing additional funds. Jai Prakash conducted a study with the objective of analyzing the role of RRBs in the economic development and revealed that RRBs have been playing a vital role in the field of rural development. Moreover, RRBs were more efficient in disbursal of loans to rural borrowers as compared to the commercial banks. Support from the state Governments, local participation and proper supervision of loans and opening urban branches were some steps, which should be taken to make RRBs' further efficient.

Reddy et al[76] conducted a study on the performance of RRBs during 1981 to 1995 and it was found that the performance in the sphere of agricultural loan was by and large satisfactory. **Satyanarayana & Rafathunnisa**[77] concluded that the proportion of term loan of RRBs has been declined during the period 1991-97 which made adverse impact on the investment pattern in agriculture sector. Saveeta and Verma Sateesh analysed the performance of banks from a profitability point of view, using various parameters. **Bapanna**[78] studied the organization and working of four

RRBs in Rajasthan. The study came to the conclusion that, there was spectacular increase in branch expansion, deposits and advances. The credit deposit ratio of RRBs was higher than that of commercial banks. The recovery performance was better in respect of non-agricultural sector compared to agricultural sector.

Abdul Noorbasha and Jyothi[79] conducted a study pertaining to the financial management pattern of Chaitanya Grameena Bank, Tenali of Andhra Pradesh. The study showed that most of RRBs were non - viable. To improve the viability of these banks, the authors suggested to allow RRBs to lend money to public bodies like Scheduled Castes and Scheduled Tribes Corporation, Housing Boards, Village Panchayats, etc. and in turn, increase their earnings. According to **Swaminathan**[80], Policy of current phase of financial liberalisation have had an immediate, direct and dramatic effect on rural credit. There has been a contraction in rural banking in general and in priority sector lending and preferential lending to the poor in particular. Chavan and Pallavi have examined the growth and regional distribution of rural banking over the period 1975-2002. Chavan's paper documents the gains made by historical underprivileged region of east, northeast and central part of India during the period of social and development banking. These gains were reversed in the 1990s: cutbacks in rural branches in rural credit-deposits ratios were the steepest in the eastern and northeastern states of India. Policies of financial liberalization have unmistakably worsened regional inequalities in rural banking in India.

Dey & Adhikari[81] articulated that the share of priority sector lending of Cachar Gramin Bank has decreased during 1992 - 2002. The bank has deviated from its laid down objective of granting higher amount of loans to priority sector in order to minimize non – performing assets (NPAs). **Golait**[82] examined different issues relating to agricultural loan in India and revealed that loan delivery mechanism to agriculture sector has been thoroughly inadequate. **Narasaiah & Ramudu**[83] studied the role of Rayalaseema Grameena Bank in Kurnool district in terms of agricultural loans from 1993-2003 and observed that the share of farm sector advance to total advance is higher than that of the share of non-farm sector. **Dilip Khankhoje and Milind Sathye**[84] have analysed the variations in the performance in terms of productive efficiency of RRBs in India and to assess whether the efficiency of these institutions has increased post-restructuring during 1993-94 or not. As none of these studies analyzed the performance after amalgamation during 2006, there is a need to carry out the present study.

Agarwal & Kumar[85] examined the advances of RRBs to agricultural and allied sector. The beneficiaries have utilised rural loan provided by these bank in various economic activities to meet their needs. **Syed Ibrahim**[86] carried out a study on the topic "Performance Evaluation of RRBs in India." In this study, it was concluded that RRBs showed a remarkable performance in the post merger period. Ishwara P, in his paper made an attempt to study the performance of RRBs during 1980 - 2009. In order to know the implications of transformation of RRBs in 2004, the study focused on financial results before and after amalgamation. **Ibrahim**[87] studied the role of RRBs in priority sector lending during 2002- 2009 and found that there is a significant growth in priority sector lending.

There are several studies concerning asset/liabilities or funds managed by banks[88]. The framework is broader because it is meant to meet, in addition to profitability, the objectives of liquidity and safety of funds as well. But, looking at from limited purpose of profit management only, it is narrower in its coverage because its scope is confined only to the framework of balance sheet, leaving out a large part of the items that go into the income and expenditure statement. It leaves out for separate treatment of problems of pricing of services, budgeting and cost control[89]. There are studies which deal with profit planning[90]. Profit planning studies are the most comprehensive managerial exercises which have applied sophisticated methods. These studies made the fullest use of the entire information system and virtually coincided with total business planning. Banks are not ready to take up any sophisticated and systematic methods either for funds management or for costing and budgeting because formal planning habits and skills have not been developed among bank executives and the control system in banks are weak and not geared up to support full - fledged planning exercises. Besides, an exercise on profit planning is not possible in the banking system at present because the information system maintained in the banks is rudimentary. It would be, therefore, considered pragmatic to think in for monitoring profitability in the banking system. We would, therefore, put both balance sheet and profit and loss accounts together.

The literature referred to spells out the areas covered by the existing studies. It brings out clearly that the studies were conducted at macro - level as they are on the working at country or state level. This merely highlights the contours of the problem rather than to present a plan for action. On the other hand, studies at the grass - roots level such as villages where they cater to the needs of their clientle are not considered useful enough because of the researchers' pre - occupation with the current fashion of model building at macro - level, which is largely divorced from the grass - roots realities. Most of the literature reviewed is sponsored by government and conducted on the objectives specified in the appointment of the committee or working group. No attempt has so far been made to grapple with the real problems at the branch level and to calculate the benefits that are actually flow to the rural poor as a result of their lending programmes. This is largely responsible for the dichotomy that exists between the national policy formulations and the objective realities obtaining at the grass - roots level, notwithstanding the declared policy of finding solutions to the problems of the general public at this level. This gap can be bridged only by bringing the realities to bear on the policy formulations at various levels of decision making. Clearly, disaggregate studies drawn from national and state levels to those of bank and branch are necessary to bring out the realities of problems faced by banks and their clientele.

There are many studies at the macro and micro level concerning RRBs at national, state and regional as reviewed above. There are studies on individual banks touching up on branch expansion, deposit mobilisation, loan operations and recovery performance. The existing studies on the specific RRBs just touched upon operational results at the bank level and completely ignored evaluative exercises at branch level. There is no specific study either at the aggregate or bank level on the financial performance, operational efficiency and viability of RRBs. They have virtually not studied in depth either at the aggregate or bank or branch level. Thus, there is an imminent need to wipe out these serious deficiencies in the research based studies on RRBs. Further, most of the Government Committees and the RBI Study Groups conducted evaluative studies at a time when RRBs were in their premature stage. As there are significant changes in the functioning of RRBs, some of the findings of the earlier studies may not hold good for the present. Added to this, even the earlier studies, most of which were conducted by official agencies revealed the great need for undertaking case studies on RRBs and to have a better evaluation of these RRBs taking into consideration their backdrop of working in different agro - climatic and socio - economic environmental conditions. There is no specific research study into the working of the SGB covering the various issues referred to earlier, as far as the knowledge and information of the researcher is concerned. Therefore, there is an urgent need to undertake an evaluative study on the SGB concerning the void referred to in the literature viz., financial viability, operational results etc. after merger.

To conclude, the ample evidence shows that profitability studies made by various bankers, economists and planners have made a number of references to the peculiar situations prevailing in India leading to decline in profitability. Further, most of these studies have been made prior to the reforms made in the banking sector and that too public sector banks. But, during the post - reform era in the banking sector, no intensive study to evaluate the performance of RRBs in general and the SGB in particular is made. Thus, the present study is made exclusively to appraise the financial performance of RRBs in general and the SGB in particular. Moreover, the proposed study makes precious suggestions for the improvement of profitability in the years to come.

4. Present study:

The present study is presented in this section.

4.1. Objective of the study:

The main objective of the present study is to evaluate the financial performance of the SGB. The specific objectives are to: (i) review the progress of the SGB in terms of branch network, deposit mix, credit deployment and recovery performance. (ii) examine the impact of variables on profit; (iii) assess the magnitude and trend in the financial profitability of the SGB; and (iv) evaluate the quantum and trend in the progress of NPAs in the SGB.

4.2. Data collection:

The main source of data used for the study is secondary in character. Basically, the information is collected from books, journals, periodicals, magazines, reports, websites etc. Further, the perceptions of managers on the NPAs are elicited.

4.3. Tools of analysis:

The present study is analysed with the help of accounting and statistical tools. The techniques used for analysis include trend analysis, common - size income statement and ratio analysis. The trend analysis of key indicators of profitability namely, total income, total expenditure, spread, burden and profit is made. Along with the trend analysis, the common size income statement analysis on the basis of the total income and total expenditure is also made. Moreover, the tools of ratio analysis are used to study, broadly, the three profitability ratios viz., spread ratio, burden ratio and profitability ratio. In addition, margin on loan business and the relationship of work fund to income, expenditure are also attempted. In the process of analysis of these ratios, statistical devices are used. Wherever possible and feasible, graphs, charts, diagrams etc. are drawn to illuminate the facts and figures.

4.4. Period of study:

The present study encompasses a ten year period from 2005 to 2014 since the second phase of reformations in the banking sector was introduced during 2006. Thus year 2005 was selected as base year for the study. The year 2014 was chosen as the concluding year of the study period owing to non - availability of latest relevant data afterwards.

4.5. Scope and limitations:

The scope of profitability is very wider and broad - based. But, with a view to achieve the objectives of the study, the present study has been divided into two parts. The first part traces the history and development of RRBs in general in India along with its operating environment and the SGB in particular. It also throws light on the recent issues relating to the banking sector. Moreover, for the theoretical understanding, the concepts of profit and profitability in relation to banking sector have been discussed. The second part deals with the profitability analysis of the SGB. There are inherent limitations. In the present study, during the course of analysis of profitability, the following limitations have been pointed out. The relevant data and information for the study have been collected from the secondary source. Hence, the study carries all the limitations inherent with the secondary data and information. Some of the data and information has been compiled and computed for the purpose of analysis of the study. During the course of compilation, some profitability ratios and percentages are also approximated. Hence, minor variations are bound to take place in the study. Though the qualitative aspect of profitability has its own importance, it has been ignored in the present study. But, only the quantitative financial data have been taken into consideration for the purpose of analysis of data. The statistical devices used for the analysis of the study have their own limitations. Thus, the findings of the preset study should be used rationally and carefully keeping in view the various limitations.

4.6. Plan of the study:

Broadly, the present study has been divided into seven chapters:
Chapter one presents an overview of RRBs in India.

Chapter two deals with the review of existing literature and research design and methodology of the study as described above.

Chapter three provides a profile of the SGB.

The deposit mix, loan operations and recovery performance of the SGB is highlighted in chapter four.

Chapter five examines the phenomenon and significance of profitability, factors influencing profitability, techniques of profitability analysis and the measurement of financial profitability in the SGB.

Sixth chapter evaluates the magnitude and trend in the growth of NPAs in the SGB.

The last chapter presents a summary of earlier chapters in the form of conclusions and suggestions for the improvement of profitability. In addition, hints for further research in future are incorporated.

References:

1. **Reed, E.W.** (1964). *The Commercial Bank Management*, A Harper International Student reprint, 1- 2.

2. **Jha, P.K.** (1982). *'Banking and Economic Growth,'* in **Subramanya K.N. (ed.)** *Modern Banking in India,* Deep and Deep publications, New Delhi, 54- 55.

3. **Ibid,** 55-56.

4. **Angadi, V.B., & Devraj, V. John.** (1983). *"Productivity and Profitability of Banks in India"*, 'Economic and Political Weekly,' 18 (48), 160- 61.

5. **"Cost of Banking Services,"** (1978). *RBI Bulletin,* 244- 45.

6. **RBI.** (1971). *Report of the Study Group on Banking Cost*, Banking Commission, Government of India, Bombay, 164- 65.

7. **IBA Bulletin.** (2003) *Special Issues*, Mumbai, 32 - 33.

8. **RBI.** *Report of the Expert Group on Simplification of Forms and Procedures to be adopted by RRB's,* Bombay, 1975; RBI, *Report of the Working Group on Simplification of Operational and Accounting Procedures,* Bombay, 1976; Government of India, *Report of the Working Group on Simplification of Application Form and Lending Procedures,* New Delhi; Ministry of Finance, 1978; RBI, *Report of the Working Group on Multi - Agency Approach in Agricultural Finance,* Bombay, 1978; and RBI, *Report of the Committee on Control Over Branches of RRB's*, Bombay. 1981.

9. **RBI.** (1978). *Report on Review Committee on RRBs*, Bombay.

10. **RBI.** (1981). *Report of the Committee to Review Arrangements for Institutional Credit for Agricultural and Rural Development*, Bombay.

11. **Agricultural Finance Corporation.** (1981). *A Study of Two RRBs*, Bombay.

12. **RBI.** (1981). *Liability of RRBs: A Study*, Bombay, Rural Planning and Credit Cell.

13. **Government of India.** (1986). *Report of the Working Group on RRBs*, Ministry of Finance.

14. **RBI.** (1990). *A Review of Agricultural Credit System in India*, Bombay.

15. **Divatia, V.V., & Venkatachalam T.R.,** (1978). *"Operational Efficiency and Profitability in Public Sector Banks,"* Reserve Bank of India Staff Papers, 3 (1), 1- 16.

16. **Soudamani Nagar.** (1979). *Regional Rural Banks: Rajasthan Experience*, Eastern Economist, 72 (24), 81- 83.

17. **Wadhva**, **C.D.** (1980). *Rural Banks for Rural Development*, Delhi, Macmillan.

18. **Patel, K.V., & Shete, N.B.** (1980). *"RRB's: Performance and prospects"*, Prajnan, 9 (1), 1- 40.

19. **Mohana Rao, L.K.** (1980). "*Impact of Programmes on Target Groups-Case Study of Regional Rural Banks*", Indian Journal of Agricultural Economics, 25 (4), 73- 77.

20. **Inu Jain**, (1980). *"Rural Credit and Regional Rural Banks"* Khadi Gramodhyog, 28 (3), 3- 5.

21. **Reddy G. R., & Suresh Kumar, D.V.** (1982) *"Regional Rural Banks and the Weaker Sections Uplift"*, Land Bank Journal, 20 (3), 73-75

22. **Panandikar, V.A.** (1982). "Regional Rural Banks", *The Economic Times*, 26th, 9- 10.

23. **Varde V.S., & Singh, S.P.,** (1982). *"Profitability Performance of RRB's"*, Prajnan, 11 (4), 247- 56.

24. **Varghese, S.K.** (1983). *"Profit and Profitability of Indian Commercial Banks in 1970's,"* Economic and Political Weekly, 7 (2), 145 - 57.

25. **Hossain, M.** (1984). *"Credit for the Rural Poor-The Grameena Bank in Bangladesh,"* Bangladesh Institute of Development Studies, (4), 43-48.

26. **Abdul Noorbasha., & Dakshina Murthy, D.** (1984). *Sulthan Chand Publishers,* 43-47.

27. **Lakshmi Narayana,V.** (1984). *"Regional Rural Banks-Problems and Prospects A Case Study,"* Financing Agriculture, 14 (2), 54-56.

28. **Singh P.K., & Upadhya, K.M.** (1984). "A Study of loan recovery of Regional Rural Banks in Bihar", Finacing Agriculture, 16 (2).

29. **Jagadish Prasad., & Sunil Kumar.,** (1985). *"Regional Rural Banks: A Study"* Kurukshetra, 33 (8), 31- 33.

30. **Prasad, B.V.S.** (1985). *"Credit and Rural bank: A Case Study,"* published M.Phil, Dissertation submitted to S.V.University, Tirupathi, 89- 91.

31. **Nagi Reddy and Ratna Kumar.** (1986). *"Credit Repayment Performance of Borrowers of Regional Rural Banks: A Case Study",* Southern Economist, 15- 17.

32. **Balishter et. al.** (1986). *"Performance of Regional Rural Banks, An evaluation of a Rural Bank in Agra District of Uttar Pradesh,"* Yojana, (9), 31-38.

33. **Varsha S. Vardhe & Singh,S.P.** (1980). *"Towards an Analytical Framework for Profit Management in Banks,"* Prajnan, 16 (3), 1069-70; and **Varsha S. Vardhe and Singh, S.P.** (1986). *"Approaches to planning in banks,"* BEM, 6 (3), 32- 33.

34. **Deshpande, D.D.** (1986). *"Bank Profitability Analysis",* BEM, 5 (3), 151- 55.

35. **Angadi V.B., & John Devraj, V.,** (1986). *"Policy Constraints and Banks Profitability",* Economic and Political weekly, 21 (24), 1081-84.

36. **Venugopal. D., & Somaskanden, V.,** (1986). *"Profitability of Nationalised Banks",* BEM, 5 (3), 101- 11.

37. **Gupta, M., & Goswami, S.,** (1986). *"Profitability and Profit Planning in Banks",* BEM, 5 (1), 92- 100.

38. **Government of India.** (1986). *Report of the Working Group on Regional Rural Banks,* New Delhi.

39. **Rehman. A.** (1986). *"Impact of Grameena Bank Intervention on the Rural power Structure",* Bangladesh Institute of Development Studies, 6 (61), 76- 79.

40. **Rehman, A.** (1987). *"Alleviation of Rural Poverty: Replicability of Grameen Bank Model,"* Grameena Bank Evaluation Project, Agriculture and Rural Development Studies, Economic and Political Weekly, 7, 29- 34.

41. **Singh, S. (1987***). "Profitability of Commercial Banks in India,"* Punjab National Bank Monthly Review, 11 (11), 20- 25.

42. **Singh, R. P.** (1988). *"Disbursement, overdues and factors Affecting Repayment Capacity of Barrowers,"* Indian Journal of Agricultural Economics, 43 (3), 37- 39.

43. **Naidu, L.K.** (1988). *"Bank Finance for Rural Artisans,"* Ashish Publishing Housing. Institute.

44. **Ramakrishnan, K.R.** (1988). *"Problems and Prospects of Regional Rural Banks"* The Banker, (43), 34- 36.

45. **Sahana Gosh.** (1988). *"Losses no justification for Removal",* Business Standard, (54), 5- 6.

46. **Rao, P.S.M**. (1988). *"Inherent Weaknesses of Regional Rural Banks",* The Hindu, Supplement, p.1.

47. **Reserve Bank of India.** (1988). *Rural Credit Planning Cell*, 67- 69.

48. **Parmar. G.D. et al.** (1988). *"Performance of Banaskantha- Mehsana Grameena Bank in Gujarat State,"* Agricultural Banker, 2 (3), 23- 25.

49. **Naidu, L.K., & Naidu, M.C.,** (1988). *Financing of Rural artisans by Regional Rural Banks-A Case Study of Rayalaseema Grameena Bank in Cuddapah District in Bank Finance For Rural Artisans* (Ed), Ashish Publishing House, 56- 58.

50. **Shete, N.B., & Karkal, G. L.,** (1989). *"Regional Rural Banks: Problems and Perspectives of Rural Credit",* Prajnan, 18(2), 131- 34.

51. **Dhabbal, A., & Bhattacharya, K.** (1989). *"Poor Recovery of Institutional Loans: An Analysis of its causes"* Indian Journal of Economics, 69 (274), 307- 10.

52. **Moin Quazi.** (1989). *"Banking and Rural Development",* Financial Express, 6-7.

53. **Hebber, A.R.K.** (1989). *"Grameena Banks - Viability No Criterion,"* The Economic Times, 5I- 52.

54. **Garg, S.** (1989). *Indian Banking: Cost and Profitability*, Annual Publications.

55. **Jain, M.K.** (1989). *Rural Banks and Rural Poor*, Printwell Publishers.

56. **Anand S.C., & Jagat Ram.,** (1989). *Handbook on RRBs*, Vision Books.

57. **Bapna, M.S.** (1989), *RRBs in Rajasthan*, Delhi, Himalaya Publishing House.

58. **Kalkundrikar, A.B.** (1990). *RRBs and Economic Development,* Delhi, Daya Publishing House.

59. **Krishnan, C.** (1990). *"Regional Rural Banks and Rural Development",* Yojana, 33 (24), 32- 34.

60. **Shete, N.B.** (1990). *"Regional Rural Banks- An Analysis,"* National Bank News Review, 6 (7), 32- 44.

61. **Velayudhan, T.K.** (1990). *"Regional Rural Banks and Rural Credit- Some Issues,"* Economic and Political Weekly, 20 (38), 157- 59.

62. **Reserve Bank of India** (1990). *Report of the Agricultural Credit Review Committee* (A Review of the Agricultural Credit System in India), New Delhi, 43-44.

63. **Balishter et.al**. (1990). *"Role of Regional Rural Banks in up-liftment of Weaker Sections-A study in Agra District of Uttar Pradesh,"* Agricultural Situation in India, New Delhi, 45 (5), 345- 49.

64. **Chauhan et.al, B.R.S.** (1991) *"Income and Savings of the Weaker Sections consequent upon Financing by Regional Rural Banks in Etwah District of Uttar Pradesh,"* Agricultural Situation in India, 45 (11), 761- 65

65. **Panda, J., & Lal, G.S.** (1991). *"A Critical Appraisal on the Profitability of Commercial Banks,"* Indian Journal of Banking and Finances, 5 (6), 12- 15.

66. **Reserve Bank of India.** (1992). *Report of the working Group on Regional Rural Banks* (Kelkar Committee), New Delhi, 24- 26.

67. **Kallu Rao, P., & Shaji Tomas,** (1992). *"Performance of the Manipur Rural Bank - An analytical Study"* Journal of Rural Development, 11 (4), 443- 59.

68. **Mishra, A.N.** (1992), *"Analysis of Profitability of Commercial Banks",* Indian Journal of Banking and Finance, 5 (3), 6- 11.

69. **Sadare, A.M.** (1992), *"Profitability in Banks",* Pigmy Economic Review, 37 (9), 20- 25.

70. **Chandra, M.** (1992), *"On Increasing Proftability of Public Sector Banks – A Note,"* Pigmy Economic Review, 38 (2), 31- 40.

71. **Kumar Raj.** (1993*). "Growth and Performance of RRBs in Haryana"* Anmol Publications.

72. **Toor, N.S.** (1993). *"Banking Business Mix and Profitability; Recent Trends in Nationalised Banks",* Punjab National Bank Monthly Review, 15 (2), 10-25.

73. **Amandeep,** (1993). *Profits and Profitability in Commercial Banks,* Deep and Deep Publication.

74. **Panandikar, V.A.** (1995). *"Regional Rural Banks",* The Economic Times, 26, 9-10.

75. **Varde Vasha Singh, S., & Sampat, P.** (1995). *"Profitability and performance of Regional Rural Banks"* Prajnan, 11 (4), 97- 98

76. **Reddy, B. R., Sakunthala, B., & Reddy, S. V.,** (1998). *"Growth and Performance of Regional Rural Banks in India,"* The Indian Journal of Commerce, 31 (2), 71-76.

77. **Satyanarayana, S., & Rafthunnisa, S.,** (2000). *"Financing of Indian Agriculture: Some Issues",* The Indian Journal of Commerce, 53 (3), 48- 53.

78. **Bapanna, M.S.** (2001). *"Regional Rural Banks in Rajasthan",* Himalaya Publishing House, 32- 35.

79. **Adbul Noorbasha., & Jyothi, M.,** (2001). *"Viablity of Regional Rural Banks- A Case Study,"* Yojana, 33, 18- 20.

80. **Swaminathan, Ramachandran, V.K., & Madhura.,** (2002), *"Rural Banking and Landless Labour Households, Institutional Reform and Rural Credit Markets in India,"* Journal of Agrarian Change, 2 (4), 502- 44.

81. **Dey, N.B., & Adhikari, K.,** (2004). *"Performance of Regional Rural Bank in Barak Valley of Assam: An Analytical Study",* Kangleipak Business Review, 3 (1), 120- 25.

82. **Golait, R.** (2007). *Current Issues in Agriculture Credit in India: An Assessment*, Reserve Bank of India.

83. **Narasaiah., & Ramudu, R.,** (2008). "Financing of Agriculture by Regional Rural Banks", Sonali Publications.

84. **Dilip Khankhoje., & Dr. Milind Sathye.,** (2008). *"Efficiency of Rural Banks: The Case of India",* International Business Research-CCSE, 1 (2).

85. **Agarwal, B., & Kumar, H.,** (2009). *Regional Rural Banks as Catalyst of Rural Development in India.* In: **Agarwal, ed., M,** *Regional Rural Banks (RRBs) in India,* New Century Publication.

86. **Syed Ibrahim,** (2010), *"Performance Evaluation of Regional Rural Banks in India",* International Business Research - CCSE, 3 (4).

87. **Ibrahim, M.** (2011). *"Role of Indian Regional Rural Banks (RRBs) in the Priority Sector Lending- An Analysis,"* International Journal of Management and Technology, 1 (1), 85- 97.

88. **James, V.** (1978). *"Bank Profitability with Regard to USA,"* in Banker in Banking.

89. **Holberton, R.M.** (1964). *"Profit Planning and Considerations in Pricing Banking Services",* Bankers monthly Magazine, **Spring, Pallian D.L., & Shirk, S.E.** (1964) in *Cost Accounting and Banking Profits*, Management Control.

90. **Ellis, C.C.** (1990). four articles in *Profit Planning of Banks with Regard to USA* in Bankers Monthly Magazine and *Successful Profit Planning for Banks,* Bank Administration **Kalkundrickars, A.B**. *Regional Rural Banks and Economic Development,* Daya Publishing House.

CHAPTER – III

PROFILE OF SAPTAGIRI GRAMEENA BANK

The profile of the Saptagiri Grameena Bank (SGB) is given in this chapter. The SGB formerly known as Sri Venkateswara Grameena Bank (SVGB) has grown in length and breadth over its long standing of over 30 years. It has appreciably mopped up the rural savings apart from borrowings and pumped them into desirable channels. The issues highlighted include genesis of the bank, operational area, objectives, functions, management, organisation, staff, branch expansion, share capital, reserves and surplus, borrowings and investment. This chapter serves as a backdrop for evaluating the financial performance of the bank.

1. Genesis:

The SVGB was established at Chittoor on 22.03.1981. It was sponsored by the Indian Bank, the lead bank of Chittoor district. The Kanaka Durga Grameena Bank (KDGB) with its head quarters at Gudivada was merged with the SVGB to form the SGB on 01.07.2006. The operational area of the former was Krishna district. It was also sponsored by the Indian Bank.

2. Operational area:

The operational area of the SGB is spread over Chittoor and Krishna districts in Andhra Pradesh (A.P). Chittoor district is located on the southern part of the state. Chittoor is the district headquarters. The district covers an extent of 15,359 sq.kms. The district is divided into three revenue divisions such as Chittoor, Madanapalli and Tirupati. There are 65 mandals in the district. It is bounded by Ananthapur district on the northwest, Kadapa district on the north, Nellore district on the northeast, Vellore and Tiruvellore districts of Tamilnadu on the south and Karnataka state on the southeast. Chittoor is on the bank of Ponnai River at the southernmost part of A.P. The city is strategically located at the junction of Bangalore - Chennai National Highway NH 4 and NH 18. The district has an area of 15,359 sq.kms. and a population of 37, 45, 875, of which 21.65 per cent is urban. Density of population is 214 per km. The literacy rate is 90.60 per cent. The district lies at the extreme south of A.P. approximately between $12^0 37^1$ - 14^0 8^1 north latitudes and $78^0 3^1$ - $79^0 55^1$ east longitudes. Thirty per cent of total geographical area is covered by forests.

Chittoor is surrounded by mango and tamarind groves. Cattle are raised in the district. Out of the total soil, red loomy constitutes 57 per cent, red sandy 34 per cent and the remaining black clay, black loamy, black sandy and red clay. The important rivers in the district are Ponnai and Swarnamukhi, which originate in Eastern Ghats. Other rivers include Kusasthali, Beema, Bahuda, Pincha, Kalyani, Araniyar and Pedderu. None of the rivers is perennial. The district is divided into 3 revenue divisions viz.,

Chittoor, Madanapalle and Tirupati and 66 Mandals. There are 14 assembly constituencies in the district.

Krishna district is located in the east coast of the state. The geographical area of the district is 8,727 sq. kms. Machlipatnam is the district headquarters. The district is divided into 4 revenue divisions viz., Gudivada, Machilipatnam, Nuziveedu and Vijayawada. There are 50 mandals in the district. It has a population of 41, 87, 841. Of which, 32.08 per cent is urban and the rest rural. Vijayawada is the commercial center of the district. The district is bounded by Khammam district on the north - west, West Godavari district on the north – east, the Bay of Bengal on the south – east, Guntur district on the south - west and Nalgonda district on the west.

The chief rivers in the district are Krishna, Muniyeru, Tammileru and Budameru. Krishna River debouches into the Bay of Bengal at Hamsala Divi and Nachugunta. The district contains small hill streams viz., Jayanthi, Kattaleru, Ippalavagu, Upputeru, Telleru, Ballaleru and Nadimeyeru. The district has no worth mentioning forests. A type of lightwood known as "Ponuku" is found on the Kondapalli hills. The wood is used for the manufacture of well-known Kondapalli toys.

The district is divided into upland and coastal areas. Kolleru Lake, one of the India's most ecologically significant wetlands, lies partly within the district. The main hill range of the district known as Kondapalli runs between Nandigama and Vijayawada with a length of 24 kms. The other important hills are Jammalavoidurgam, Mogalrajapuram and Indrakiladri hills. The famous Kanakadurga temple stands on the Indrakiladri hills at Vijayawada. There are three types of soils. The black cotton forms 57.60 per cent, sand clay loams 22.30 per cent and red loams 20.10 per cent.

Natural gas and crude oil is extensively found offshore on the coastal belt. Small deposits of diamond are available. Limestone is a major mineral extracted in the district. Sand quarrying for construction is extracted from Krishna and Munneru rivers. The climatic conditions are extreme nature with hot summers and cold winters. They may be classified as tropical.

3. Objectives:

The main objective behind the establishment of the SGB could be summarised as under: (i) to develop the rural economy by providing resources for the development of agriculture, trade, commerce, industry and other productive activities in the rural areas, credit and other facilities particularly to small and marginal farmers, agricultural labourers, rural artisans and small entrepreneurs and for matters connected therewith and incidental thereto; (ii) to take the banking to the doorstep of rural areas particularly to hitherto unbanked rural areas; (iii) to make available institutional credit to weaker sections of the society who had far little or no access to cheap institutional loans and had been depending on private moneylenders; (iv) to mobilise rural savings and channelise them for supporting productive activities in rural areas; (v) to create a supplementary channel for flow of credit from central money market to rural areas and refinance; (vi) to create employment opportunities in rural areas; and (vii) to bring down the cost of purveying credit to rural areas.

4. Functions:

One of the main reasons for the backwardness of rural India is indebtedness of farmers. There is a well-known saying, which is true in our country. "The Indian rural people particularly Indian farmer is born in debt; lives in debt; and dies in debt." The rural people depend on non - institutional sources of credit such as landlords, moneylenders, traders, commission agents and relatives. They exploit them in several ways by levying high rates of interest. As a result, farmers are unable to pay their debt. The debt of farmers increases. This is collectively known as "rural indebtedness". This could only be avoided by providing institutional credit. However, it is noticed that the commercial banks extend benefits mostly to the richer sections in the rural society. Moreover, the savings mobilised from the rural areas have flown into urban and metropolitan areas and have not met the needs of weaker sections of rural community. To overcome these, state – sponsored, region based and rural – sponsored and region based and rural – oriented commercial banks called "Regional Rural Banks (RRBs)" which are popularly called as "Poor man's bank" and "Small Banks of Small Men" came during 1975. RRBs basically perform all the banking functions. It is desirable to perform certain non - banking functions such as constructing and maintaining godowns, supply of agricultural inputs, lease out agricultural and other equipment, provide marketing assistance etc.

The SGB primarily covers small and marginal farmers, landless labourers, rural artisans, small traders and other weaker sections of rural society. It meets the credit needs and to a limited extent sanctions consumption loans. The main function of the SGB is to provide credit and banking facility to the rural people. It also extends non - banking facility to the rural population. The main functions include to: (i) mobilise local savings by means of various types of deposits; (ii) implement programmes for the supervised credit tailored to the needs of individual farmers; (iii) provide short and medium - term credit for agriculture and other purposes to rural producers and long - term loans to agriculturists as agent of land development bank; (iv) undertake various ancillary banking services to local people such as remittance of funds, acceptance of insurance premium, safe deposit lockers etc; (v) set up and maintain godowns; (vi) undertake supply of inputs and agricultural and retail equipment to farmers as agents and in appropriate cases equipment leasing; (vii) extend assistance in the marketing of agricultural and other products through marketing institutions; and (viii) help in the overall development of villagers in the operational area. Thus, the SGB should cater to the credit needs of medium and small cultivators fully in the rural Chittoor and Krishna districts.

5. Management:

The management of the SGB is vested in the Board of Directors, consisting of nine Directors including the Chairman. Of these, two each are nominees of the government of India, government of A.P. and the Indian Bank, one each of the Reserve Bank of India (RBI) and the National Bank for Agriculture and Rural Development (NABARD). The Chairman is the chief executive of the bank. The supervision and monitoring is in the hands of the NABARD and the regulatory functions are looked after by the RBI. Inspection is undertaken by the NABARD instead of the RBI. Apart from this, regular inspections are undertaken by the Indian Bank. Policy – decisions relating to organisational matters and loaning operations are in the hands of the Steering Committee of RRBs and in many cases in consultation with the Government of India.

The Board of Directors is the supreme authority in the SGB with regard to general superintendence, direction and management of affairs. The central government has the power to increase the number of members of the Board up to a maximum of 15 and also prescribe the manner in which the additional number is filled in. The Central government appoints the Chairman of the Board for a maximum period of 5 years and the Chairman holds the office during the pleasure of Central government. A person is eligible for reappointment as the Chairman. Chairman is a full time officer of the bank and is responsible for managing the affairs of the SGB subject to the superintendence, control and direction of the Board of Directors. This body is vested with general superintendence, direction and management of affairs and business of the SGB[1].

It is specifically laid down in the Ordinance that in discharging its function, "the Board should act on business principles and should have due regard to public interest". Further, the SGB discharges such functions as directed with regard to matters of policy involving public interest as the Central Government may give, after consultation with the RBI. The Sponsor Bank, Indian Bank assists the SGB in the initial years of its functioning by deputing its officers and other employees to it for managing its day to day business activities[2].

6. Organisation:

Organisation is of immense important to a banking institution as it is to any other business organisation. "Organisation implies structuring and integrating activities of a group of people performing different functions for achieving specific objectives of the enterprise"[3]. The employee performs the task with the help of others and distribute it. Then with the aid and assistance of others, he achieves the objectives. But in this process, if he is to avoid and choose, he must define the respective responsibilities and duties of his subordinates, assign them powers and know their limitations and must also explain them that to whom they are answerable. Thus, the term organisation may be said to refer to a system or structure that enables people to work together and effectively. In any such structure, there are three basic elements, namely, division of labour, source of authority and relationship between various components[4].

An organisational structure of the SGB is shown in **Figure 3.1**. There may be variations depending on staff strength, volume of business, area of coverage, number of branches, local priorities etc. The Chairman is the chief executive of the bank. Board of Directors is the top management authority in the SGB. The Chairman is assisted by a General Manager / Administrative Officer. Various functional departments at Head office are headed by the officer of the rank of senior manager. To facilitate effective control of Head office on the branches, separate area offices were established. These are manned by Area Managers, who are equivalent to senior managers in Head office. An Area Office looks after 25 - 35 branches. Branches are headed by

Fig 3.1: <u>Organisational Structure of SGB</u>:

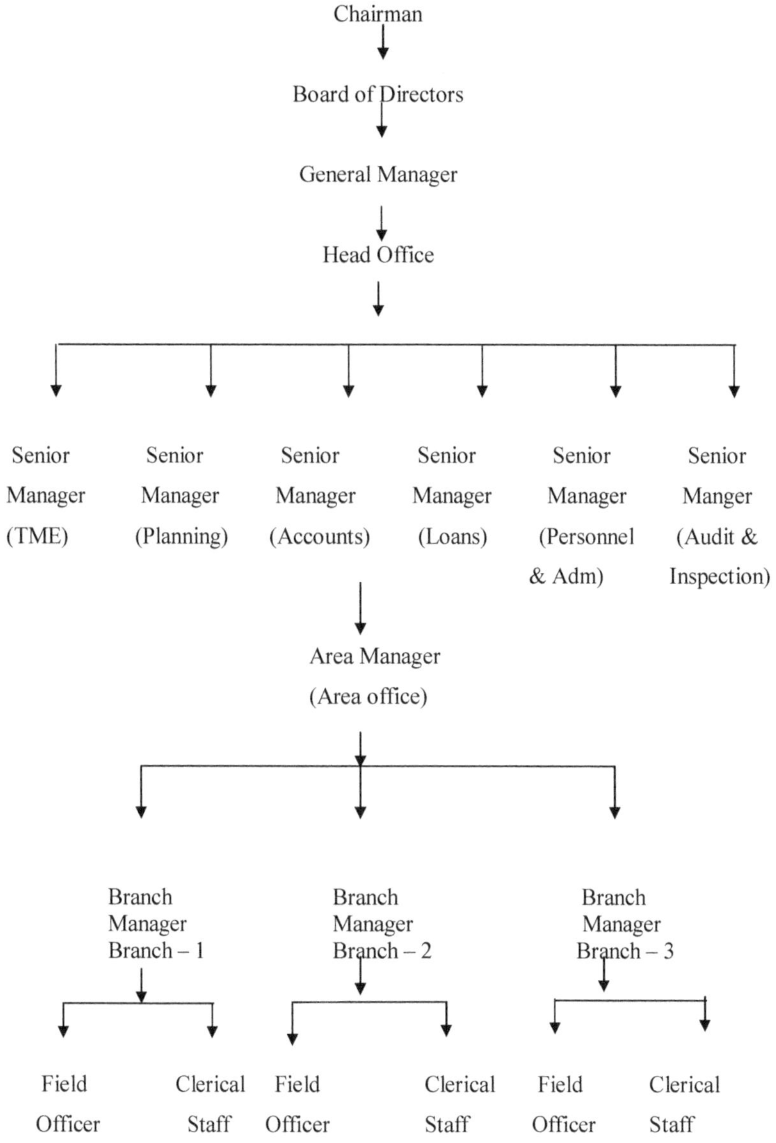

Chairman

↓

Board of Directors

↓

General Manager

↓

Head Office

↓

| Senior Manager (TME) | Senior Manager (Planning) | Senior Manager (Accounts) | Senior Manager (Loans) | Senior Manager (Personnel & Adm) | Senior Manger (Audit & Inspection) |

↓

Area Manager
(Area office)

↓

| Branch Manager Branch – 1 | Branch Manager Branch – 2 | Branch Manager Branch – 3 |

| Field Officer | Clerical Staff | Field Officer | Clerical Staff | Field Officer | Clerical Staff |

Source: Field survey.

Branch Managers, who in turn are assisted by Field Officers and 2 - 3 clerks in large branches.

7. Staff:

The effective functioning of any institution will definitely be influenced by the attitude of the staff who mans the institute. The right attitude of the staff would certainly boost its image. This is valid in the case of the SGB, in which the staff plays an important role in extending the benefit of rural banking to the poorest of the rural poor. Initially, the bank has depended on the sponsor bank for personnel requirements. Subsequently, it recruited its own staff. The organisational hierarchy of the SGBs consists of the Chairman, General Manager, Development Manager, Inspectors, Section Officers, Branch Managers, Technical and Ministerial Staff. The Branch Managers are in - charge of branches and discharge functions in accordance with the directions / instructions from the Head Office. However, discretionary powers with regard to purchase beyond the prescribed amount and maintenance of minimum cash balance are vested with Branch Managers. They are expected to exercise discretions very judiciously.

The details of staff in the SGB during 2005 - 14are furnished in the **Table 3.1.** The officers were 257 in 2005 as compared to 393 in 2014. There were 75 office assistants in 2005 as against 236 in 2014. This is so because the number of office assistants increased due to rise in the number of branches and volume of business in the Head Office. There is almost an increasing trend in it. The office attendants were 186 in 2005 which come down to 47 in 2014. When all the categories of employees are put together, the staff was 518 in 2005 whilst it was 676 in 2014. In the meanwhile, there are variations. On an average, per year, officers, office assistants and office attendants stood at 301.5, 148.6 and 116.7 during the period. It may be

Table 3.1: Staff Pattern in SGB during 2005 - 14

Year	Officers	Office Assistants	Office Attendants	Total
2005	257	75	186	518
2006	253	75	183	511
2007	259	108	148	515
2008	258	114	133	505
2009	265	134	123	522
2010	302	165	122	589
2011	327	150	102	579
2012	332	237	73	642
2013	369	192	47	608
2014	393	236	47	676
Average	301.50	148.60	116.70	566.80

Source: Collected from the relevant Annual Report of the SGB, Chittoor.

concluded that the employee strength had gone up due to branch expansion, volume of business etc., Further, among the staff, officers rank first throughout the period without any exception.

8. Branch expansion:

Branch expansion became essential to meet the financial requirements of the people in the rural areas. These are underbanked and unbanked areas.

The policy of branch expansion was mainly based on spatial gaps, potentialities, viability and licensing policy of the RBI / NABARD. Mainly, branches are necessary to provide banking facilities to the people at proper places and at the right time. At present, the most effective way to make the farmers bank minded is to spread branches to the nook and corner of the country. Hence, one of the important indicators of highlighting the role of banks is the extent of branch network. One of the objectives underlying the SGBs scheme is that credit should be extended to remote rural areas, particularly to unbaked and underbanked centres by establishing branches. This calls for a wide network of branches spread over the area of operation. The SGB was started with a branch at Chittoor on 22.03.1981 and has opened 6 branches in the same year. The **Table 3.2** shows branch expansion in the SGB during 2005 - 14. The number of branches were 75 during 2005. No branch was opened till 2006.

During 2007, in terms of decision to amalgamate RRBs sponsored by the same bank in the state, Government of India notified the formation of the SGB by amalgamating the KDGB with the SVGB. After amalgamation, the number of branches stood at 103 since 28 were transferred from the KDGB. Seventy five branches are located in Chittoor district and 28 branches in Krishna district. Out of the branches, three are extension counters and four satellite branches. It can be observed that six branches were established in 2013 and the number of branches was 157. In the following year, six branches were opened. Thus the number of branches stood at 163 at the end of 2014. It may be concluded that the branch expansion programme in the SGB is slow in the beginning, absent in the middle and faster at the end. This

Table 3.2: Branch Expansion in SGB during 2005 - 14

Year	No. of branches opened / transferred during the year	Total no. of branches
2005	-	75
2006	-	75
2007	28*	103
2008	6	109
2009	18	127
2010	4	131
2011	13	144
2012	7	151
2013	6	157
2014	6	163

Note : * Transferred from the erstwhile Kanaka Durga Grameena Bank.

Source: Relevant Annual Reports of SGB, Chittoor.

is the result of policy and uncertainity about the continuation of the SVGB and the KDGB.

The location – wise classification of branches of the SGB is furnished in the **Table 3.3.** Of the total branches, rural branches are 58, semi - urban 11 and urban 6 during 2005. There was no change in the number of urban, semi - urban and rural branches as no branch was started during 2006. With the merger of the KDGB with the SVGB, the rural, semi - urban and urban branches stood at 78, 15 and 10 respectively. In the next year, six branches were opened in the rural areas. Thus rural branches stood at 84 during 2008. No branch was started in semi - urban and urban locations in the same year.

Table 3.3 Location- wise Classification of Branches of SGB during 2005 - 14

Year	Rural	Semi - urban	Urban	Total
2005	58	11	6	75
2006	58	11	6	75
2007	78	15	10	103
2008	84	15	10	109
2009	86	26	15	127
2010	88	28	15	131
2011	99	30	15	144
2012	103	36	12	151
2013	107	38	12	157
2014	111	40	12	163

Source: As in Table 3.1

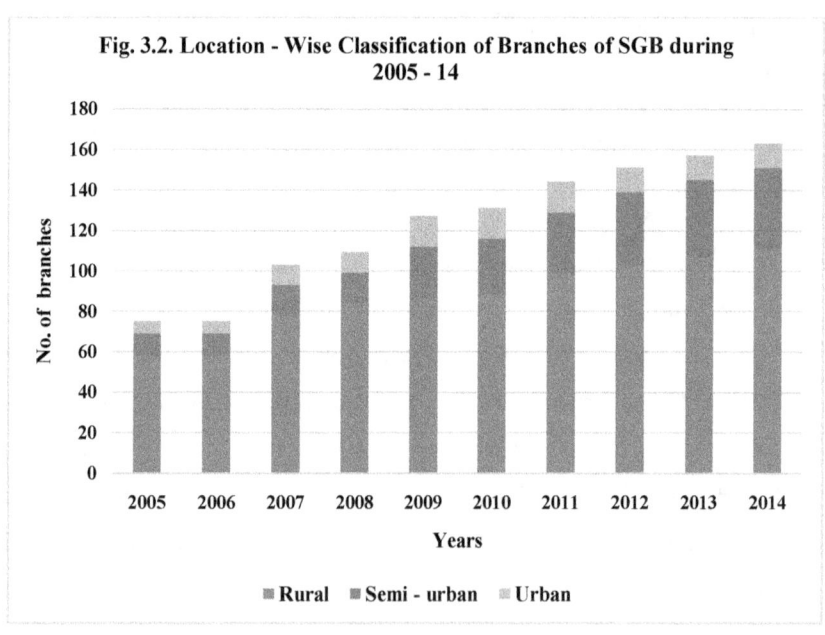

Fig. 3.2. Location - Wise Classification of Branches of SGB during 2005 - 14

Source: Table 3.3

During 2014, the rural, semi - urban and urban branches stood at 111, 40 and 12 respectively. It may be concluded that a little over 77 per cent of branches were located in rural areas, 14 per cent in semi - urban locations and the rest in urban areas. These are shown in **Figure 3.2**. The bank has accorded priority for establishing branches in rural unbanked and underbanked centres. This is in tune with the declared policy of the government.

9. Resources:

The resources of the SGB are described in the following pages. The resources are its own funds, deposits mobilised from public and borrowings from sponsored bank, the NABARD, other institutions and banks. The mobilisation of deposits is discussed in the following chapter.

9.1 Own funds:

Share capital forms an integral part of owned funds. It is the base for the volume of business and guiding principle to borrow funds. The share capital is the cost free fund, which acts as a cushion in its operations and helps in achieving viability. It amounts to a small fraction of total deposits and borrowings of a bank. In terms of section 5 of RRBs Act 1976, the authorised capital of the SGB is Rs. 500 lakhs divided into 5 lakhs fully paid up shares of Rs. 100/- each. This was contributed by government of India, Indian Bank and government of A.P. in the ratio of 50: 35: 15 respectively. The share capital of the SGB was Rs. 100 lakhs during 2005 as against Rs. 200 lakhs during 2014 (see **Table 3.4**). There is no increase in share capital during 2005 and 2006. It has gone up to Rs.200 lakhs in 2007 and remained as such till 2014. Its share in the total owned fund was 3.60 per cent in 2005 as compared to 0.76 per cent in 2014. In the meantime, there are fluctuations. Its proportion has decreased due to increase in the other elements of owned fund. The share capital deposit was Rs. 1,462.29 lakhs in 2005 as against Rs 1,577.05 lakhs in 2014. In percentage terms, the former

Table 3.4 Owned funds of SGB during 2005 - 14

(Rs. lakhs)

Year	Share capital	Share capital deposit	Reserves and surplus	Total
2005	100.00 (3.60)	1,462.29 (52.69)	1,213.22 (43.71)	2,775.51 (100)
2006	100.00 (3.06)	1,462.29 (44.78)	1,702.92 (52.16)	3,265.21 (100)
2007	200.00 (3.07)	1,577.05 (24.18)	4,744.85 (72.75)	6,521.90 (100)
2008	200.00 (2.70)	1,577.05 (21.25)	5,643.24 (76.05)	7,420.29 (100)
2009	200 (2.37)	1,577.05 (18.66)	6,674.69 (78.97)	8,451.74 (100)
2010	200 (1.95)	1,577.05 (15.41)	8,456.46 (82.64)	10,233.51 (100)
2011	200 (1.55)	1,577.05 (12.24)	11,109.18 (86.21)	12,886.23 (100)
2012	200 (1.20)	1,577.05 (9.44)	14,921.31 (89.36)	16,698.36 (100)
2013	200 (0.93)	1,577.05 (7.33)	19,729.07 (91.74)	21,506.12 (100)
2014	200 (0.76)	1,577.05 (5.99)	24,571.32 (93.25)	26,348.37 (100)

Note : Figures in brackets indicate the percentage total.

Source: As in Table 3.1

and latter formed 52.69 and 5.99 sequentially. There is a gradual decrease in its account. This is due to increase in the proportion of reserves and surplus. Another source of owned funds for the SGB is the creation of reserves and surplus. This depends on the adequacy of net profits earned. A strong reserve base reflects the financial stability of the bank and reposes confidence among the members. Reserves facilitate the bank write off bad debts and to meet unforeseen contingencies. The reserves and surplus has gradually gone up from Rs. 1,213.22 lakhs in 2005 to Rs. 24,571.32 lakhs in 2014. In relative terms, it has progressively increased from 43.71 per cent to 93.26 per cent in the aforesaid period. It may be noted that the proportion of reserves and surplus was less during 2005. Afterwards, it has risen to register the highest at the end of 2014. The total owned funds were Rs. 2,775.51 lakhs in 2005. It has progressively increased to reach the highest at Rs. 26,348.37 lakhs during 2014. There is no decline in any one of the years.

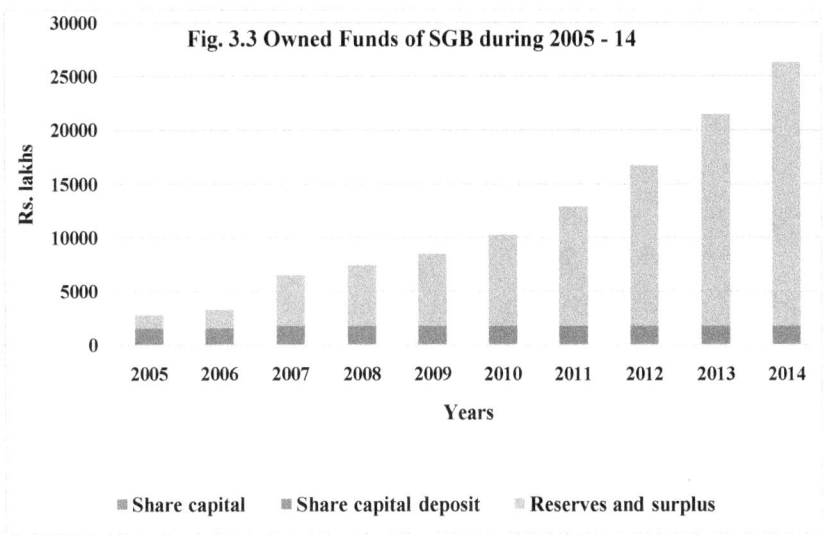

Source: Table 3.4

95

The funds are depicted in **Figure 3.3.** It may be concluded that the share capital is almost static in the period. The share capital deposit has remarkably declined as against an increase in reserves and surplus. The total owned fund has gone up nearly five times in the period under reference. Thus the bank has recorded a spectacular progress in the matter of mobilising own resources on the principle of survival of the fittest.

9.2 Borrowings:

Borrowings and refinance are important sources of finance for the SGB in view of small capital base and inadequate deposit mobilisation and reserves and surplus. Borrowings and refinance are obtained from the NABARD, the Indian Bank and the Industrial Development Bank of India (IDBI). The bank avails refinance from the NABARD under schematic lending, automatic pattern and general line of credit. The Indian Bank provides refinance to the extent of eligible advances apart from differential rate of interest (DRI) scheme. The SGB has borrowed Rs. 9,341.05 lakhs in 2005 as against Rs. 101,204.03 lakhs in 2014 (**see Table 3.5**). There is a gradual growth in borrowings except 2014. Of the sources of borrowing, Indian bank, the sponsored bank of the SGB has made available funds to a tune of Rs. 29.59 lakhs in 2005 as against Rs. 8,927.92 lakhs during 2014. There are violent fluctuations in the contribution of sponsored bank to the SGB. In the total funds borrowed by the SGB, the share of sponsored bank was less than 1 per cent in four years. It was negligible in 2008 and 2013. In the remaining years, the proportion was in the order of 6.27 – 8.11 per cent. The NABARD has provided Rs. 9,341.05 lakhs in 2005 as compared to Rs. 101,204.03 lakhs during 2014. The borrowed funds are depicted in **Figure 3.4.** It may be summed up that the borrowings of the bank have almost progressively increased many times in the period. Further, contribution of the NABARD has increased more than 11 times in 2014 over 2005. On the

Table 3.5 Details of Borrowed Funds of SGB during 2005 - 14 (Rs. lakhs)

Year (1)	Sponsored bank (2)	NABARD (3)	Total (4)	% of col. (2) to col. (4) (5)
2005	29.59	9,341.05	9,470.64	0.32
2006	2.00	13,502.26	13,504.26	0.01
2007	1,802.37	21,546.75	23,349.12	7.72
2008	0.01	32,485.74	32,485.75	0.00
2009	1.90	36,745.00	36,746.90	0.01
2010	195	55,905.30	56,100.30	0.35
2011	5,000.00	64,082.85	69,082.85	7.24
2012	6,000.00	89,712.99	95,712.99	6.27
2013	0.01	116,004.18	116,004.19	0.00
2014	8,927.92	101,204.03	110,131.95	8.11

Source: As in Table 3.1

Fig. 3.4 Details of Borrowed Funds of SGB during 2005 - 14

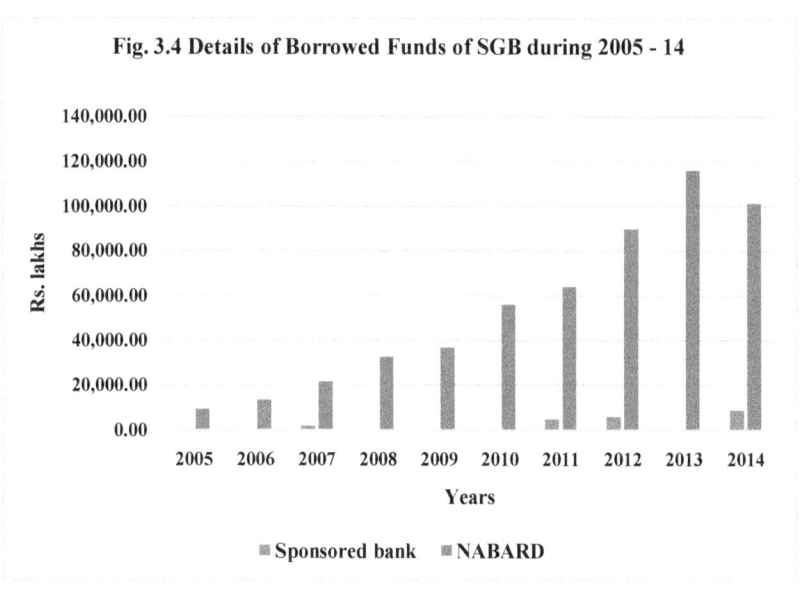

Source: Table 3.5

other hand, the proportion of sponsored bank has declined. This is also in consonance with the avowed objectives of RRBs.

The **Table 3.6** shows a comparative picture of borrowed and owned funds of the SGB. The total funds mobilised were Rs. 12,146.20 lakhs in 2005. These have steadily increased to reach Rs. 137,510.31 lakhs during 2013 except a decrease in 2014. In these years, there is a marginal increase. In the total funds, owned funds have accounted for 22.85 per cent during 2004 as compared to 19.31 per cent during 2014. The owned and borrowed

Table 3.6: Owned and Borrowed Funds of SGB during 2005 - 14

(Rs. lakhs)

Year (1)	Owned (2)	Borrowed (3)	Total (4)	% of col. (2) to col. (4) (5)
2005	2,775.51	9,370.64	12,146.20	22.85
2006	3,265.21	13,504.26	16,769.57	19.47
2007	6,521.90	23,349.12	29,871.02	21.83
2008	7,420.29	32,485.75	39,906.04	18.59
2009	8,451.74	36,746.90	45,198.64	18.70
2010	10,223.51	56,100.30	66,323.81	15.41
2011	12,886.23	69,082.85	81,969.08	15.72
2012	16,698.36	95,712.99	112,411.35	14.85
2013	21,506.12	116,004.19	137,510.31	15.64
2014	26,348.37	110,131.95	136,480.32	19.31
Average	67,858.62	124,107.53	67,876.87	18.24

Source   : As in Table 3.1

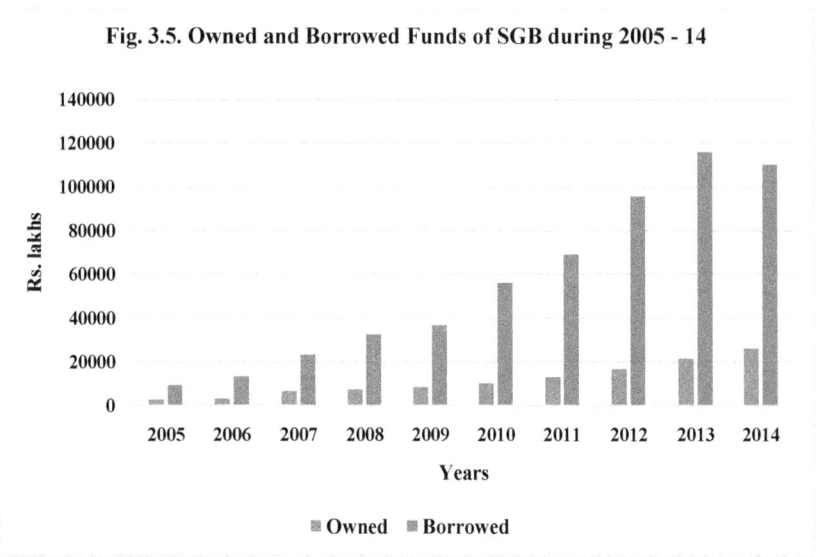

Fig. 3.5. Owned and Borrowed Funds of SGB during 2005 - 14

Source: Table 3.6

funds are graphically presented in **Figure 3.5.** In the meantime, the fluctuations are noticeable. The remaining is accounted for borrowed funds. It may be inferred that, out of the total funds at the disposal of the SGB, borrowed funds constituted more than 77 per cent during the period under study. In future, the bank has to put concerted efforts to increase the contribution of owned funds. The dependence on external sources is not advisable in the long run.

The investment pattern of the SGB is reported in the **Table 3.7** and **Figure 3.6.** It can be observed that the bank has invested its funds in different kinds of securities along with disbursement of loans to borrowers directly as well as indirectly. Of the avenues of investment, the bank has not invested a single rupee in other approved securities during 2009 - 2014. In the initial period, it varied between Rs. 150 lakhs and Rs. 50 lakhs. These securities in the total investment have formed 1.41 per cent in 2005 and 0.26 per cent in 2008. The investment in government securities was Rs. 9,229.24

lakhs in 2005 vis - à - vis Rs. 58,872.39 lakhs in 2014. There is no decline in any one of the years. In relative terms, these have varied between 86.74 per cent and 94.88 per cent in the period. In the meantime, there are to and fro changes. The investment in debentures and bonds was Rs. 1,033.80 lakhs during 2005 with 9.72 per cent as against Rs. 100 lakhs during 2014 with

Table 3.7 Investments of SGB during 2005 - 14

(Rs. lakhs)

Year	Government securities	Other approved securities	Debentures and bonds	Others	Total
2005	9,229.24	150.00	1033.80	227.42	10,640.46
	(86.74)	(1.41)	(9.72)	(2.13)	(100)
2006	9,469.24	100.00	677.50	284.57	10,531.31
	(89.92)	(0.95)	(6.43)	(2.70)	(100)
2007	15,308.72	125.00	895.00	430.13	16,758.85
	(91.35)	(0.75)	(5.34)	(2.56)	(100)
2008	17,864.94	50.00	603.50	506.34	19,024.78
	(93.90)	(0.26)	(3.17)	(2.67)	(100)
2009	23,169.68	0	537	734.56	24,441.24
	(94.80)	(0.00)	(2.20)	(3.01)	(100)
2010	31,781.75	0	365	846.62	32,993.37
	(96.33)	(0.00)	(1.11)	(2.56)	(100)
2011	36,041.13	0	265	1,375.47	37,681.60
	(95.65)	(0.00)	(0.70)	(3.65)	(100)
2012	41,067.14	0	125	1,955.63	43,147.77
	(95.18)	(0.00)	(0.29)	(4.53)	(100)
2013	46,185.66	0	10,082.84	2,290.09	58,558.59
	(78.87)	(0.00)	(17.22)	(3.91)	(100)
2014	58,872.39	0	100	3,076.35	62,048.74
	(94.88)	(0.00)	(0.16)	(4.96)	(100)

Note : Figures in brackets indicate the percentage total.
Source: As in Table 3.1

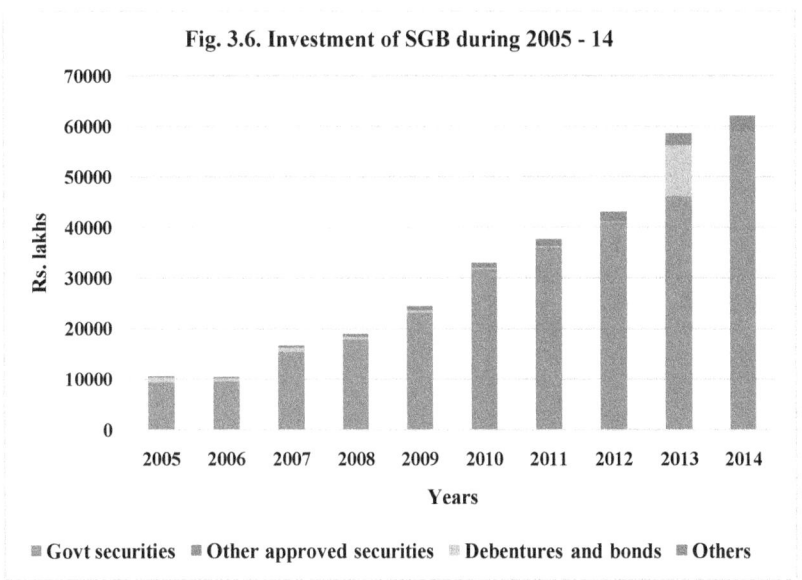

Fig. 3.6. Investment of SGB during 2005 - 14

■ Govt securities ■ Other approved securities ▨ Debentures and bonds ■ Others

Source: Table 3.7

0.16 per cent. The total investments have gradually gone up from Rs. 10,640.46 lakhs in 2005 to Rs. 62,048.74 lakhs in 2014. It can be concluded that among the sources of parking of funds, government securities ranked first followed by others, debentures and bonds and approved securities.

10. Working funds:

The average working funds of the SGB during 2005 - 2014 is reported in the **Table 3.8.** A look at the Table reveals that the working funds were Rs. 56,576.80 lakhs in 2005. These have progressively increased to reach Rs. 383,837.00 lakhs in 2014. Though there is an increase in absolute figures, there are wild fluctuations in relative terms. The variation was in the range of 3.11 – 52.02 per cent. It may be concluded that there is a remarkable growth in the working funds during the year. However, there are fluctuations in the yearly increment. Besides, the bank has raised sizeable amount from the

Table 3.8: Average Working Funds of SGB during 2005 – 14

(Rs. lakhs)

Year	Amount	% of change
2005	56,576.80	-
2006	64,019.97	13.16
2007	97,324.14	52.02
2008	100,349.41	3.11
2009	127,516.62	27.07
2010	161,943.66	27.00
2011	215,115.62	32.83
2012	270,162.00	25.59
2013	348,044.00	28.83
2014	383,837.00	10.28

Source: As in Table 3.1.

public by introducing several kinds of deposits. This results in the promotion of savings and banking habit among the rural clientele. The loans and advances and profits are significantly related to deposits. The analysis of deposits along with advances is presented in the next chapter.

References:

1. Buat, N.S. (1999). *Rural Banking in India,* Bombay, Himalaya Publishing Company, 121-22.

2. RBI Bulletin. (1976). p. 61.

3. Karnel., & Gopal., (1997). *Perspectives in Indian Banking,* Bombay, Popular Prakashan, 86.

4. Parikh, M. G., and others, (1980). *Commercial Banking,* Bombay, Vora and Company Publishers Pvt. Ltd., 173-74.

CHAPTER – IV

DEPOSIT MOBILISATION AND LOAN OPERATIONS

An attempt is made in this chapter to analyse the trend in the mobilisation of deposits, loan operations, credit – deposit ratio (CDR), business and recovery performance of the Saptagiri Grameena Bank (SGB). This serves as a backdrop for the evaluation of financial performance of the SGB. The issues focussed are yearly growth in deposits, deposit mix, targets and achievements of deposit, disbursement of loans, yearly coverage of priority and non – priority sectors, small farmers / marginal farmers / agricultural labourers, scheduled castes (SCs)/ scheduled tribes (STs), minorities, level of achievement, outstanding advances, business, CDR and recovery efficiency at aggregate and sector - wise.

1. Deposit mobilisation:

The most important source of resource for commercial banks is the mobilisation of deposits. Deposits mobilised by Regional Rural Banks (RRBs) play a key role not only as an important source of fund but also acts as an instrument for promoting savings and banking habits among the rural people. The resources of any bank largely depend on the quantum of deposits that it mobilises from different sources. RRBs, therefore, have to strive hard for mobilisation of deposits. They have even to make special efforts for this purpose. The loans and advances and profits of a bank are significantly related to its deposits.

Deposit is the raw material of banking industry which turns into a final product in the form of credit. Thus, banks create utility in the process of manufacturing credit. The survival of a bank, therefore, much depends on the deposits mobilised by it. The resources of any bank rarely depend on the quantum of deposits it mobilises from different sources. Since savings of the community form a source of deposit, banks have a greater responsibility of motivating people with surplus funds to keep them in the form of deposits. In this process, banks contribute to the progress of capital formulation in a country by activising the savings of the community. Deposit mobilisation is, thus, a significant activity of a bank in the context of economic development. The efficiency of a credit agency, to a larger extent, depends upon its ability to mobilise the savings of the community in the form of deposits.

All RRBs accept different types of deposits from the public as follows: current account; savings bank deposits; fixed (or) term deposits; recurring deposits; and others. Current deposits are the cheapest source of fund to banks, but they require a high amount of liquidity. Current deposits are generally operated by the business class. The savings deposits are meant to encourage saving habits in the people and so a nominal interest is paid on such deposits. These deposits can be encouraged by opening branches in different parts of the country. Fixed deposits are more costly for the banks because the highest rate of interest is paid on them. The only advantage to the bank on such deposits is that they can lend such funds on long - term basis. The fixed deposits are highly influenced by the rate of interest. However, saving and fixed deposits are more popular with the rural clientele as compared with the current and recurring deposits. RRBs, therefore, have to strive hard for the mobilisation of deposits. They have even to make special efforts for this purpose. Thus, deposits have a greater significance not only for RRBs but also for the development of the rural economy. However, in order to help RRBs effectively and enable them to compete with other banks, they have been permitted to allow half a per cent more interest on deposits when compared to commercial banks in the country.

Since the SGB has been brought into existence to meet the credit requirements of weaker sections of the society and its own funds are limited and so also its access to refinance facilities from the National Bank for Agriculture and Rural Development (NABARD), the Industrial Development Bank of India (IDBI) and Indian bank, the importance of deposits from public as the main source of funds cannot be over emphasised. The larger the amount of funds it can mobilse, the better its position could be to lend to the needy. It is pertinent to add that the amount of deposits with the bank shall indicate not only its ability to contribute towards development of the area by extending financial assistance for economic activities but also the level of confidence which the public reposes to it. Unlike lending, which is restricted to the specific target group, there is no restriction in respect of avenues for mobilisation of deposits. Deposits can be mobilised from the public at large at the rates of interest as prescribed by RBI from time to time.

1.1. Trend in deposit accretion:

The SGB has introduced several types of deposit schemes keeping in view the poorer sections in its operational area. The deposits have attracted small depositors in a big way. Their encouraging response has resulted in an impressive trend in the growth of deposits. The aggregate number of deposit accounts which stood at Rs. 334,000 lakhs in 2005 has progressively increased to Rs.1256,518 lakhs by the end of 2014 (see **Table 4.1.**). The year to year changes are noticeable. The increment was in the range of 4.61 –

54.03 per cent. The growth in accounts during 2007 was remarkable due to amalgamation of the Kanakadurga Grameena Bank (KGB) with the Sri Venkateswara Grameena Bank (SVGB). The deposits mobilised have increased from Rs.35,295.80 lakhs in 2005 to Rs.252,363.50 lakhs in 2014. Like accounts, there are variations in the yearly increase without any decline. The level of addition was in the range of 4.62 – 67.93 per cent during the

Table 4.1: Trend in Deposit Mobilisation of the SGB during 2005 - 14

(Rs. lakhs)

End Dec.	Number of accounts	% of change	Amount	% of change	Amount per		
					Branch	Employee	Per capita (Rs.)
2005	334,000	-	35,295.80	-	470.61	85.46	10,567.60
2006	349,400	4.61	36,925.95	4.62	492.35	90.73	10,568.39
2007	538,166	54.03	62,008.53	67.93	602.02	121.59	11,522.19
2008	652,808	21.30	77,779.80	25.43	713.58	154.02	11,914.65
2009	652,808	0.00	97,785.51	25.72	769.96	187.33	14,979.21
2010	825,354	26.43	124,397.41	27.21	949.60	213.37	15,072.01
2011	873,779	5.87	155,361.64	24.89	1,078.90	268.33	17,780.41
2012	954,193	9.20	185,229.44	19.22	2,692.62	633.31	19,412.16
2013	1139,942	19.47	213,467.36	15.24	3,083.47	796.22	18,726.16
2014	1256,518	10.23	252,363.50	18.22	3,555.39	857.29	20,084.35
Average	757,696.80		124,061.49		1,440.85	340.77	15,062.72
S.D.	310,558.58		75,521.22		1,184.74	301.01	3768.27
C.V. (%)	40.99		60.87		82.22	88.33	25.02
CAGR (%)	14.17		21.74		22.41	25.93	6.63
't' cal	7.715**		5.195**		3.846**	3.579**	12.64**

Note: S.D. : Standard deviation

C.V. : Coefficient of variation

CAGR : Compound annual growth rate

** : Indicates significant at 1 per cent level

Source: Relevant issues of the SGB, Annual Report, Chittoor.

period. The average deposits per branch were Rs.470.61 lakhs in 2005 as compared to Rs.3,555.39 lakhs in 2014. There is a gradual increase in it without any decrease.

The amount of deposit per employee increased progressively from Rs. 85.46 lakhs to Rs 857.29 lakhs during the aforesaid period. A similar trend exists in per capita deposits. These have constituted Rs.10,567.60 in 2005 while Rs.20,084.35 in 2014. On an average, per year, number of accounts, amount, branch per branch, per employee and per capita stood Rs. 757,696.80 lakhs, Rs.124,061.49 lakhs, Rs. 1,440.85 lakhs, Rs. 340.77 lakhs and Rs. 15,062.72 during the period sequentially. Coefficient of variation in the case of branch per employee is 88.33 per cent indicating more variability and less consistency. It is 25.02 per cent in the case of per capita which shows less variability and more consistency. Growth rate analysis shows the higher growth rate in the case of branch per employee 25.93 per cent and in per capita, it is low at 6.63 per cent. The calculated value of 't' is more than the corresponding critical value at one per cent level. Hence, it is significant at one per cent level. It may be concluded that there is a notable increase in per capita, per employee and per branch deposits. The number of accounts and amounts has shown a growing trend. The bank achieved a satisfactory progress due to opening of branches and sustained efforts of employees. This has resulted in broad basing the deposit mix. The bank has made concerted efforts to mobilise saving by bringing rural public into the banking fold. Thus, it has built up a special image and landmark in deposit mobilisation.

1.2 Deposit mix:

The deposit mix in the SGB during 2005 - 14 is furnished in the **Table 4.2.** Among the deposits, savings deposits, in terms of accounts ranked first. For example, in terms of accounts, these were in the range of 73.95 - 87.52 per cent during 2005 - 14. With regard to amount, their share was in the order of 25.69 – 31.69 per cent in the same period. The term deposits constituted 19.91 per cent in 2005 as against 12.50 per cent in 2014. There

Table 4.2: Structure of Deposits in the SGB during 2005 – 14 (Figures lakhs)

Year	ACCOUNTS			AMOUNTS		
	Savings deposits	Current deposits	Term deposits	Savings deposits	Current deposits	Term deposits
2005	260,363.00 (77.95)	7,138 (2.14)	66,496 (19.91)	9,556.66 (27.08)	6,337.35 (17.95)	19,401.79 (54.97)
2006	305,822.00 (87.52)	6,907 (1.97)	36,699 (10.51)	11,410.30 (30.90)	5,567.54 (15.07)	19,948.11 (54.03)
2007	433,598 (80.57)	3,956 (0.74)	100,612 (18.69)	18,551.92 (29.92)	6,017.49 (9.70)	37,439.12 (60.38)
2008	505,593 (77.45)	50,985 (7.81)	96,230 (14.74)	22,488.30 (28.91)	2,896.70 (3.72)	52,394.80 (67.37)
2009	505,593 (77.45)	50,985 (7.81)	96,230 (14.74)	30,984.48 (31.69)	1,258.27 (1.29)	65,542.76 (67.37)
2010	610,355 (73.95)	52,186 (6.32)	162,813 (19.73)	34,522.23 (27.75)	1,321.78 (1.06)	88,553.40 (71.19)
2011	743,342 (85.07)	3,425 (0.39)	127,012 (14.54)	48,300.85 (31.09)	1,400.07 (0.90)	105,660.72 (68.01)
2012	816,882 (85.61)	3,673 (0.39)	133,688 (14.00)	49,842.00 (26.91)	1,547.56 (0.84)	133,839.88 (72.25)
2013	989,219 (86.78)	3,950 (0.35)	146,773 (12.87)	58,572.17 (27.44)	1,582.97 (0.74)	153,312.22 (71.82)
2014	1095,174 (87.16)	4,234 (0.34)	157,110 (12.50)	64,821.14 (25.69)	1,705.61 (0.68)	185,836.75 (73.64)
Average	626,594.10 (74.16)	18,743.90 (2.61)	105,716.70 (13.23)	33,949.34 (26.03)	2,329.80 (3.40)	84,252.78 (60.57)
S.D.	279,824.78	22,563.59	40,672.61	19,690.18	2135.30	57,623.10
C.V. (%)	44.66	120.38	36.20	56.41	72.05	66.85
CAGR (%)	15.45	-5.09	8.98	21.10	-12.30	25.35
't' cal	7.08**	2.63*	8.74**	5.61**	4.39**	4.73**

Note: Figures in brackets indicate the percentage to total
        S.D.   : Standard deviation
        C.V.   : Coefficient of variation
       CAGR : Compound annual growth rate
        *   : Indicates significant at 5 per cent level
        **   : Indicates significant at 1 per cent level
Source : As in Table 4.1.

are variations in the yearly share during the period. For instance, 2006 registered the lowest at 10.51 per cent whereas 2005 the highest at 19.91 per cent. In respect of amount, these deposits have ranked the first place throughout the period with more than 55 per cent share. Their share was in the order of 54.03 – 73.64 per cent in the period. The current deposits came last in both the accounts and amount. For instance, in accounts, their share proportion was 2.14 per cent in 2005 as compared to 0.34 per cent in 2014. A contrary situation prevails in terms of amount. These deposits formed 17.95 per cent in 2005 as against 0.68 per cent in 2014. The number of savings deposit accounts is relatively more because of the compulsion that every person has to open an account, the moment he becomes a borrower of the bank. It infers that the bank has introduced deposit oriented loaning scheme. On an average, per year, savings deposits, current deposits and term deposits stood at Rs. 33,949.34 lakhs, Rs.2,329.80 lakhs, Rs.84,252.78 lakhs respectively during the period. Coefficient of variation in term deposit is 72.05 per cent indicating more variability and less consistency. It is 40.99 per cent in savings deposits which shows less variability and more consistency. The CAGR is the higher in term deposit at 25.35 per cent whereas current deposit is lesser at -12.30 per cent. The calculated value of 't' is more than the corresponding critical value at one per cent level. Hence, it is significant at one per cent level.

It may be concluded that the demand of savings deposits declined in terms of accounts while a negligible decrease in amount. The term deposits though ranked second in respect of accounts occupied the first place in amount. The current deposits are comparatively not significant. The increasing importance of term deposits in terms of amount may be attributed to such factors as increased level of income of the public in the operational area; improved economic standards; change in the attitude of public;

declining trend in the prices of real estate, etc. Thus the bank possesses a greater term deposit base. This has result in stability in deposit mobilisation and lending. It is so because these deposits give necessary time for advancing loans. The change in the deposit mix is a sign of healthy development of the SGB in the matter of deposit accretion.

1.3. Accomplishments:

A look at the **Table 4.3** reveals that the targets in deposit mobilisation were unfulfiled in all years except 2006, 2007, 2008, 2010, 2011 and 2014. **Figure 4.1** presents this clearly. The percentage of achievement in these years was 117.25, 105.69, 100.49, 100.97, 100.72 and 100.14 respectively. Among the target unfulfiled years, the achievement was the highest (96.93 per cent) in 2012 followed by 2013 (94.87 per cent), 2009 (93.13 per cent) etc. The least accomplishment was 85.26 per cent in 2005. In a way, the achievement registered in six years indicates the sign of underestimating the potential of the bank in the field of deposit mobilisation and increase in the level of income of depositors. The targets could not be reached in four years due to difficult agricultural situation in the operational area of the bank. On an overall appraisal, the performance of the SGB in the matter of fulfilment of targets can be considered to be unsatisfactory.

The increase in deposits may be due to: expansion of branches, development plans, growth of banking habit and rise in the income of the rural public. There are also other contributory factors such as awareness among the rural people to open accounts, personal contact with the staff, half a per cent higher interest in the SGB as compared to commercial banks, innovative deposit schemes, loan facility against fixed deposits, location of branches at unbanked and underbank centres and availability of insurance. However, in certain years, growth in deposits declined due to drought conditions. The rural clients withdraw their money to meet their necessities. Later on, deposits once again increased due to good harvest. The progress in

Table 4.3: Targets and Achievements of SGB in Deposit Mobilisation during
2005 – 14

(Rs. lakhs)

Year	Target	Actual	% of achievement
2005	41,400.00	35,295.80	85.26
2006	42,400.00	49,713.35	117.25
2007	58,670.00	62008.53	105.69
2008	77,400.00	77,779.80	100.49
2009	105,000.00	97,785.51	93.13
2010	123,200.00	124,397.41	100.97
2011	154,251.00	155,361.64	100.72
2012	191,100.00	185,229.45	96.93
2013	225,000.00	213,467.36	94.87
2014	252,000.00	252,363.50	100.14
Average	127,042.10	125,340.24	99.55
S.D.	76,152.27	73,974.31	
C.V. (%)	59.94	59.02	
CAGR (%)	19.80	21.74	
't' cal	5.28**	5.36**	

Note: S.D.   : Standard deviation

C.V.   : Coefficient of variation

CAGR : Compound annual growth rate

**   : Indicates significant at 1 per cent level

Source: As in Table 4.1

112

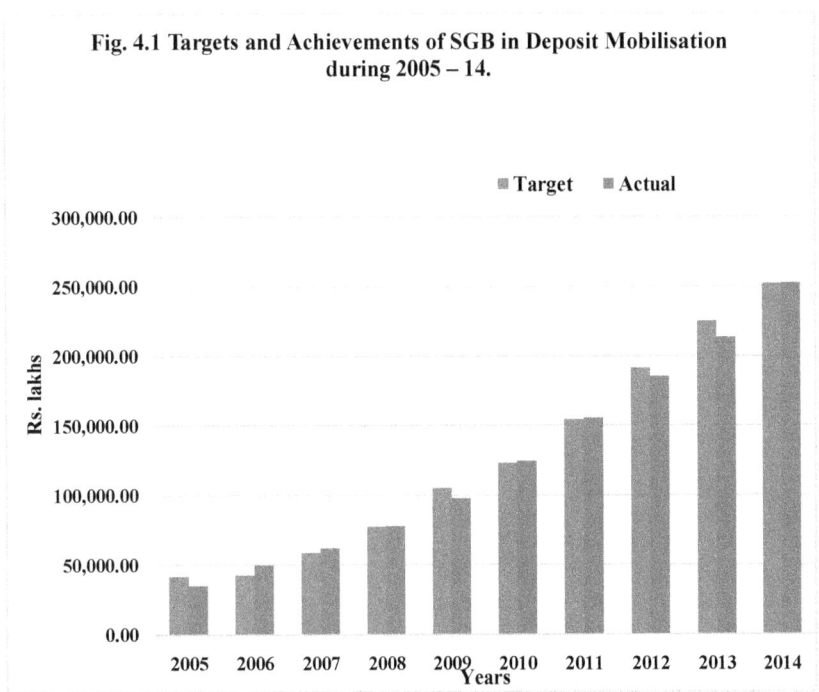

**Fig. 4.1 Targets and Achievements of SGB in Deposit Mobilisation
during 2005 – 14.**

Source: Table 4.3

the number of accounts has declined when compared to amount. This is due

to the fact that small depositors have withdrawn their savings in the SGB.

Such depositors were large in number. On an average, per year, targets and

actuals in deposit mobilisation stood Rs. 1,27,042.10 lakhs, Rs. 1,25,340.24

lakhs serially during the period. Coefficient of variation in target is 59.94 per

cent indicating more variability and less consistency. It is 59.02 per cent in

case of actuals which shows less variability and more consistency. The

CAGR in actuals is 21.74 per cent and in targets 19.80 per cent. The

calculated value of 't' is more than the corresponding critical value at one

per cent level. Hence, it is significant at one per cent level. It may be said

that despite increase in deposits, yet the progress in deposits is not

commensurate with the potential of the area. If systematic and sustained

113

efforts were made, a much larger amount could have been procured from the general public.

2. Credit operations:

The resources are to be gainfully employed so that not only the cost of raising funds is adequately met but additional income is generated. As such, resources have to be judiciously and effectively utilised in conformity with the guidelines issued. Meeting the credit requirement of weaker sections of the society for undertaking productive economic activities for increasing their income stakes paramount claim on the funds of RRBs. However, all the funds available with the bank cannot be used for lending. Some funds are pre - empted and are required to be used to meet statutory requirements of liquidity while a part of the fund is used for creating fixed assets. Besides, some funds are necessarily blocked in the form of cash to meet the requirements of depositors. The Head Office fixes the quantum of cash on hand required to be maintained at the level of branch with a view to avoid unnecessary holding of idle cash and at the same time avoiding any inconvenience to the clientele arising out of inadequate cash.

Now - a - days, the function of any bank is not just mopping up of deposits and lending to the needy public, but it should involve in the overall development of its operational area. This is more so in the case of the SGB. It should accelerate integrated rural development by providing adequate and timely credit. This depends upon the coverage of activities; reaching occupational target groups; extent of deployment of credit to priority sector; assistance rendered to weaker sections for their upliftment; participation in the implementation of government sponsored anti - poverty programmes; level of utilisation of locally mobilised deposits in the operational area etc. Therefore, an attempt is made in this section to assess how far the SGB has participated in accelerating the rural development in its operational area. The loan operations of the bank are discussed here in terms of trend in growth, term - wise, sector - wise, etc. The targets and achievements in credit expansion are also covered.

For the purpose of speedy attainment of rural development, the SGB has extended credit for a varied range of activities by covering the target groups in its operational area. It has participated in the implementation of several government sponsored schemes since its inception. The loan operations of the SGB are presented in this section. The credit deployment pattern of the SGB shows that the benefits of its various schemes of advances have percolated to a large number of beneficiaries. Keeping in line with the importance attached to rural development, the bank has achieved considerable progress in providing finance to farming community, weaker sections and others in the rural areas.

2.1. Credit disbursement:

A glance at the **Table 4.4** shows disbursement of loans in the SGB during 2005 - 14. It can be observed that the bank disbursed Rs. 27,650.38 lakhs in 2005 and progressively increased year after year to reach Rs. 215,628.33 lakhs at the end of 2014. There is a remarkable increase in 2007 over 2006 due to amalgamation of KDGB with the SVGB. There is no decline in the amount disbursed in any year except in 2014. The advances for priority sector reveal the same trend. During 2005, Rs. 21,669.70 lakhs were disbursed under priority sector as compared to Rs. 179,742.84 lakhs in 2014. There is a gradual growth in the amount disbursed every year except 2014 during the reference period. In the case of non - priority sector, there are fluctuations in the yearly disbursement. A little over Rs. 5,980.68 lakhs was disbursed during 2005 as compared to Rs. 35,885.49 lakhs during 2014. The share of priority sector in the total disbursement was 78.37 per cent in 2005 as against 83.36 per cent in 2014. There is a gradual increase in the share of priority sector except 2014. The remaining is accounted for non – priority sector. In other words, the proportion of non - priority sector has declined

Table 4.4: Sector – wise Disbursement of Loans in the SGB during 2005 - 14

(Rs. lakhs)

Year (1)	Priority sector (2)	Non - priority sector (3)	Total (4)	% of col (2) to col (4) (5)
2005	21,669.70	5,980.68	27650.38	78.37
2006	29,149.11	5,485.84	34634.95	84.16
2007	65,059.70	8,531.22	73590.92	88.41
2008	73,744.44	15,764.20	89508.64	82.39
2009	101,121.34	7,355.12	108,476.46	93.22
2010	131,190.00	16,625.00	147,815.00	88.75
2011	144,952.08	27,566.40	172,518.48	84.02
2012	179,545.37	42,060.63	221,606.00	81.02
2013	208,258.33	44,054.59	252,312.92	82.54
2014	179,742.84	35,885.49	215,628.33	83.36
Average	113,443.29	20,930.92	134,374.21	84.62
S.D.	65,540.03	15,254.10	79,911.70	
C.V. (%)	57.77	72.88	59.47	
CAGR (%)	23.56	19.62	22.80	
't' cal	4.82**	4.00**	4.71**	

Note: S.D.   : Standard deviation
            C.V.   : Coefficient of variation
            CAGR : Compound annual growth rate
            **   : Indicates significant at 1 per cent level
Source: As in Table 4.1

from 21.63 per cent in 2005 to 16.64 per cent in 2014. This is due to the fact that there is no directed lending to non - priority sector. On an average, per year, priority sector and non – priority sector stood Rs. 1,13,443.29 lakhs and Rs. 20,930.92 lakhs during the period. Coefficient of variation in non – priority sector is 72.88 per cent indicating more variability and less consistency. It is 57.77 per cent in the case of priority sector which shows less variability and more consistency. The CAGR in priority sector advances was 23.56 per cent whereas non – priority sector is 19.62 per cent, which are significant at one per cent level.

It may be concluded that the priority sector accounts for a lions share in the total loans disbursed during the period. Further, its share has increased as against a decline in the non - priority sector which reflects the government policy. The banks are advised to disburse more than 50 per cent of loans to priority sector. There are clear variations in the disbursement of credit during the period. Keeping in view the objectives laid down, the SGB has made available funds for several purposes.

Under priority - sector lending, the bank has disbursed loans for different purposes as presented in the **Table 4.5.** Among the purposes, short - term agricultural loans accounted for a major share ranging between 78.97 per cent and 57.70 per cent during 2005 - 14. Agriculture has claimed a lion's share in the total advances disbursed. This is due to the fact a large proportion of population in the operational area was depending on it. Others ranked second. Their proportion has accounted for 2.35 per cent in 2005 as against 17.99 per cent in 2014. Self Help Groups (SHGs) ranked third. Their proportion was in the order of 13.45 – 20.22 per cent. Allied agri - term

Table 4.5: Segregation of Loans Disbursed under Priority - Sector in SGB during 2005 – 2014 (Rs. lakhs)

Year	STAL	ATL	AATL	SHGs	SSI	SL	Others	Total
2005	17,112.12 (78.97)	258.09 (1.19)	189.89 (0.88)	-	42.57 (0.20)	3,557.03 (16.41)	510.00 (2.35)	21,669.70 (100)
2006	22,003.27 (75.49)	350.35 (1.20)	659.45 (2.26)	-	14.66 (0.05)	5,544.84 (19.02)	576.54 (1.98)	29,149.11 (100)
2007	43,668.97 (74.57)	622.79 (1.06)	12,429.79 (21.23)	-	672.15 (1.15)	528.81 (0.90)	637.19 (1.09)	58,559.70 (100)
2008	49,024.60 (66.48)	465.74 (0.63)	21,357.40 (28.96)	-	476.66 (0.65)	955.60 (1.30)	1,464.44 (1.98)	73,744.44 (100)
2009	50,348.04 (49.79)	1,021.37 (1.01)	2,134.48 (2.11)	17,127.26 (16.94)	499.94 (0.49)	720.43 (0.71)	29,269.82 (28.95)	101,121.34 (100)
2010	71,423.35 (54.44)	1,401.25 (1.07)	2,154.65 (1.64)	21,545.75 (16.42)	630.95 (0.48)	1,031.75 (0.79)	33,002.30 (25.16)	131,190.00 (100)
2011	77,521.93 (53.48)	2,480.00 (1.71)	1,937.44 (1.34)	29,306.00 (20.22)	573 (0.40)	1041 (0.72)	32,092.71 (22.14)	144,952.08 (100)
2012	105,943.88 (59.01)	858.55 (0.48)	3,145.46 (1.75)	30,276.36 (16.86)	643 (0.36)	434.18 (0.24)	38,243.94 (21.30)	179,545.37 (100)
2013	133,095.90 (63.91)	1,372.00 (0.66)	3,623.55 (1.74)	28,004.18 (13.45)	609 (0.29)	990.45 (0.48)	40,563.25 (19.48)	208,258.33 (100)
2014	103,717.58 (57.70)	562.55 (0.31)	994.59 (0.55)	32,359.74 (18.00)	721.55 (0.40)	9,057.22 (5.04)	32,329.61 (17.99)	179,742.84 (100)
Average	67,385.96 (63.38)	939.27 (0.93)	4,862.67 (6.25)	15,861.93 (10.19)	488.35 (0.45)	2,386.13 (4.56)	20,868.98 (14.24)	112,793.29 (100)
S.D.	38,035.81	672.06	6,762.80	14,331.17	253.31	2,858.21	17,565.74	66,103.01
C.V. (%)	56.44	71.55	139.08	90.35	51.87	119.78	84.17	58.61
CAGR (%)	19.74	8.10	18.01	6.57	32.71	9.80	51.43	23.56
't' cal	3.54**	3.19**	2.07*	2.80*	3.64**	2.32*	2.92**	3.48**

Note: Figures in brackets indicate the percentage of total
STAL : Short term agri – loans; ATL: Agri – term loans; AATL: Allied agri - term loans; SSI: Small Scale Industries; SL : Small Loans
S.D. : Standard deviation; C.V. : Coefficient of variation; CAGR : Compound annual growth rate; * : Indicates significant at 5 per cent level
** : Indicates significant at 1 per cent level; Source: As in Table 4.1

loans (AATL) ranked fourth. Their proportion was in the order of 0.55 - 28.96 per cent. The small loans (SL) constituted 5.04 per cent in 2014 as compared to 16.41 per cent in 2005. Agri - term loans (ATL) were in the frequency of 0.31 – 1.71 per cent. The small scale industries (SSI) formed 0.20 per cent in 2005 as against 0.40 per cent in 2014. The consumption loans were sanctioned for the benefit of economically weaker sections of society. Though there was a greater demand for small loans, its share has submerged. Thus the bank has disbursed loans under priority - sector for varied purposes.

Since agriculture is predominant in the operational area, loans for agriculture and allied-agricultural activities formed more than 95 per cent of total disbursement in the period. Of them, short – term agricultural loans (STAL) constitute more than 55 per cent except 2009. The loans for SSIs, others and small advances are significant. On an average, per year, STAL, ATL, AATL, SHGs, SSI, SL and others stood Rs. 67,385.96 lakhs, Rs.939.27 lakhs, Rs. 4,862.67 lakhs, Rs.15,861.93 lakhs, Rs. 488.35 lakhs, Rs. 2,386.13 lakhs and Rs. 20,868.98 lakhs serially during the period. Coefficient of variation in AATL is 139.08 per cent indicating more variability and less consistency. It is 51.87 per cent in the case of SSI, which shows less variability and more consistency. The CAGR was higher at 51.43 per cent in others and lower at 6.57 per cent in SHGs. The CAGR is significant in the loans to STAL, ATL, SSI and others at one per cent level whilst at 5 per cent level in AATL, SHGs and SL. It may be concluded that the loan delivery is in accordance with the state policy of the government as well as needs of the operational area.

The share of non - agricultural activities is indicative of the fact that the scope for non - farm loans in the rural areas was limited. Therefore, the SGB could lay aside only small amount of loanable funds for this purpose. It is to be noted that the trend in allied - agricultural activities is different from others. The allied - agricultural activities include sheep - rearing, poultry, dairy, sericulture etc. An important feature which deserves attention to be paid in this context is that there was no disbursement of loans for SHGs till 2008. During 2009 and 2014, it was more than 16 per cent. As regards disbursement to SSIs, the performance is not impressive. It seems that industrial activities that have a lot of potential to develop in the operational area have not been seriously taken care of by the SGB. The credit disbursement for industrial growth is awfully disproportionate. There is no doubt that proportionally higher amount of credit should be disbursed to agricultural sector, but in a operational area like this, which is basically a drought prone area, a large chunk of credit is desired to be flown towards rural industry. In such agro - climatic conditions that prevail all over the operational area, the potentiality for developing industry seem to be more. But, if credit does not flow to this sector adequately, the potential for developing industrial activity remains untapped. Therefore, the goal of rural development through rural industrialisation may not be visualised soon.

One of the laudable objectives behind the setting up of the SGB is to uplift the weaker sections of the rural community like Scheduled Castes (SCs), Scheduled Tribes (STs), Backward Castes (BCs) and minorities by extending them the required credit facilities. Since the beginning, the bank has been making efforts to introduce new schemes tailored to the needs of weaker sections of rural community. Hence, it is necessary to study to what extent these communities have been provided with financial assistance from the SGB. By and large, a majority of public in the operational area are

SCs/STs/BCs. Since inception, the SGB has been providing credit to these communities aiming to bring them above the poverty line. The disbursement of loans under priority sector for various kinds of borrowers is furnished in the **Table 4.6.** Out of different categories of borrowers, weaker sections occupied the first place followed by women, SCs, STs and minority communities. An amount of Rs. 11,275.25 lakhs were distributed to weaker sections in 2005 vis - à - vis Rs. 1,66,082.22 lakhs in 2014. Their share in the total disbursement was in the range of 71.22 - 87.37 per cent during the period. The amount made available to women was Rs. 3,672.50 lakhs in 2006 while Rs. 49,460.84 lakhs in 2014. These have formed 13.79 per cent and 21.86 per cent in the former and latter sequentially. There are ups and downs in the meantime. Loans disbursed to SCs and STs was Rs. 1,345.25 lakhs in 2005 as compared to Rs. 9,806.03 lakhs during 2014. In other words, their proportion was between 3.62 per cent and 11.53 per cent in the aforesaid period. The minorities were provided with Rs. 284.90 lakhs during 2005 while Rs. 950.62 lakhs during 2014. Over the 10 year period, the account of minorities has declined in both the absolute figures and percentage terms. Contrary to it, the share of women increased in absolute figures as well as relative terms. A similar trend can be observed in the case of weaker sections. On an average, per year, weaker sections, women, SCs/STs and minorities stood Rs. 95,781.80 lakhs, Rs. 28,298.02 lakhs, Rs. 5,908.58 lakhs and Rs. 546.00 lakhs serially during the period. Coefficient of variation in women is 70.04 per cent indicating more variability and less consistency. It is 50.02 per cent in SCs/STs which shows less variability and more consistency. The CAGR in weaker sections was 30.86 per cent and minorities 12.81 per cent. They are significant at one per cent level. It may be summed up that priority was accorded to weaker sections. There is a growing importance to women. This is in consonance with the declared policy of the government.

Table 4.6 Categorisation of Loans Issued under Priority Sector in the SGB

during 2005 – 2014

(Rs. lakhs)

Year	Weaker sections	Women	SCs / STs	Minorities	Total
2005	11275.25 (87.37)	-	1,345.25 (10.42)	284.90 (2.21)	12,905.40 (100)
2006	19,382.82 (72.80)	3,672.50 (13.79)	3,069.54 (11.53)	498.69 (1.87)	26,623.55 (100)
2007	29,245.78 (74.41)	5,535.02 (14.08)	3,947.62 (10.04)	577.36 (1.47)	39,305.78 (100)
2008	63,977.00 (71.22)	21,785.00 (24.25)	3,976.00 (4.43)	90.00 (0.10)	89,828.00 (100)
2009	83,526.87 (74.05)	24,135.45 (21.40)	4,831.26 (4.28)	301.46 (0.27)	112,795.04 (100)
2010	123,254.65 (72.41)	39,535.25 (23.23)	6,985.35 (4.10)	445.35 (0.26)	170,220.60 (100)
2011	136,014.78 (72.42)	44,319.43 (23.60)	7,020.48 (3.74)	470.16 (0.25)	187,824.85 (100)
2012	157,018.00 (73.87)	47,016.00 (22.12)	7,702.00 (3.62)	810.00 (0.38)	212,546.00 (100)
2013	168,040.58 (74.03)	47,520.66 (20.93)	10,402.22 (4.58)	1,031.44 (0.45)	226,994.90 (100)
2014	166,082.22 (73.39)	49,460.84 (21.86)	9,806.03 (4.33)	950.62 (0.42)	226,299.71 (100)
Average	95,781.80 (74.60)	28,298.02 (18.53)	5,908.58 (6.11)	546.00 (0.77)	130,534.38 (100)
S.D.	62,230.52	19,820.85	2,955.60	302.60	84,975.24
C.V. (%)	64.97	70.04	50.02	55.42	65.10
CAGR (%)	30.86	29.70	21.97	12.81	33.17
't' cal	4.87**	4.52**	6.32**	5.71**	4.86**

Note: Figures in brackets indicate the percentage total.

      S.D. : Standard deviation

      C.V. : Coefficient of variation

      CAGR : Compound annual growth rate

      ** : Indicates significant at 1 per cent level

Source: As in Table 4.1

Analysis of disbursement of loans and advances of the SGB shows that the bank was able to disburse a sizeable portion of loans for the purpose of crops, consumption, SSIs, etc. But the disbursement for consumption purposes is inadequate and, therefore, borrowers divert a part of loans taken by them for productive purposes to consumption activities. The credit flow to SCs/ STs is much lower than the credit flow to other castes. Even though they constitute more than 22 per cent, the credit disbursement to them is far below it. The relatively more bias to others can be explained in terms of accessibility to the SGB and possession of land. If at all, credit worthiness is to be regarded as the criterion of providing credit, then apart from ownership of land, there may be other criterion that can determine the credit worthiness of the individual. For example, an individual may not possess land but he is able to start a small scale unit, the prospect of which might ensure his credit worthiness. If the second criterion is accorded importance, the credit flow may not be such a disproportionate level across caste groups. Advances are directed towards land - based activities. In accordance with the policy, the SGB has taken active steps to extend credit to SCs/ STs on easy terms and given priority in expediting sanction. In future, the bank should direct its efforts towards deployment of funds to SCs/ STs rather than simply covering the beneficiaries.

The targets and accomplishments of the SGB in the disbursement of credit during 2005 - 14 are presented in the **Table 4.7.** The targets have gradually increased from Rs. 27,220 lakhs in 2005 to Rs. 280,000 lakhs in 2014. There is a gradual growth in the amount disbursed every year during the reference period. A similar trend emerges in the amount actually disbursed. The disbursement stood at Rs. 27,650.38 lakhs in 2005 whereas Rs. 215,628.33 lakhs in 2014. There is a steady growth in the period. The percentage of actual to achievement was 101.58 per cent in 2005 as

Table 4.7: Targets and Achievements of the SGB in Credit Disbursement during 2005 - 2014

(Rs. lakhs)

Year	Target	Actual	% of col (3) to col (2)
(1)	(2)	(3)	(4)
2005	27,220.00	27,650.38	101.58
2006	34,500.00	34,634.95	100.39
2007	57,113.69	73,590.92	128.85
2008	80,000.00	89508.64	111.89
2009	130,000.00	108,476.46	83.44
2010	146,000.00	147,815.00	101.24
2011	170,000.00	172,518.48	101.48
2012	203,000.00	221,606.00	109.17
2013	251,000.00	252,312.92	100.52
2014	280,000.00	215,628.33	77.01
Average	137,883.37	134,374.21	101.56
S.D.	88,945.00	79,911.70	
C.V. (%)	64.51	59.47	
CAGR (%)	26.25	22.80	
't' cal	4.90**	5.32**	

Note: S.D. : Standard deviation
    C.V. : Coefficient of variation
    CAGR : Compound annual growth rate
    **   : Indicates significant at 1 per cent level
    NA   : Not Available
Source: As in Table 4.1.

compared to 77.01 per cent in 2014. The accomplishment was more than estimate in all the years except 2009 and 2014. The year 2007 achieved the highest accomplishment at 128.85 per cent. Among the target fulfiled years, it was the least at 100.39 per cent in 2006. In the rest of the period, it varied between 100. 52 per cent and 128.85 per cent during the period. On an average, per year, targets and actuals in credit disbursement stood Rs. 1,37,883.37 lakhs and Rs. 1,34,374.21 lakhs during the period. Coefficient of variation in targets is 64.51 per cent, which indicates more variability and less consistency. It is 59.47 per cent in the case of actuals which shows less variability and more consistency. The CAGR in targets was 26.25 per cent whereas in actuals, it was 22.80 per cent. These are significant at one per cent level. It may be inferred that the targets were overfulfiled in all the years except 2009 and 2014 without any exception. In the first three years, they are remarkable. This may be due to the fact that it was fixed at low level. In certain years, targets were just achieved due to drought situation coupled with over confidence while setting up the targets in those years. It can be attributed to under estimation of credit needs of clientele or efficient mechanism of credit delivery system adopted by the bank. On the other hand, it may be due to competition from other banks or lethargic attitude of employees. The aforesaid analysis indicates that the bank has successfully participated in the bank implementation of government programmes since the achievements in credit deployment are satisfactory and above 100 per cent.

2.2 Outstanding advances:

The progress of outstanding advances of the SGB during 2005 - 14 is provided in the **Table 4.8** and depicted in **Figure 4.2.** It can be observed that the advances have gone up gradually from Rs. 35,556.67 lakhs in 2005 to Rs. 3,27,165.40 lakhs in 2014. Though there is a gradual increase, there are fluctuations in the yearly increment. The percentage of progress was the highest at 55.66 in 2007 while the lowest at 18.52 in 2006. The advances per branch have also gone up progressively from Rs. 474.06 lakhs in 2005 as against Rs. 3,555.39 lakhs in 2014. Similarly the amount per employee has

125

Table 4.8: Progress of Outstanding Advances the of SGB during 2005-14

(Rs. lakhs)

Year	Total	% of change	Per branch	Per employee
2005	35,556.67	-	474.06	68.64
2006	42,142.82	18.52	995.65	199.13
2007	65,600.22	55.66	1,238.92	250.21
2008	83,655.86	27.52	1,481.06	319.67
2009	111,389.93	33.15	1,647.05	400.72
2010	138,461.84	24.30	2,006.56	450.87
2011	175,474.83	26.73	2,297.48	571.39
2012	221,356.31	26.15	2,692.62	633.31
2013	270,637.26	22.26	3,083.47	796.22
2014	327,165.40	20.89	3,555.39	857.29
Average	147,144.11	28.35	1,947.23	454.75
S.D.	99,710.27		968.61	258.54
C.V. (%)	67.76		49.74	56.85
CAGR (%)	24.05		22.32	28.72
't' cal	4.67**		6.36**	5.57**

Note: S.D. : Standard deviation
      C.V. : Coefficient of variation
      CAGR : Compound annual growth rate
      **   : Indicates significant at 1 per cent level
Source: As in Table 4.1

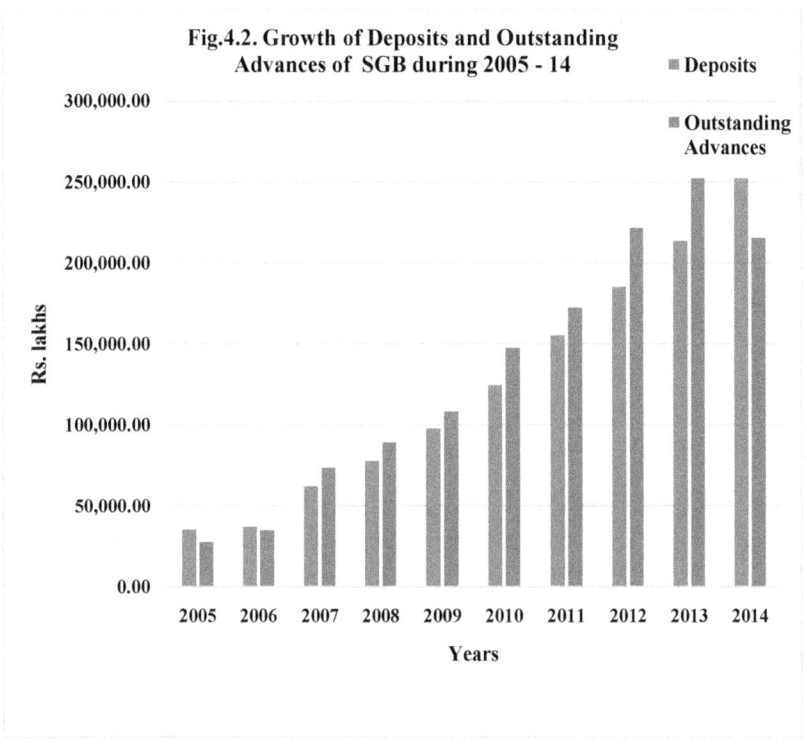

Fig.4.2. Growth of Deposits and Outstanding Advances of SGB during 2005 - 14

Source: Tables 4.1 and 4.8

also increased from Rs. 68.64 lakhs in 2005 as compared Rs. 857.29 lakhs in 2014. The outstanding advances total, mean per year, amount per branch and amount per employee stood Rs. 1,47,144.11 lakhs, Rs. 1,947.23 lakhs and Rs. 454.75 lakhs serially during the period. Coefficient of variation in total outstanding advances is 67.76 per cent indicating more variability and less consistency. It is 56.85 per cent in case of amount per employee which shows less variability and more consistency. The CAGR per employee was higher at 28.76 per cent and lower at 22.32 per cent in the amount per branch which are significant at one per cent level. It may be concluded that there is a gradual increase in outstanding advances in aggregate, per branch and per employee. Further, there are variations in the yearly addition. This is common because the disbursement and recovery of loans depend on several uncontrollable factors. Consequently, there are fluctuations in the advances outstanding. The overall average performance was quite encouraging. It is not known as to why in one particular year there was a sudden increase in the outstanding amount and for the remaining years, there was a declining trend. This may be the result of over enthusiasm and likely better prospects envisaged by the bank or recession in the software industry or may also be due to government policy and programme.

The **Table 4.9** reveals the classification of outstanding advances of the SGB into priority and non - priority sectors. **Figure 4.3** explains it graphically. The amount under priority - sector has increased from Rs. 29,582.37 lakhs in 2005 to Rs. 2,95,252.13 lakhs in 2014. There is no decline in any one of the years but there are fluctuations in the yearly addition. In the case of non - priority sector, the outstanding advances were Rs. 5,974.30 lakhs in 2005 as compared to Rs. 31,913.27 lakhs in 2014. There is no progressive growth throughout the period. It declined in 2006, 2011 and 2014. In the total advances, priority – sector has constituted 83.20 per cent in 2005 as against 90.25 per cent in 2014. On an average, per year, priority and non – priority sectors stood Rs. 1,25,908.81 lakhs and Rs. 21,235.31 lakhs sequentially during the period. Coefficient of variation in priority sector is 71.85 per cent indicating more variability and less consistency. It is 51.29 per cent in non – priority sector, which shows less variability and more consistency. The CAGR in the former was 25.87 per cent while latter 18.24 per cent, which are significant at one per cent level. It may be summed up that there is a continuous growth in the priority - sector advances. Further, the share of priority - sector was in the range of 77 - 90 per cent. It means that the bank has followed the guidelines and channelled majority of its funds towards priority - sector as desired by the government.

Table 4.9: Sector - wise Distribution of Outstanding Advances of SGB during 2005 – 14

(Rs. lakhs)

Year (1)	Priority sector (2)	Non - priority sector (3)	% of col (2) to total (4)
2005	29,582.37	5,974.30	83.20
2006	37,360.81	4,782.01	88.65
2007	56,479.64	9,120.58	86.10
2008	64,063.72	19,592.14	76.58
2009	87,806.01	23,583.92	78.83
2010	108,476.58	29,985.26	78.34
2011	150,373.67	25,101.16	85.70
2012	192,089.93	29,266.38	86.78
2013	237,603.22	33,034.04	87.79
2014	295,252.13	31,913.27	90.25
Average	125,908.81	21,235.31	84.22
S.D.	90,462.84	10,892.53	
C.V. (%)	71.85	51.29	
CAGR (%)	25.87	18.24	
't' cal	4.40**	6.17**	

Note: S.D.   : Standard deviation
     C.V.   : Coefficient of variation
     CAGR : Compound annual growth rate
     **   : Indicates significant at 1 per cent level
Source: As in Table 4.1

The share of non - priority sector never exceeded 25 per cent during the period under study.

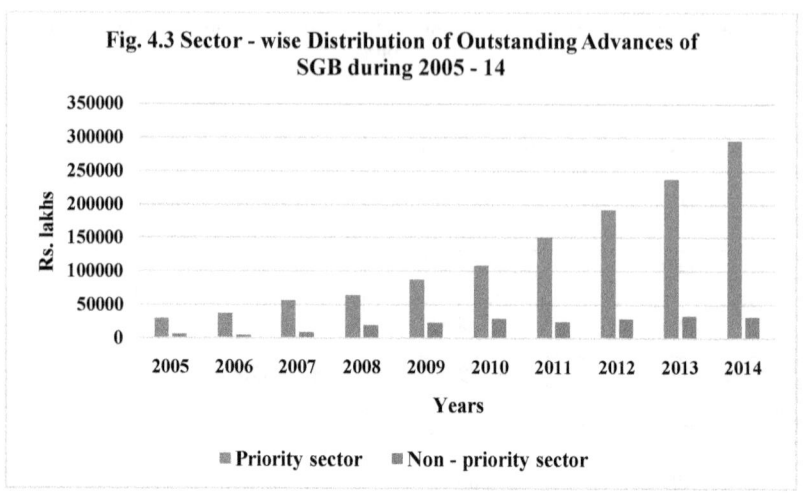

Fig. 4.3 Sector - wise Distribution of Outstanding Advances of SGB during 2005 - 14

Source: Table 4.9

The SGB, as pointed out earlier, has been established for helping the rural poor in general and the low income groups in particular. The low income groups include small and marginal farmers, landless labour, rural artisans, small businessman etc. These categories have more indebtedness when compared to their asset owning position. In fact, they are born in debt, live in debt and die in debt. Since they do not possess anything to show as security, they are denied credit by cooperatives and commercial banks. As already stated, the SGB has been established to meet the credit requirements of these groups of people without insisting upon any security. The performance of the bank will be judged by taking into consideration to what extent these target groups are covered. The SGB has reached all the specified categories of target groups of its operational area.

Target group - wise classification of outstanding advances of the SGB during 2005 – 14 is furnished in the **Table 4.10.** Of the total outstanding advances, SCs/ STs were provided with Rs. 3,476.28 lakhs or 10.46 per cent during 2005 when compared to Rs. 21,550.33 lakhs or 6.97 per cent during 2014. There are fluctuations in the yearly percentage during the period. Women were provided with Rs. 21,897 lakhs in 2008 while Rs. 87,970.16

lakhs in 2014. These have formed 23.43 per cent in 2008 and 28.45 per cent in 2014. There are to and fro changes in the meantime. The outstanding advances of SFs/ MFs/ ALs was Rs. 28,502.35 lakhs in 2005 whereas Rs. 1,95,008.24 lakhs in 2014. There are wide fluctuations in absolute as well as relative terms during the period under reference. In the total outstanding advances, their share was in the frequency of 57.38 – 86.60 per cent. The amount outstanding with minorities was Rs. 1,275.04 lakhs during 2005 whilst Rs. 4,652.12 lakhs in 2014. In relative terms, these have formed 3.83 per cent and 1.50 per cent. Out of the total borrowers, SFs/ MFs/ ALs occupied the first place. The women ranked second, SCs/ STs ranked third and minorities last. There is a significant increase in the proportion of women while just rise in the share of SFs/ MFs/ ALs. A converse situation prevails in the case of minorities. It is interesting to note that the share of SFs/ MFs/ ALs is more as compared to the share of other groups in each year. It is distressing to note that the SCs and STs have not received much attention from the bank. In most of the years, their share was unimaginably low. But their proportion ought to have been higher since they deserve considerable attention of the bank.

The aforesaid kind of skewed pattern of outstandings across the various groups of weaker sections of rural society is found to have emerged, possibly due to the variation in the coverage of population under each category. The mean amounts, per year, SCs/ STs, SFs/ MFs/ ALs, minorities and women stood Rs. 13,489.24 lakhs, Rs. 100,023.35 lakhs, Rs. 2,716.82 lakhs and Rs.40,635.30 lakhs serially during the period. Coefficient of variation in women is 82.56 per cent, indicating more variability and less consistency. It is 44.12 per cent in the case of minorities, which shows less variability and more consistency. The CAGR in SFs/ MFs/ ALs was higher at 21.20 per cent whereas minorities lower at 13.82 per cent. These are significant at one per cent level. It is evident that there is a growth in the share of all he categories except minorities. The beneficiary - wise break of advances implies that the advances were concentrated in SFs / MFs / ALs.

Table 4.10: Target Group-wise Classification of Outstanding Advances of SGB during 2005 – 14 (Rs. lakhs)

Year	SCs/ STs	SFs/ MFs/ ALs	Minorities	Women	Total
2005	3,476.28 (10.46)	28,502.35 (85.71)	1,275.04 (3.83)	---	33,253.67 (100)
2006	4,459.15 (10.45)	36,561.03 (85.71)	1,635.54 (3.84)	---	42,655.72 (100)
2007	5,785.45 (10.27)	48,765.87 (86.60)	1,763.82 (3.13)	---	56,315.14 (100)
2008	6,731.48 (7.21)	62,897.85 (67.32)	1,902.10 (2.04)	21,897.00 (23.43)	93,428.43 (100)
2009	12,841.77 (9.48)	80,138.75 (59.16)	2,297.49 (1.69)	40,176.45 (29.67)	135,454.46 (100)
2010	18,452.35 (9.52)	123,254.55 (63.58)	2,603.65 (1.34)	49,535.64 (25.56)	193,846.19 (100)
2011	19,610.75 (9.95)	113,058.62 (57.38)	2,840.00 (1.44)	61,520.66 (31.23)	197,030.03 (100)
2012	20,724.00 (8.68)	145,016.00 (60.76)	3,688.00 (1.55)	69,252.00 (29.01)	238,680.00 (100)
2013	21,260.82 (7.91)	167,030.21 (62.14)	4,510.39 (1.68)	76,001.12 (28.27)	268,802.54 (100)
2014	21,550.33 (6.97)	195,008.24 (63.07)	4,652.12 (1.50)	87,970.16 (28.45)	309,180.85 (100)
Average	13,489.24 (8.60)	100,023.347 (63.76)	2,716.82 (1.73)	40635.303 (25.90)	156864.70 (100)
S.D.	7,652.61	57,532.35	1,198.57	33,550.42	99,062.87
C.V. (%)	56.73	57.52	44.12	82.56	63.15
CAGR (%)	20.01	21.20	13.82	14.92	24.98
't' cal	5.57**	5.50**	7.17**	3.83**	

Notes : Figures in brackets indicate the percentage to total.
  S.D. : Standard deviation
  C.V. : Coefficient of variation
  CAGR : Compound annual growth rate
  ** : Indicates significant at 1 per cent level
Source: As in Table 4.1

Thus they have benefited more than any other group of weaker sections. This could be due to the fact that the total number of beneficiaries considered for providing credit is extremely lower than any other group of weaker section. However, the issue that emerges from such observation is that whether the

132

disbursement per individual is to be regarded as sufficient condition for self - sustenance of individual activity.

3. Business and credit deposit ratio:

The business per branch in the SGB has continuously risen from Rs. 474.06 lakhs in 2005 to Rs. 3,555.39 lakhs in 2014(**see Table 4.11**). Here business means loans and advances. There is no decline in any one of the years but there are variations in the yearly increment. Similarly business per employee had gone up from Rs. 68.64 lakhs to Rs. 857.29 lakhs in the same period. The ratio between credit and deposit reveals the possibilities of utilisation of available deposits in the form of credit. Higher percentage of CDR shows more benefits to society through credit mechanisation in the context of rural areas or it reveals how much the SGB has helped the rural development through credit. The lesser percentage of CDR shows the lesser benefits to the society through its credit mechanisation and deposit mobilisation in the context of rural areas. The CDR has been regarded an indicator of the SGBs performance in credit operations. On an average, per year, business per branch, business per employee and CDR stood Rs. 1,947.23 lakhs, Rs. 454.75 lakhs and Rs. 114.23 lakhs respectively during the period. The CV per employee is 56.85 per cent, indicating more variability and less consistency. In CDR, it is less, which shows less variability and more consistency. The CGAR in the business per employee was 28.72 per cent and 2.55 per cent in CDR. These are significant at one per cent level.

The CDR was more than 100 per cent during 2005 and 2014 (**see Table 4.11**). It reflects that the deposits mobilised by the SGB were fully locally deployed in this period. It means deposits were not distributed as advances in the non - operational area of the bank in all the 10 years. It may be inferred that there is a growth in the business per branch and employee throughout the period. The phenomenon of CDR is a welcome one. In these ten years, the collected urban savings were deployed in its operational area.

This was because of lesser development of banking habit among the locals. Apart from this, a commensurately higher cash holding habit of the rural clientele of the SGB was also responsible for this. The CDR was relatively higher in the SGB due to fact that it was not only relying on deposit but also on borrowings from other banks and its main object was to provide financial supports to the rural public. The bank deployed all the locally mobilised deposits in its operational area in all these years. The bank availed itself of the refinance facility through borrowings from the Indian Bank, the IDBI and the NABARD to meet deployments over deposits. But in the long run, it may not be good on the part of the bank to depend on others for advancing loans to needy people in its operational area. The lowering CDR should be viewed as a slight improvement in the banking habit of rural borrower and not entirely as a matter of change in policy alone. The performance of the bank in deposit mobilisation and credit deployment is undoubtedly praiseworthy. These are reflected in the CDR. The present loan operation is

Table 4.11: Business and CDR of SGB during 2005 – 14 (Rs.lakhs)

| Year | Business per | | C D R (%) |
	Branch	Employee	
2005	474.06	68.64	100.74
2006	995.65	199.13	114.13
2007	1,238.92	250.21	105.79
2008	1,481.06	319.67	107.56
2009	1,647.05	400.72	113.91
2010	2,006.56	450.87	111.31
2011	2,297.48	571.39	112.95
2012	2,692.62	633.31	119.50
2013	3,083.47	796.22	126.78
2014	3,555.39	857.29	129.64
Average	1,947.23	454.75	114.23
S.D.	968.61	258.54	9.01
C.V. (%)	49.74	56.85	7.89
CAGR (%)	22.32	28.72	2.55
't' cal	6.36**	5.57**	40.08**

Note: **S.D.** : Standard deviation; **C.V.** : Coefficient of variation
CAGR : Compound annual growth rate ; ** : Indicates significant at 1 per cent level;
Source: As in Table 4.1

134

in conformity with the avowed goals of the bank. Keeping in view rural development, the SGB has made dedicated efforts to provide easy and timely credit to farm and non - farm sectors in the operational area.

4. Recovery performance:

Recycling of funds is one of the major determinant factors of credit expansion. It is a function of recovery of advances. Recovery of loans means realisation of advance scheduled to be repaid by borrowers. Recovery of advances is a source of mobilisation of funds for future operations. If recovery is low, banks will have to arrange additional funds through deposit mobilisation or borrowings for carrying on the existing/ potential business. Higher the recovery of loans, greater is the effectiveness of lending at a given level of funds. The speedy recovery and deployment of credit accelerate the pace of rural development. Recovery of loans plays a pivotal role in the upliftment of the weakest of the weak. Credit supervision constitutes an integral part of credit deployment function. It has to be ensured that the credit disbursed is used for the avowed purpose. Then it enables the borrower to repay the loan out of income generated in time as per schedule. Given credit should result in income generation and building up of repaying capacity. In the literature, it is held that the recovery performance makes a financial institution more viable and self - sustainable.

The SGB had spread far and wide in the operational area. The credit deployed by it had also increased several folds. A wide variety of rural clientele with divergent socio - economic - political and educational background became borrowers of this bank for equally varied range of purposes. In order to cater to the requirements of the rural public, the SGB has tried to equip itself suitably. Notwithstanding the attempts, there appears to be a growing gulf between the SGB on the one hand and the borrowers on the other. It is observed in the first chapter that there exists a wide gap between the amount demanded and the recovery in most of RRBs at the macro level. It reflects the failure on the part of the borrowers to make prompt repayment of advances. It also shows that the recovery drives adopted by RRBs were defective. As a result, collection was poor and a huge amount existed as overdues. If the overdues rise out of proportion, the loanable funds at the disposal of the SGB would dry up and thereby bring down the pace of rural development. The deteriorating situation arising out of non - repayment of loans has not received the attention it deserves. If this aspect moves out of control, the lending function would be drastically affected. The SGB has, therefore, to be careful while offering financial assistance and take every precaution to ensure timely recovery of advances.

The SGB is not a philanthropic organisation to grant loans to the needy people. It is an institution dealing in accepting money, granting interest on deposits and lending money to the needy at a stipulated rate of interest for a stipulated period. The borrowers are required to repay the principal amount of loan along with the amount of accrued interest as per the repayment schedule. Proper functioning of these activities results in the flow of funds from and into the bank. Thus, recovery of loans advanced to the needy has a direct bearing on the economic survival, efficiency and prosperity of the bank. The inadequate or non - recovery of loans inhibits the ability of the rural banking system to recycle its funds. Non - payment of bank dues by a section of borrowers would only mean denying the benefit to other borrowers. Poor performance in the matter of recovery also cripples the capacity of the SGB to draw refinance from apex institution because bank's eligibility criteria are now linked with its recovery performance.

The SGB fixes the repayment schedule in such a manner as to make it convenient to the borrower based on his repaying capacity and income generation. In order to supervise the credit effectively, the bank has recruited field supervisors. Despite the best efforts put forth by the SGB, the overdues have grown unabated year after year. In view of the importance of credit expansion, the recovery performance and overdues of the SGB are analysed in this section. The emphasis is laid on demand, collection and overdues. The demand is arrived at by the SGB based on the advances made in each year. The causes for mounting overdues are believed to be manifold. It would be a fruitful exercise, if these causes are sorted out and analysed. With this end in view, the researcher has collected the views of the field level staff on the matters relating to recovery efficiency and overdues. This helps in formulating relevant strategies or incorporating measures to contain the growth of overdues further by improving the recovery rate in the years to come.

4.1 Trend:

Analysis of yearly demand, collection and overdues of the SGB are presented in the **Table 4.12** and exhibited in **Figure 4.4.** The percentage of recovery to demand has increased from 86.61 in 2005 to 87.42 in 2014. There is a gradual growth during the period except 2007, 2009, 2010, 2012 and 2014. The recovery was the highest at 93.39 per cent in 2006. In absolute figures, the collection has progressively increased from Rs. 14,956.38 lakhs in 2005 to Rs. 2,04,190.99 lakhs in 2014. The overdues which stood at Rs. 2,313.34 lakhs in 2005 have risen to Rs. 29,381.50 lakhs in 2014 with relative ups and downs. These were maximum at Rs. 29,381.50 lakhs in 2014. It is happy to note that the recovery performance was quite impressive and showed a growing trend. On the other hand, overdues rose year after year despite the best efforts put forth by the SGB to keep it as low as possible. On an average, per year, demand, recovery and overdues stood Rs. 88,303.23 lakhs, Rs. 77,595.43 lakhs and Rs. 10,704.81 lakhs sequentially during the period.

Table 4.12: Yearly Recovery Performance of SGB during 2005 - 14

(Rs. lakhs)

Year (1)	Demand (2)	Recovery (3)	Overdues (4)	% col (3) to col (2) (5)
2005	17,269.72	14,956.38	2,313.34	86.61
2006	18,292.53	17,082.91	1,209.62	93.39
2007	38,666.51	32,805.87	5,860.64	84.96
2008	51,919.06	46,349.11	5,569.95	89.27
2009	54,521.77	47,650.63	6,871.14	87.40
2010	73,885.61	62,103.85	11,751.76	84.05
2011	91,941.50	81,329.03	10,612.47	88.46
2012	128,792.84	1,12,125.13	16,667.71	87.06
2013	174,170.28	1,57,360.36	16,809.92	90.35
2014	233,572.49	2,04,190.99	29,381.50	87.42
Average	88,303.23	77,595.43	10,704.81	87.87

Source: As in Table 4.1

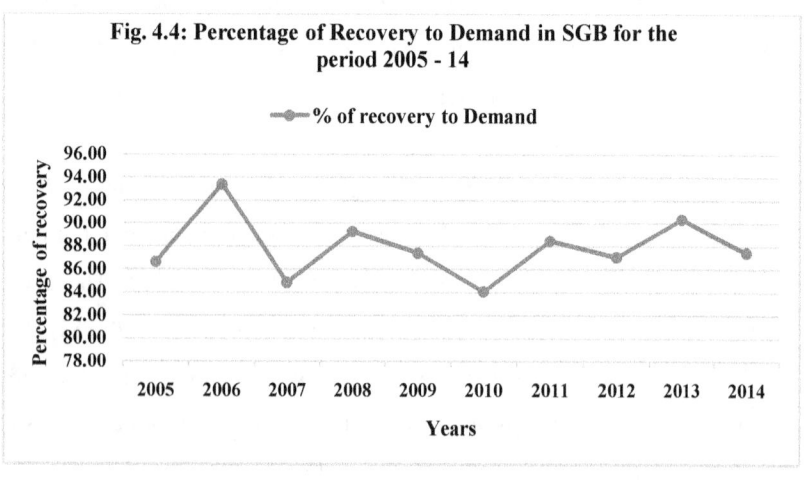

Fig. 4.4: Percentage of Recovery to Demand in SGB for the period 2005 - 14

Source: Table 4.12

138

4.2 Farm sector:

Recovery of credit in the farm sector of the SGB during 2005 - 14 is furnished in the **Table 4.13.** The proportion of recovery to demand was 85.97 per cent in 2005 as against 84.85 per cent in 2014. In the meantime, there are fluctuations in the yearly recovery rate. The recovery efficiency has reached an all time high at 94.23 per cent in 2006. The amount demanded

Table 4.13: Recovery of Loans in Farm Sector of SGB during 2005 – 14

(Rs. lakhs)

Year (1)	Demand (2)	Recovery (3)	Overdues (4)	% of col (3) to col (2) (5)
2005	14,616.91	12,566.26	2,050.65	85.97
2006	14,370.15	13,540.92	829.23	94.23
2007	31,805.93	26,694.96	5,110.97	83.93
2008	35,444.63	31,076.75	4,367.88	87.68
2009	35,838.59	30,307.39	5,531.20	84.57
2010	31,806.66	23,731.42	8,075.24	74.61
2011	40,374.33	33,932.04	6,442.29	84.04
2012	65,959.08	54,437.75	11,521.33	82.53
2013	86,542.03	80,846.63	5,695.40	93.42
2014	1,48,133.91	1,25,691.52	22,442.39	84.85
Average	50,489.22	43,282.56	7,206.66	85.58

Source: As in Table 4.1

has gone up from Rs. 14,616.91 lakhs in 2005 as compared to Rs. 1,48,133.91 lakhs in 2014. In the collection also, there is a like trend. The overdue amount was Rs. 2,050.65 lakhs in 2005 as against Rs. 22,442.39 lakhs in 2014. On an average, per year, demand, recovery and overdues stood Rs. 50,489.22 lakhs, Rs. 43,282.56 lakhs and Rs. 7,206.66 lakhs respectively during the period. It may be concluded that the recovery performance has improved in the SGB during the study period.

4.3. Non - farm sector:

The **Table 4.14** shows the recovery efficiency of the SGB in the non - farm sector during 2005 to 2014. This is also evident from the **Figure 4.5.** The recovery performance was 90.10 per cent in 2005 and reached 91.88 per cent in 2014 with relative ups and downs. It was highest at 92.83 per cent in 2009 while it was lowest at 87.32 per cent in 2013. Overdues account for the rest. In absolute terms, demand has increased from Rs. 2,652.81 lakhs in 2005 as compared to Rs. 85,438.58 lakhs in 2014. There is a continuous growth in it except 2014 when there was a decline. A similar trend exists in the case of loans recovered. The recovery stood at Rs. 2,390.12 lakhs in 2005 relative to Rs. 78,499.47 lakhs in 2014. In the overdue amount also, there are fluctuations in the yearly amount. On an average, per year, demand, recovery and overdues stood Rs. 37,814.01 lakhs, Rs. 34,315.86 lakhs and Rs. 3,498.15 lakhs serially during the period. It may be concluded that the recovery performance in the non - farm loans of the SGB showed on improvement over the period. It can be observed that the recovery rate in the

Table 4.14 Recovery of Advances in Non-farm Sector of SGB during 2005 - 14

(Rs. lakhs)

Year (1)	Demand (2)	Recovery (3)	Overdues (4)	% of col (3) to col (2) (5)
2005	2,652.81	2,390.12	262.69	90.10
2006	3,922.38	3,541.99	380.39	90.30
2007	6,860.58	6,110.91	749.67	89.07
2008	16,474.43	15,272.36	1,202.07	92.70
2009	18,683.18	17,343.24	1,339.94	92.83
2010	42,078.95	38,402.43	3,676.52	91.26
2011	51,567.17	47,396.99	4,170.18	91.91
2012	62,833.76	57,687.38	5,146.38	91.81
2013	87,628.25	76,513.73	11,114.52	87.32
2014	85,438.58	78,499.47	6,939.11	91.88
Average	37,814.01	34,315.86	3,498.15	90.92

Source: As in Table 4.1

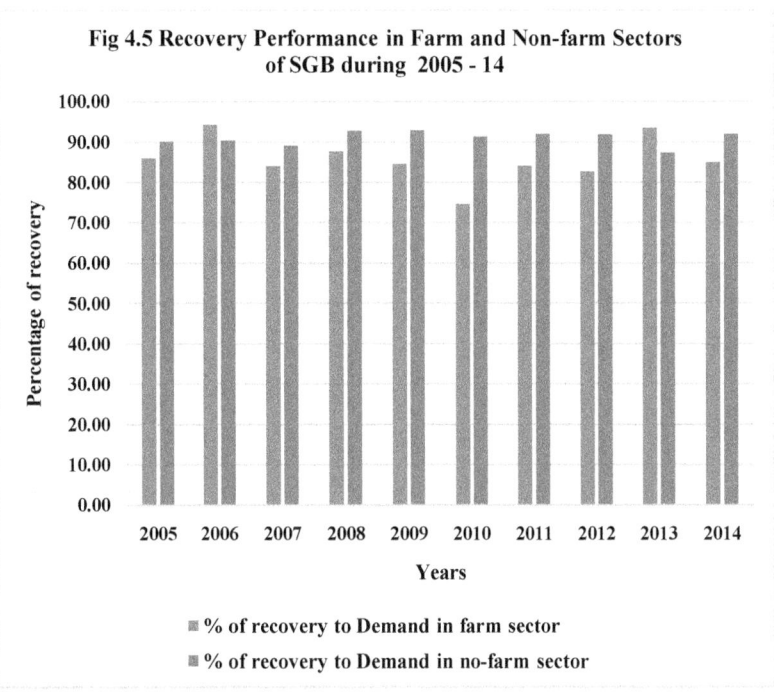

Fig 4.5 Recovery Performance in Farm and Non-farm Sectors of SGB during 2005 - 14

Source: Table 4.13 and 4.14

farm sector is favourable in four years when compared to non - farm sector. In otherwords, the recovery efficiency was highest in the farm sector during 2006 and 2014. In the remaining period, a contrary situation prevails. It may be summed up that the non - farm sector ranked first in six years while the farm sector occupied the first place in four years.

CHAPTER – V
FINANCIAL PERFORMANCE

Viability has a direct bearing on the efficiency of any bank. Viability, along with other factors, is to a large extent determined by the relationship between expenditure and income. Performance of any credit organisation should be evaluated from the angle of task dimension, that is, socio-economic objectives for which it is created. RRBs were launched with much fanfare some 40 years ago to help the rural poor. Their growth has raised the hope that they will in all probability force to reckon with development activity. Being specially created to cater to the needs of the weaker sections of society, profit cannot be the sole motive of RRBs. Nevertheless, the fact remains that no financial institution can incur loss over a long period of time. The trends on this horizon do indicate that they are today in the red. It is equally necessary to ensure that the social objectives do not provide an umbrella to the inefficiency and therefore, an appraisal of working of credit institution must be based both on the fulfilment of social objectives as well as its financial viability. A credit institution is considered to be viable, if it attains a level of business which gives income that would enable it to meet not only all the expenses, but also help it to build up a minimum reserve over a period of time. Further, it is to be noted that the economic viability of RRBs is absolutely necessary to improve the economic well - being of the rural poor.

Financial strength is a necessary prerequisite for the survival and growth of any organisation. This is valid for the Saptagiri Grameena Bank (SGB) as it is for any other institution. The SGB, to be efficient must have sound financial position which enables it to run smoothly and render valuable service effectively to its customers. In fact, the quality of its services to a considerable extent depends on its financial base. It should strive to maintain a reasonable balance between income and expenditure with a due provision for payment of interest and generation of internal resources. It is in this context, the financial performance of the SGB is analysed to identify its financial strength and weaknesses.

1. Income generation:

The sources of income of the SGB include interest earned on advances outstanding, deposits kept with sponsored bank, the Reserve Bank of India (RBI), other banks, discounts, commission, exchange, brokerage and miscellaneous receipts. When all the sources of income are put together, it has progressively increased from Rs. 4,549.79 lakhs in 2005 to Rs. 41,642.90 lakhs in 2014 without any decline (**see Table 5.1**). The year to year fluctuations are in the range of 6.90 – 61.87 per cent in the aforesaid period. The interest income was Rs. 4,389.75 lakhs in 2005 as compared to Rs. 40,173.62 lakhs in 2014. The trend in its increase is similar to that of total income. In the total income, the share of interest income was in the range of 95.36 – 96.67 per cent. The non - interest income was Rs. 160.04 lakhs in 2005 as against Rs. 1,469.28 lakhs in 2014. The non - interest income is insignificant when compared to interest income. The income of the SGB is given in **Figure 5.1.** On an average, per year, interest, non - interest income amount and total income stood Rs. 17,526.21 lakhs, Rs. 712.39 lakhs and Rs. 18,238.60 lakhs during the period sequentially. Coefficient of variation (CV) is the highest in interest income (72.98 per cent) followed by total income (72.83 per cent) and non –interest income (70.12 per cent). The compound annual growth rate (CAGR) was 24.781 per cent, 24.783 per cent and 24.821 per cent in interest income, total income and non - interest income respectively which are significant at one per cent level. The calculated value of 't' is more than the corresponding critical value at one per cent level. Hence, it is significant at one per cent level. It may be concluded that the bank has substantially earned income in the reference period. The interest income outweighs non - interest income. This is in tune

Table 5.1 Income of the SGB during 2005 - 14

(Rs. lakhs)

Year	Interest income	Non-interest income	Total	% of change	% of col (3) to col (4)
(1)	(2)	(3)	(4)	(5)	(6)
2005	4,389.75	160.04	4,549.79	-	96.48
2006	4,701.62	162.29	4,863.91	6.90	96.66
2007	5,841.48	263.12	6,104.60	25.51	95.69
2008	9,423.68	458.05	9,881.73	61.87	95.36
2009	12,008.29	546.82	12,555.11	27.05	95.64
2010	16,346.42	562.58	16,909.00	34.68	96.67
2011	20,744.88	990.09	21,734.97	28.54	95.44
2012	27,282.36	1,054.31	28,336.67	30.37	96.28
2013	34,350.00	1,457.35	35,807.35	26.36	95.93
2014	40,173.62	1,469.28	41,642.90	16.30	96.47
Average	17,526.21	712.39	18,238.60		
S.D.	12,791.26	499.55	13,283.34		
C.V. (%)	72.98	70.12	72.83		
CAGR (%)	24.781	24.821	24.783		
't' cal	4.33**	4.51**	4.34**		

Note: S.D.   : Standard deviation

C.V.   : Coefficient of variation

CAGR : Compound annual growth rate

**   : Indicates significant at 1 per cent level

Source   : Relevant issues of the SGB, Annual Report, Chittoor.

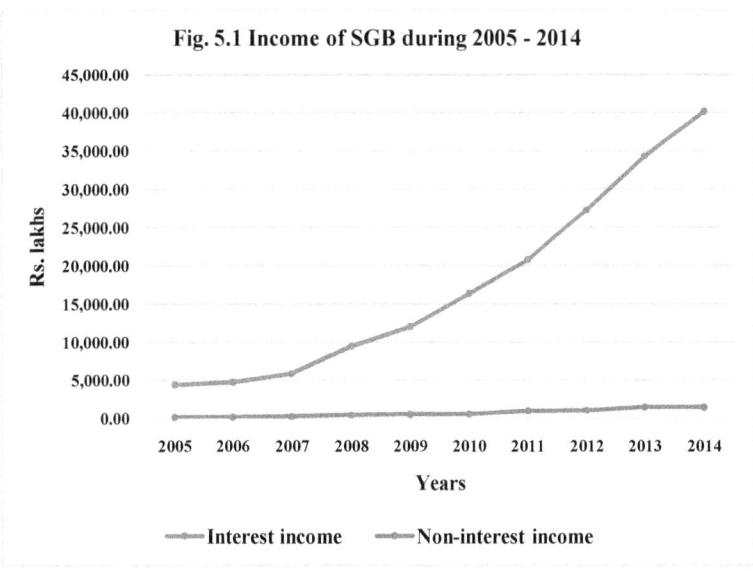

Fig. 5.1 Income of SGB during 2005 - 2014

Source: Table 5.1

with the nature of business undertaken by SGB. Further, more than 95 per cent of total income of the bank is from interest source.

The classification of interest income of the SGB is provided in the **Table 5.2.** Among the sources of interest income, interest/discount on advances/outstanding bills ranks first. The interest/discount was Rs. 35,754.90 lakhs in 2014 as compared to Rs. 3,303.32 lakhs in 2005. In percentage terms, it constituted 89.00 and 75.25 in the same period sequentially. The income on investments ranked second place. Income under this source was as low as Rs. 877.33 lakhs in 2005 whilst Rs. 4,189.21 lakhs in 2014. The income from investments was in the order of 10.43 – 19.99 per cent during the period. The share interest on balances with banks formed 4.76 per cent in 2005 as against 0.57 per cent in 2014. Interest on balances with banks occupied the third place. The interest earned to volume of business of the bank was 6.20 per cent in 2005 while 6.23 per cent in 2014.

145

Table 5.2: Classification of Interest Income of the SGB during 2005 - 14

(Rs. lakhs)

Year	Interest/ discount on advances/ bills	Income on investments	Interest on balances with banks	Total	Ratio of interest earned to	
					Volume of business	Working fund
2005	3,303.32 (75.25)	877.33 (19.99)	209.10 (4.76)	4,389.75 (100)	6.20	7.76
2006	3,855.29 (82.00)	767.14 (16.32)	79.19 (1.68)	4,701.62 (100)	5.95	7.34
2007	4,685.45 (80.21)	912.54 (15.62)	243.49 (4.17)	5,841.48 (100)	4.58	6.00
2008	7,741.67 (82.15)	1,326.18 (14.07)	355.83 (3.78)	9,423.68 (100)	5.84	9.39
2009	9,840.50 (81.95)	1,714.15 (14.27)	453.64 (3.78)	12,008.29 (100)	5.74	9.42
2010	13,972.22 (85.48)	2,105.77 (12.88)	268.43 (1.64)	16,346.42 (100)	6.22	10.09
2011	17,806.26 (85.83)	2,677.72 (12.91)	260.90 (1.26)	20,744.88 (100)	6.27	9.64
2012	23,780.13 (87.16)	3,439.25 (12.61)	62.98 (0.23)	27,282.36 (100)	6.71	10.10
2013	29,572.69 (86.09)	4,537.99 (13.21)	239.32 (0.70)	34,350.00 (100)	7.10	9.87
2014	35,754.90 (89.00)	4,189.21 (10.43)	229.51 (0.57)	40,173.62 (100)	6.23	10.47
Average	15,031.24 (85.76)	2,254.73 (12.86)	240.24 (1.37)	17,526.21 (100)		
S.D.	11,430.23	1,399.43	114.78	12,791.26		
C.V. (%)	76.04	62.07	47.78	72.98		
CAGR (%)	26.89	16.92	0.94	24.78		
't' cal	4.16**	5.10**	6.61**	4.33**		

Note: Figures in brackets indicate the percentage to total
      S.D. : Standard deviation
      C.V. : Coefficient of variation
    CAGR : Compound annual growth rate
      ** : Indicates significant at 1 per cent level
Source: As in Table 5.1.

It reflects that the lending operations of the bank have declined during the period. The ratio of interest earned is related to working fund of a bank. Therefore, it is analysed here. The interest earned to working fund ratio is calculated by dividing the former by the latter and expressed in percentage terms. This ratio is computed to ascertain the rate at which the SGB earns income by way of interest through lending funds. This ratio has declined from 7.76 per cent in 2005 to 10.47 per cent in 2014. It was highest at 10.47 per cent in 2014 while lowest at 6.00 per cent in 2007. On an average, per year, interest/discount on advances/outstanding bills, income on investments and interest on balances with banks stood at Rs. 15,031.24 lakhs, Rs. 2,254.73 lakhs, Rs. 240.24 lakhs respectively during the period. The degree of variation was least in interest on balances with banks (47.78 per cent) followed by income on investments (62.07 per cent) while interest/discount on advances/bills, the highest 76.04 per cent. The overall variation in total interest income is 72.98 per cent. The CAGR was 0.94 per cent, 16.92 per cent, 24.78 per cent and 26.89 per cent in interest on balances with banks, income on investments, total interest income and interest/discount on advances/bills respectively. These are significant at one per cent level. The fluctuating trend reveals that there is a disproportionate growth in the interest earned and working fund. It signifies that of the 10 years, the initial period earned the least interest as a percentage of working fund whereas the recent past earned the highest. It means that the last years proved to be the most efficient in utilising working funds at its command.

It may be summed up that, of the sources of interest income, interest/discounts on advances outstanding and bills ranks first with more than 75 per cent. Further, interest on balances with banks occupied second place while income on investments occupied third place. This reflects the business of the bank. In this context, it may be pointed out that the main activity of the banks is disbursement of loans along with discounting of bills. The trend in the interest earned ratio is heartening.

The **Table 5.3** reveals the categorisation of non - interest income of the bank. It can be observed that commission, exchange and brokerage were Rs. 102.92 lakhs in 2005 when compared to Rs. 196.47 lakhs in 2014. The rest is miscellaneous income, which was Rs. 57.12 lakhs in 2005 vis - à - vis Rs. 1,272.81 lakhs in 2014. In the total non – interest income, commission, exchange and brokerage was in the range of 13.37 - 64.31 per cent and the remaining, miscellaneous income. The non - interest income to volume of business ratio was 0.23 per cent in 2005 as against 0.25 per cent during 2014. The other income ratio registered the trend similar to interest earned ratio. The non - interest income to working fund ratio is calculated to determine the rate of non - interest income in working fund. From the view point of profitability, non - interest income of the bank is considered as an important factor. This is so because the quantum of burden is reduced if non - interest income increases. Thus banks have to lay much emphasis to increase non - interest income so as to have higher profitability. The ratio of non - interest income to working fund fluctuated between 0.25 per cent and0.46 per cent over the period under study. The variation in this ratio over the period was characterised by difference in the growth rates of non - interest income and working fund. On an average, per year, commission, exchange and brokerage and miscellaneous income stood Rs. 190.62 lakhs, Rs. 521.77 lakhs serially during the period. The degree of variation was least in commission, exchange and brokerage (33.68 per cent) followed by miscellaneous income (88.45 per cent). The overall variation in total non - interest income is 70.12 per cent. The CAGR in miscellaneous income was 36.39 per cent and commission, exchange and brokerage 6.68 per cent. They are significant at one per cent level. It may be inferred that the commission,

Table 5.3: Distribution of Non - Interest Income of the SGB during 2005 – 14 (Rs. lakhs)

Year	Commission, exchange & brokerage	Miscellaneous	Total	Ratio of non - interest income to	
				Volume of business (%)	Working fund (%)
2005	102.92 (64.31)	57.12 (35.69)	160.04 (100)	0.23	0.28
2006	98.56 (60.73)	63.73 (39.27)	162.29 (100)	0.21	0.25
2007	120.77 (45.90)	142.35 (54.10)	263.12 (100)	0.21	0.27
2008	218.06 (47.61)	239.99 (52.39)	458.05 (100)	0.28	0.46
2009	271.37 (49.63)	275.45 (50.37)	546.82 (100)	0.26	0.43
2010	196.04 (34.85)	366.54 (65.15)	562.58 (100)	0.21	0.35
2011	250.84 (25.34)	739.25 (74.66)	990.09 (100)	0.30	0.46
2012	189.27 (17.95)	865.04 (82.05)	1,054.31 (100)	0.26	0.39
2013	261.89 (17.97)	1,195.46 (82.03)	1,457.35 (100)	0.30	0.42
2014	196.47 (13.37)	1,272.81 (86.63)	1,469.28 (100)	0.25	0.38
Average	190.62 (26.76)	521.77 (73.24)	712.39 (100)		
S.D.	64.20	461.50	499.55		
C.V. (%)	33.68	88.45	70.12		
CAGR(%)	6.68	36.39	24.82		
't' cal	9.41**	3.58**	4.51**		

Note: Figures in brackets indicate the percentage to total
   S.D. : Standard deviation
   C.V. : Coefficient of variation
   CAGR : Compound annual growth rate
   ** : Indicates significant at 1 per cent level
Source: As in Table 5.1.

exchange and brokerage account for a lion's share in the non – interest income of the SGB. It was more than half in 2 years and miscellaneous income in the rest of the period. Further, the non – interest income ratio shows a declining trend which is unwelcome from the view point of profitability of the bank. Furthermore, the percentage of working fund in the non - interest income has declined during the period.

2. Expenditure:

The main heads of expenditure of the SGB are interest paid and operating expenses. A look at the **Table 5.4** reveals that the aggregate expenditure of the SGB had gradually increased from Rs. 4,383.98 lakhs in 2005 to Rs. 34,242.58 lakhs in 2014. In the year 2006, it declined at 0.25 per cent. In the rest of the years, there was an increase. It varied between 17.67 per cent and 65.03 per cent. Interest paid on deposits mobilised from the public and on borrowings constitute the bulk of total interest cost. The interest paid and operating expenses show a similar trend. The interest paid was Rs. 26,586.19 lakhs in 2014 as compared to Rs. 2,542.82 lakhs in 2005. As the business expanded and the resources were mobilised on an increasing scale, the interest payment also increased correspondingly. The proportion of interest paid in the total expenditure was in the order of 57.87 - 79.16 per cent. Similarly, operating expenses were Rs. 1,142.36 lakhs and Rs. 5,366.39 lakhs in the latter and former respectively. The operating expenses constituted between 15.67 per cent and 38.86 per cent in the reference period. The provisions and contingencies were Rs. 698.80 lakhs in 2005 whilst Rs. 2,290.00 lakhs in 2014. The provisions and contingencies formed 2.44 – 15.94 per cent in the study period. The provisions for investments were Rs. 275 lakhs in 2013 whilst Rs. 17.44 lakhs in 2008. There is no

Table 5.4: Expenditure of the SGB during 2005 – 14 (Rs. lakhs)

Year (1)	Interest paid (2)	Operating expenses (3)	Provisions & contingencies (4)	Provision for investments (5)	Total (6)	% of change (7)
2005	2,542.82 (58.00)	1,142.36 (26.06)	698.80 (15.94)	-	4,383.98 (100)	0
2006	2,530.84 (57.87)	1,699.54 (38.86)	142.80 (3.27)	-	4,373.18 (100)	-0.25
2007	3,062.00 (59.50)	1,684.03 (32.72)	400.00 (7.77)	-	5,146.03 (100)	17.67
2008	5,647.07 (66.50)	2,127.74 (25.06)	700.00 (8.24)	17.44 (0.21)	8,492.25 (100)	65.03
2009	8,269.32 (75.40)	2,298.24 (20.95)	400.00 (3.65)	-	10,967.56 (100)	29.15
2010	10,612.48 (74.14)	3,001.49 (20.97)	700.00 (4.89)	-	14,313.97 (100)	30.51
2011	13,011.24 (73.28)	4,595.12 (25.88)	-	150.00 (0.84)	17,756.36 (100)	24.05
2012	17,748.70 (78.35)	4,150.31 (18.32)	553.00 (2.44)	200.00 (0.88)	22,652.01 (100)	27.57
2013	22,824.57 (79.16)	4,652.80 (16.14)	1,080.00 (3.75)	275.00 (0.95)	28,832.37 (100)	27.28
2014	26,586.19 (77.64)	5,366.39 (15.67)	2,290.00 (6.69)	-	34,242.58 (100)	18.76
Average	11,283.52 (74.65)	3,071.80 (20.32)	696.46 (4.61)	64.24 (0.43)	15,116.03 (100)	
S.D.	8,654.22	1,500.92	638.96	103.90	10,590.56	
C.V. (%)	76.70	48.86	91.74	161.73	70.06	
CAGR (%)	26.45	16.73	12.60	31.76	22.82	
't' cal	4.12**	6.47**	3.45**	1.95*	4.51**	

Note: Figures in brackets indicate the percentage to total
      S.D.   : Standard deviation
      C.V.   : Coefficient of variation
    CAGR : Compound annual growth rate
       *   : Indicates significant at 5 per cent level
      **   : Indicates significant at 1 per cent level

Source : As in Table 5.1.

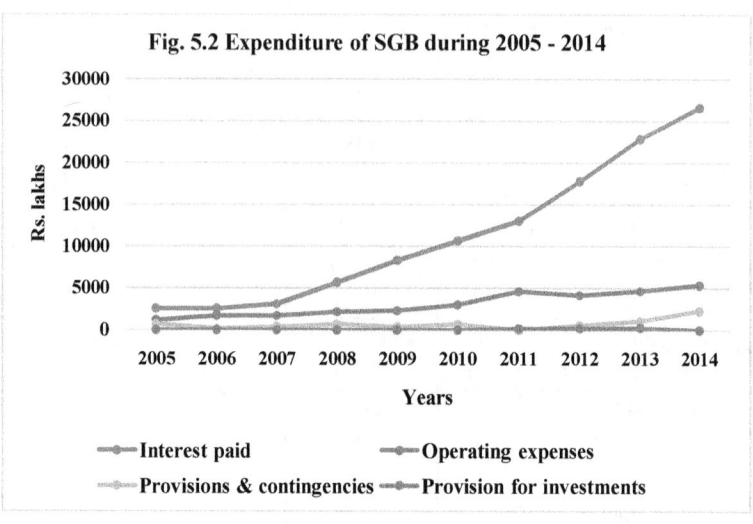

Fig. 5.2 Expenditure of SGB during 2005 - 2014

Source: Table 5.4

provision for investments during 2005, 2006, 2007, 2009, 2010 and 2014. In the rest of the period, they are in the range of 0.21 – 0.95 percent. On an average, per year, interest paid, operating expenses, provisions and contingencies and provision for investments stood Rs. 11,283.52 lakhs, Rs.3,071.80 lakhs, Rs. 696.46 lakhs, and Rs. 64.24 lakhs serially during the period. The C.V. in the provision for investments was the highest at 161.73 per cent followed by provisions and contingencies (91.74 per cent), interest paid (76.70 per cent) and total expenditure 70.06 per cent. Inconsistency in operating expenses was 48.86 per cent. The CAGR was 31.76 per cent in the provision for investments and lower at 12.60 per cent in the provisions and contingencies. The CAGR is significant in interest paid, operating expenses, provisions and contingencies at one per cent level whilst at 5 per cent level in provision for investments. It may be concluded that the total expenditure has increased during the period. Of the total expenditure, interest expended accounts for a lion's share with more than 58 per cent. It can be observed that the operating expenses had declined in percentage terms, though there was an increase in their magnitude. They came second in the order followed by provisions and contingencies. This can be attributed to the fact that the increase in interest charges had completely outweighed the increase in establishment charges. The increase in the total expenditure mainly owed to increase in interest paid on deposits and borrowings and not so much on account of growth in establishment expenses. **Figure 5.2** presents this clearly.

Efforts can be made to reduce the interest charges by resorting to various cheap sources of finance. Interest is paid on various types of deposits secured from the public and the borrowings from various agencies including the RBI and sponsor bank. Since the rate of interest differs among various types of deposits and purposes and sources of borrowing, the bank can think of raising funds from those deposits and sources which carry relatively lower rate of interest. In this context, an earlier observation may be recalled that short term deposits which carry nil interest had a meagre share in the total deposits of the SGB. Hence, it can be reiterated that canvassing may be launched on a vigorous scale to mobilise them in order to minimise interest charges.

The interest paid by SGB is segregated into interest paid on deposits and borrowings. It can be observed from the **Table 5.5** that the interest paid on deposits was more than that of interest paid on borrowings. The interest expended on deposits constituted Rs. 2,102.09 lakhs in 2005 and it was Rs. 18,219.15 lakhs in 2014. The interest paid on borrowings formed Rs. 440.73 lakhs and Rs. 8,367.04 lakhs in the former and latter respectively. Out of the total amount of interest paid, interest paid on deposits was 82.67 per cent in 2005 as compared to 68.53 per cent in 2014. The rest was paid as interest on borrowings. It can be noticed that the interest paid on borrowings has grown faster than the interest paid on deposits. The interest paid to volume of business ratio was 3.59 per cent in 2005 as compared to 4.59 per cent in 2014. In the meantime, there are fluctuations in the yearly ratio. The year 2007 registered the lowest at 2.40 per cent while in 2013 the highest at 4.71 per cent.

Interest paid is related to working fund of a bank. Hence, interest paid to working fund is considered to evaluate profitability. To obtain the interest paid to working fund ratio, interest expended by a bank is divided by working fund and expressed as a percentage. This ratio explains as to what per cent of working fund of a bank constitutes the interest cost. There is a fluctuating declining trend in the ratio of interest expended to working fund during the study period. It was 4.49 per cent in 2005 as compared to 6.93 per cent in 2014. It was the highest at 6.93 per cent in 2014 while the lowest at 3.15 per cent in 2007. The variation may be due to fluctuations in the interest payment and rise in the volume of working fund. In other words, there may be disproportionate progress in interest payments and working funds with volatility. It may be summed up that the interest paid on deposits was more than that of interest paid on borrowings. However, the growth in the latter is relatively more than that of the former. The trend in the interest paid ratio is disheartening. It means that the volume of business has grown more than that of the interest paid during the reference period. There is a definite increasing trend in the interest paid on deposits and borrowings.

A close look at the **Table 5.5** reveals that the rise is primarily due to the change in the deposit mix and the proportion of deposits and borrowing to the total fund. On an average, per year, deposits and borrowings stood Rs. 7,769.73 lakhs and Rs. 3,513.79 lakhs serially during the period. The C.V. in borrowings was 81.26 per cent indicating more variability and less

Table 5.5: Segregation of Interest paid by the SGB during 2005 – 14

(Rs. lakhs)

Year	Deposits	Borrowings	Total	Ratio of interest paid to	
				Volume of business (%)	Working fund (%)
2005	2,102.09 (82.67)	440.73 (17.33)	2,542.82 (100)	3.59	4.49
2006	1,898.45 (75.01)	632.39 (24.99)	2,530.84 (100)	3.20	3.95
2007	2,224.42 (72.65)	837.58 (27.35)	3,062.00 (100)	2.40	3.15
2008	3,877.33 (68.66)	1,769.74 (31.34)	5,647.07 (100)	3.50	5.63
2009	5,743.48 (69.46)	2,525.84 (30.54)	8,269.32 (100)	3.95	6.48
2010	7,339.05 (69.15)	3,273.43 (30.85)	10,612.48 (100)	4.04	6.55
2011	8,842.62 (67.96)	4,168.62 (32.04)	13,011.24 (100)	3.93	6.05
2012	12,147.23 (68.44)	5,601.47 (31.56)	17,748.70 (100)	4.37	6.57
2013	15,303.50 (67.05)	7,521.07 (32.95)	22,824.57 (100)	4.71	6.56
2014	18,219.15 (68.53)	8,367.04 (31.47)	26,586.19 (100)	4.59	6.93
Average	7,769.73 (68.86)	3,513.79 (31.14)	11,283.52 (100)	3.83	5.64
S.D.	5,802.76	2,855.47	8,654.22	0.69	1.31
C.V. (%)	74.68	81.26	76.70	18.10	23.25
CAGR (%)	24.10	34.23	26.45	2.49	4.42
't' cal	4.23**	3.89**	4.12**	17.47**	13.60**

Note: Figures in brackets indicate the percentage to total
   S.D.   : Standard deviation
   C.V   : Coefficient of variation
   CAGR : Compound annual growth rate
   **   : Indicates significant at 1 per cent level
Source : As in Table 5.1 and 5.9

consistency. It was 74.68 per cent in deposits which shows less variability and more consistency. The CAGR in borrowings was 34.23 per cent and deposits 24.10 per cent. They are significant at one per cent level. In fact, while long term deposits have increased considerably during the period, there is a marginal increase in the medium term deposits and no increase in short term deposits. Further, the proportion of borrowings to deposits increased significantly. The declining trend in the ratio of interest paid to working fund can be attributed to higher growth in interest payments as compared to working fund. More than 70 per cent of interest was paid for the deposits mobilised from the public and the residual on borrowed funds.

The **Table 5.6** furnishes the details of distribution of operating expenses of the SGB. Of the categories of expenditure incurred, emoluments to employees constituted the highest followed by other expenses. The emoluments to employees were Rs. 3,657.66 lakhs during 2014 vis - à - vis Rs. 980.23 lakhs in 2005. In percentage terms, these have formed 68.16 – 85.81 per cent in the former and latter respectively. Similarly, other expenses were Rs. 1,708.73 lakhs and Rs. 162.13 lakhs in the former and latter sequentially. These were in the range of 14.19 – 32.10 per cent during 2005 – 14. The growth in other expenses is far ahead of emoluments to man - power. Though emoluments increased in the aforesaid period, its share declined. The ratio of man - power expenses to volume of business ratio had decreased from 1.38 per cent to 0.63 per cent during 2005 - 14 serially. It shows that the turnout of employees has improved when compared to expenses incurred on them. The other establishment expenses to volume of business ratio also revealed an identical trend with relative ups and downs. It was 0.23 per cent in 2005 where as 0.29 per cent in 2014.

The ratio of non - interest expenditure to working fund is ascertained to know how much percentage of working fund is being spent towards non - interest costs. The ratio of non - interest expenses to working fund were 2.02 per cent in 2005 as compared to 1.40 per cent in 2014. This ratio was the highest at 2.65 per cent in 2006 whereas the lowest at 1.34 per cent in 2013. There is a decreasing trend with ups and downs in the percentage of non - interest expenses to working fund due to fluctuations in non - interest expenditure and continuous increase in the working fund. It implies that there is no better control over non - interest expenditure in relation to working fund. On an average, per year, expenses towards employees and other establishment expenses stood Rs. 2,256.97 lakhs and Rs. 814.83 lakhs during the period. The C.V. in other establishment expenses was 64.67 per cent, which indicates more variability and less consistency. It was 43.89 per cent in the case of expenses towards employees, which shows less variability and more consistency. The CAGR was 26.56 per cent, 16.73 per cent and 14.07 per cent in other establishment expenses, total non – interest expenses and expenses towards employees respectively. These are significant at one per cent level. It may be inferred that though emoluments to employees were higher relative to other operating expenses, the progress in the latter exceeds the former. Further, there is a decline in the employees' expenses ratio as well as other expenses ratio. These are welcome from the view point of performance of the bank. Furthermore, more than 70 per cent non – interest expenditure was towards employees and the rest other establishment charges.

Table 5.6 Segregation of Operational (Non - interest) expenses of the SGB during 2005 - 14

(Rs. lakhs)

Year	Expenses towards employees	Other establishment expenses	Total	Ratio of non-interest expenses to working fund (%)	Ratio of employee expenses to volume of business (%)	Ratio of other establish-ment expenses to volume of business (%)
2005	980.23 (85.81)	162.13 (14.19)	1,142.36 (100)	2.02	1.38	0.23
2006	1,336.72 (78.65)	362.82 (21.35)	1,699.54 (100)	2.65	1.69	0.46
2007	1,328.10 (78.86)	355.93 (21.14)	1,684.03 (100)	1.73	1.04	0.28
2008	1,667.03 (78.35)	460.71 (21.65)	2,127.74 (100)	2.12	1.03	0.29
2009	1,708.99 (74.36)	589.25 (25.64)	2,298.24 (100)	1.80	0.82	0.28
2010	2,263.37 (75.41)	738.12 (24.59)	3,001.49 (100)	1.85	0.86	0.28
2011	3,513.61 (76.46)	1,081.51 (23.54)	4,595.12 (100)	2.14	1.06	0.33
2012	2,954.62 (71.19)	1,195.69 (28.81)	4,150.31 (100)	1.54	0.73	0.29
2013	3,159.36 (67.90)	1,493.44 (32.10)	4,652.80 (100)	1.34	0.65	0.31
2014	3,657.66 (68.16)	1,708.73 (31.84)	5,366.39 (100)	1.40	0.63	0.29
Average	2,256.97 (73.47)	814.83 (26.53)	3,071.80 (100)	1.86	0.99	0.30
S.D.	990.52	526.92	1,500.92	0.40	0.34	0.06
C.V. (%)	43.89	64.67	48.86	21.32	33.91	19.74
CAGR (%)	14.07	26.56	16.73	-3.61	-7.55	2.57
't' cal	7.21**	4.89**	6.47**	14.84**	9.33**	16.02**

Note: Figures in brackets indicate the percentage to total

        S.D.   : Standard deviation

        C.V   : Coefficient of variation

    CAGR : Compound annual growth rate

        **   : Indicates significant at 1 per cent level

Source : As in Table 5.1.

A glance at the **Table 5.7** shows the distribution of other operating expenses of the SGB. Out of all the other operating expenses of the bank, miscellaneous categories constituted the highest followed by rent, taxes and lighting, depreciation and repairs, printing and stationary and so on. In the total other operating expenses, the proportion of miscellaneous categories was in the range of 12.59 – 49.44 per cent. The share of rent, taxes and lighting was in the order of 11.28 – 22.53 per cent. The percentage of printing and stationary varied between 4.06 and 9.12. The advertisement and publicity have gradually increased from Rs. 1.02 lakhs in 2005 to Rs. 9.84 lakhs in 2014. It constituted less than one per cent throughout the period. Depreciation and repairs formed in the frequency of 15.40 – 45.95 per cent. The fee expended registered less than 5 per cent leaving 2007. The percentage of fee varied between 1.87 and 9.40. The postage, telephone and telegrams charges accounted for 10.39 per cent in 2005 as against 4.71 per cent in 2014. The share of insurance was in the frequency of 2.01 – 20.25 per cent. On an average, per year, rent, taxes and lighting, printing and stationary, advertisement and publicity, depreciation and repairs, fee, postage, telephone and telegrams, insurance and others stood Rs. 125.96 lakhs, Rs. 43.44 lakhs, Rs. 3.65 lakhs, Rs. 263.77 lakhs, Rs. 23.57 lakhs, Rs. 50.34 lakhs, Rs. 33.61 lakhs and Rs. 270.48 lakhs during the period. The C.V. in rent, taxes and lighting was 82.11 per cent followed by advertisement and publicity (74.61 per cent), depreciation and repairs (73.50 per cent), others (69.94 per cent), fee (61.07 per cent), postage, telephone and telegrams (59.40 per cent). Inconsistency in printing and stationary was the least at 52.15 per cent. The CAGR in others was 39.69 per cent whereas in insurance, 4.13 per cent. These are significant at one per cent level. It may

Table 5.7 Distribution of Other Operating Expenses of the SGB during 2005 - 14

(Rs. lakhs)

Year	Rent, taxes & lighting	Printing & stationery	Advertise-ment & Publicity	Depreciation & repairs	Fee	Postage, telephone & telegrams	Insurance	Others
2005	33.73 (20.80)	14.79 (9.12)	1.02 (0.63)	35.72 (22.03)	6.77 (4.18)	16.85 (10.39)	32.83 (20.25)	20.42 (12.59)
2006	43.24 (11.92)	16.17 (4.46)	1.24 (0.34)	166.70 (45.95)	6.78 (1.87)	20.02 (5.52)	42.82 (11.80)	65.85 (18.15)
2007	58.67 (16.48)	22.97 (6.45)	1.34 (0.38)	90.70 (25.48)	33.45 (9.40)	23.88 (6.71)	8.21 (2.31)	116.71 (32.79)
2008	65.24 (14.16)	29.49 (6.40)	1.81 (0.39)	136.02 (29.52)	15.65 (3.40)	32.43 (7.04)	11.89 (2.58)	168.18 (36.50)
2009	84.97 (14.42)	39.97 (6.78)	2.52 (0.43)	166.07 (28.18)	16.24 (2.76)	37.34 (6.34)	11.82 (2.01)	230.32 (39.09)
2010	109.04 (14.77)	67.12 (9.09)	3.69 (0.50)	113.69 (15.40)	18.92 (2.56)	37.23 (5.04)	23.51 (3.19)	364.88 (49.44)
2011	161.19 (14.90)	43.87 (4.06)	5.26 (0.49)	456.45 (42.20)	25.80 (2.39)	93.90 (8.68)	50.12 (4.63)	244.92 (22.65)
2012	150.04 (12.55)	53.90 (4.51)	4.70 (0.39)	437.18 (36.56)	20.94 (1.75)	82.12 (6.87)	51.17 (4.28)	395.64 (33.09)
2013	168.50 (11.28)	74.22 (4.97)	5.12 (0.34)	552.50 (37.00)	39.04 (2.61)	79.17 (5.30)	54.58 (3.65)	520.31 (34.84)
2014	385.02 (22.53)	71.94 (4.21)	9.84 (0.58)	482.70 (28.25)	52.09 (3.05)	80.41 (4.71)	49.19 (2.88)	577.54 (33.80)
Average	125.96 (15.46)	43.44 (5.33)	3.65 (0.45)	263.77 (32.37)	23.57 (2.89)	50.34 (6.18)	33.61 (4.13)	270.48 (33.19)
S.D.	103.43	22.66	2.73	193.87	14.39	29.90	18.39	189.17
C.V. (%)	82.11	52.15	74.61	73.50	61.07	59.40	54.70	69.94
CAGR (%)	27.57	17.14	25.44	29.74	22.64	16.92	4.13	39.69
't' cal	3.85**	6.06**	4.19**	4.31**	5.23**	5.32**	5.80**	4.52**

Note: Figures in brackets indicate the percentage to total
     S.D. : Standard deviation;   C.V : Coefficient of variation;   CAGR : Compound annual growth rate
     ** : Indicates significant at 1 per cent level
Source : As in Table 5.1.

be summed up, that the relative share of each of other operating expenses of the SGB varied in the period.

3. Working results:

Profit cannot and should not be the main criterion for an institution established to meet certain social objectives. But it does not mean that such institution should totally divorce the principle of economic viability. Such institutions should become economically liable in course of time. These call for achieving break-even as early as possible. The financial results of working of some of RRBs do show that they have a potential and capability to attain financial viability and become profit - making institutions. Further, RRBs have to put this right on higher business, if they are to earn profits to build up efficient credit delivery and supervision system and required bad debt and other reserves. It is held that RRBs should act as the rural wings of the public sector banks so that losses incurred by them can be absorbed by sponsor banks through higher rate of interest on their lending activities in other areas. The viability issue of RRBs would receive proper attention only when we make RRB as a subsidiary of sponsor bank. Notwithstanding this, the performance of some of RRBs in the country indicates that their working results are encouraging. Against this background, the income and expenditure of the SGB is analysed and presented in the **Table 5.8** and **Figure 5.3.**

In order to fully comprehend financial situation in which the SGB finds itself, it may be useful to study the working results. The bank has earned a gross profit of Rs. 165.81 lakhs in 2005 as compared to Rs. 7,400.32 lakhs in 2014. It can be observed that the SGB had earned profit in all the years except 2005. This is so because the bank has created unprecedentedly higher amount for provisions and contingencies. The net -

profit has increased from Rs. 347.93 lakhs in 2006 to Rs. 5,110.32 lakhs in 2014 with relative ups and downs. Mean per year, in total income, total expenditure, gross profit, provisions and contingencies and net profit stood Rs. 18,238.60 lakhs, Rs. 15,116.03 lakhs, Rs. 3,122.57 lakhs, Rs. 696.46 lakhs and Rs. 2,426.11 lakhs serially during the period. The C.V. in net profit was 97.50 per cent indicating more variability and less consistency. It was 70.06 per cent in the case of total expenditure which shows less variability and more consistency. The CAGR in gross profit was highest at 46.21 per cent and lowest at 12.60 per cent in the provisions and contingencies which are significant at one per cent level. The primary cause for this may be the speedy recruitment of staff and opening of a large number of branches. Another reason was reduction in the lending rate on advances without any corresponding reduction in the rate of interest. Instead, the rate of interest on different types of deposits was raised. Later on, the bank was able to reap higher profits due to improved business. On an overall basis, the profits tend to increase due to rise in lending rate; exercise of vigorous control over expenditure and availability of refinance under various schemes at comparatively lower rates of interest. The fluctuations in the profit are due to changes in certain years. For example, despite reduction in the rate of interest on advances, increase in the rate of interest on deposits, the bank earned profits almost throughout the study period The major factors that enabled the bank to have these achievements are: planned deployment of funds; effective case management; impressive growth of advances; increase in the business without proportionate rise in man - power; comparatively favourable interest rate structure with total exemption from interest - tax; control over expenditure and avoiding the seepage of income; proper profit planning; apart from economy measures undertaken at the corporate level.

Table 5.8 Profit and Loss of the SGB during 2005 - 14

(Rs. lakhs)

Year	Total income	Total expenditure	Gross profit (2-3)	Provisions & contingencies	Net profit (4-5)
(1)	(2)	(3)	(4)	(5)	(6)
2005	4,549.79	4,383.98	165.81	698.8	-532.99
2006	4,863.91	4,373.18	490.73	142.8	347.93
2007	6,104.60	5,146.03	958.57	400	558.57
2008	9,881.73	8,492.25	1,389.48	700	689.48
2009	12,555.11	10,967.56	1,587.55	400	1,187.55
2010	16,909.00	14,313.97	2,595.03	700	1,895.03
2011	21,734.97	17,756.36	3,978.61	0	3,978.61
2012	28,336.67	22,652.01	5,684.66	553	5,131.66
2013	35,807.35	28,832.37	6,974.98	1,080.00	5,894.98
2014	41,642.90	34,242.58	7,400.32	2,290.00	5,110.32
Average	18,238.60	15,116.03	3,122.57	696.46	2,426.11
S.D.	13,283.34	10,590.56	2,712.77	638.96	2,365.56
C.V. (%)	72.83	70.06	86.24	91.74	97.50
CAGR (%)	24.78	22.82	46.21	12.60	30.83
't' cal	4.34**	4.51**	3.64**	3.45**	3.24**

Note: S.D. : Standard deviation
      C.V : Coefficient of variation
      CAGR : Compound annual growth rate
      ** : Indicates significant at 1 per cent level
Source : As in Table 5.1 and 5.4.

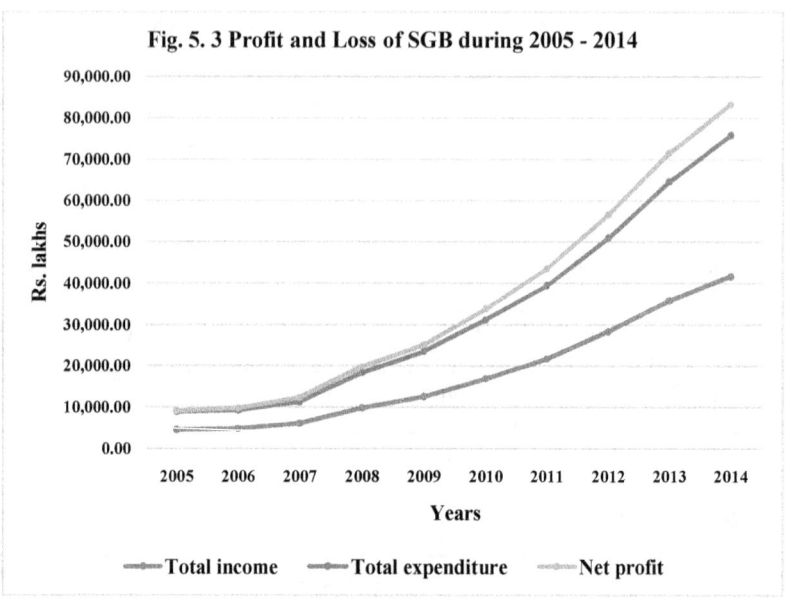

Fig. 5. 3 Profit and Loss of SGB during 2005 - 2014

Source: Table 5.8

The bank should make efforts to increase its productivity of operations and resort to cheaper means of re - finance and depend more on its deposits in the hinterland.

The net profit to total assets ratio is arrived at dividing profit by assets and expressed in percentage terms. The ratio of profit to working fund is derived at dividing net - profit by working fund and expressed in percentage terms. This ratio explains as to what proportion of working fund is earned as net - profit. In other words, it determines the level of resource use efficiency to enhance profit. Profit to total income ratio shows the share of profit to total income. The ratio of profit to total deposit reveals what percentage of deposit is earned as profit. The ratio of profit in relation to total assets, working fund, total income and total deposit is reported in the **Table 5.9.**

164

The profit in total assets has declined from 1.04 per cent in 2005 to 0.70 per cent in 2014 with to and fro changes. It was the highest at 1.16 per cent in 2012 while the lowest at 0.27 per cent in 2009. It infers that there is no corresponding movement between net - profit and total assets employed in the SGB during the period.

There is a declining trend in the ratio of net – profit to working fund with relative ups and downs in the period under reference. It formed 1.23 per cent in 2005 as against 1.33 per cent in 2014. In the meantime, there are volatile fluctuations. The year 2012 reported the maximum at 1.90 per cent whereas the minimum at 0.54 per cent in 2006. The profit as a percentage of working fund has declined in the earlier period as compared to recent one. The efficiency of the bank has increased over the period. The **Table 5.9** discloses the fluctuating trend in the ratio of net – profit to total income of the bank. It was 11.71 per cent in 2005 vis - à - vis 12.27 per cent in 2014. In the intervening period, the ups and downs are noticeable. It recorded the highest percentage at 18.31 in 2011 whilst the lowest at 6.98 in 2008. This poor performance may be attributed to introduction of prudential norms in the SGB. It can be observed that the ratio of profit in relation to total deposit reflects a decreasing trend as in the case of others. The ratio was 1.51 per cent in 2005 to 2.02 per cent in 2014 with to and fro changes. This has registered the highest at 2.77 per cent in 2012 whereas the lowest at 0.89 per cent in 2008. On an average, per year, ratio of profit to total assets, working fund, total income and total deposits stood 0.71 per cent, 1.19 per cent, 12.08 per cent and 1.71 per cent sequentially during the period. The C.V. in the ratio of profit to total deposits was 44.87 per cent, 42.72 per cent in working fund, 40.97 per cent in total assets and 35.01 per cent in total income. The

Table 5.9 Ratio of Profit in Relation to total Assets, Working Fund, Total Income and Total Deposit in the SGB during 2005 - 14

(%)

Year	Ratio of profit to			
	Total assets	Working fund	Total income	Total deposits
2005	1.04	1.23	11.71	1.51
2006	0.61	0.54	7.15	0.94
2007	0.57	0.57	9.15	0.90
2008	0.54	0.69	6.98	0.89
2009	0.27	0.93	9.46	1.21
2010	0.38	1.17	11.21	1.52
2011	0.89	1.85	18.31	2.56
2012	1.16	1.90	18.11	2.77
2013	0.97	1.69	16.46	2.76
2014	0.70	1.33	12.27	2.02
Average	0.71	1.19	12.08	1.71
S.D.	0.29	0.51	4.23	0.77
C.V. (%)	40.97	42.73	35.01	44.87
CAGR (%)	-3.91	0.80	0.47	2.98
't' cal	9.02**	7.40**	9.03**	7.05**

Note: S.D. : Standard deviation
     C.V   : Coefficient of variation
     CAGR : Compound annual growth rate
     **   : Indicates significant at 1 per cent level
Source: As in Table 5.1 and 5.4.

CAGR was -3.91 per cent in total assets. It was 0.47 per cent, 0.80 per cent and 2.98 per cent in total income, working fund and total deposits respectively. They are significant at one per cent level. It implies that the SGB had utilised its deposits more efficiently and therefore, generated the relatively higher profits. It may be concluded that there is a downward trend in the ratio of net - profit to assets, total income, working fund and total deposits.

The interest coverage ratio of the SGB is furnished in the **Table 5.10.** The interest coverage ratio was 0.79 times in 2005 while 1.19 times in 2014. In the meantime, there are noticeable variations. It registered the lowest at 0.79 times in 2005 while the highest at 1.31 times in 2011. It never crossed 1.5 times in any one of the years under reference. This ratio shows that the interest charges have increased at a galloping pace without a corresponding increase in the net - profit. Hence, it decreased in the period. This ratio can be improved by relying more on deposits which carry relatively lower rate of interest, so that the interest charges will be considerably minimised. The mean net profit before interest and interest paid stood Rs. 13,709.64 lakhs, and Rs.11,283.52 lakhs serially during the period. The C.V. in net profit before interest was 79.66 per cent, which indicates more variability and less consistency. It was 76.70 per cent in the case of interest paid, which shows less variability and more consistency. The CAGR in net profit before interest was 31.76 per cent whereas interest paid at 26.45 per cent. These are significant at one per cent level. On the other hand, to maximise the net –

Table 5.10 Interest Coverage Ratio of the SGB during 2005 - 14

(No. of times)

Year	Net profit before interest	Interest paid	Interest coverage ratio
2005	2,009.83	2,542.82	0.79
2006	2,878.77	2,530.84	1.14
2007	3,620.57	3,062.00	1.18
2008	6,336.55	5,647.07	1.12
2009	9,456.87	8,269.32	1.14
2010	12,507.51	10,612.48	1.18
2011	16,989.85	13,011.24	1.31
2012	22,880.36	17,748.70	1.29
2013	28,719.55	22,824.57	1.26
2014	31,696.51	26,586.19	1.19
Average	13,709.64	11,283.52	1.16
S.D.	10,921.76	8,654.22	0.14
C.V. (%)	79.66	76.70	12.47
CAGR (%)	31.76	26.45	4.20
't' cal	3.97**	4.12**	25.36**

Note: **S.D.** : Standard deviation
   C.V : Coefficient of variation
   CAGR : Compound annual growth rate
   ** : Indicates significant at 1 per cent level
Source : As in Table 5.4 and 5.8.

profit before interest, the bank should encourage such types of loans which carry comparatively higher rate of interest.

4. Spread:

Spread (S) is the difference between interest and discounts received (R) and interest paid on deposits and borrowings (K). Thus S = (R − K). The trend of spread gives a better idea to judge the profitability of banks business of intermediation. Bank acquires funds through deposits and borrowings and in return they promise to pay interest. Bank acquires assets such as loans and investments, for which they receive interest. The difference between what the banks pay for funds and what they get for funds is 'spread'. Thus, spread plays a major role in determining the profitability of a bank. Hence, for the purpose of analysing the profitability of the SGB, the trend of spread for the study period is described.

The spread has steadily increased from Rs. 1,846.93 lakhs in 2005 to Rs. 13,587.43 lakhs in 2014 except a decline in 2009 (**see Table 5.11**). The decrease was 1.00 per cent in 2009 over its previous year. In the remaining period, the variation in the increment of growth was in the order of 17.53 – 53.36 per cent. The ratio of spread to working fund is computed by dividing spread by working fund and shown in percentage figures. In other words, it can also be obtained by deducting the ratio of interest paid to working fund from the ratio of interest earned to working fund. This ratio is ascertained to evaluate the performance of the SGB in terms of profitability. The ratio of spread to working fund was the highest at 3.54 per cent in 2014 whilst the lowest at 2.86 per cent in 2007. The analysis of trend of spread to working fund ratio reveals that the SGB in the initial period of study was able to earn more income by way of spread at a higher rate as compared to that of recent period in the study era. The analysis of trend of spread during the ten year period shows that the bank was able to earn income by way of spread at a higher rate in the recent past. From the view point of profitability, there is a growth during the period. The ratio of spread to volume of business was 2.61 per cent in 2005 as compared to 2.34 per cent in 2014. On an average, per year, interest income and interest paid stood Rs. 17,526.21 lakhs, and Rs. 11,283.52 lakhs respectively during the period. The C.V. in interest paid was

Table 5.11 Spread Ratio of the SGB during 2005 - 14

(Rs. lakhs)

| Year | Interest income | Interest paid | Spread | % of change | Ratio of spread to | |
					Volume of business (%)	Working fund (%)
2005	4,389.75	2,542.82	1,846.93	0	2.61	3.26
2006	4,701.62	2,530.84	2,170.78	17.53	2.75	3.39
2007	5,841.48	3,062.00	2,779.48	28.04	2.18	2.86
2008	9,423.68	5,647.07	3,776.61	35.87	2.34	3.76
2009	12,008.29	8,269.32	3,738.97	-1.00	1.79	2.93
2010	16,346.42	10,612.48	5,733.94	53.36	2.18	3.54
2011	20,744.88	13,011.24	7,733.64	34.87	2.34	3.60
2012	27,282.36	17,748.70	9,533.66	23.28	2.34	3.53
2013	34,350.00	22,824.57	11,525.43	20.89	2.38	3.31
2014	40,173.62	26,586.19	13,587.43	17.89	2.34	3.54
Average	17,526.21	11,283.52	6,242.69		2.32	3.37
S.D.	12,791.26	8,654.22	4,155.48		0.26	0.29
C.V. (%)	72.98	76.70	66.57		11.03	8.62
CAGR (%)	24.78	26.45	22.09		-1.05	0.81
't' cal	4.33**	4.12**	4.75**		28.67**	36.71**

Note: **S.D.** : Standard deviation
      C.V : Coefficient of variation
      CAGR : Compound annual growth rate
      ** : Indicates significant at 1 per cent level
Source : As in Table 5.1 and 5.4.

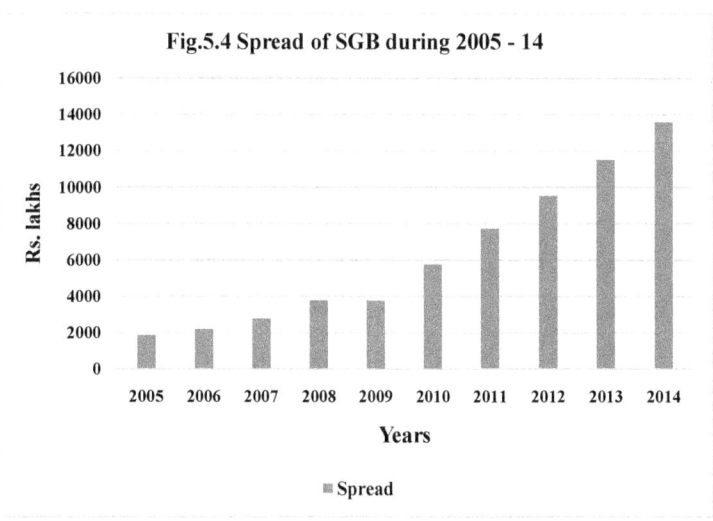

Fig.5.4 Spread of SGB during 2005 - 14

Source: Table 5.11

76.70 per cent followed by interest income (72.98 per cent). Inconsistency in spread was 66.57 per cent. The CAGR was 26.45 per cent, 24.78 per cent and 22.09 per cent in interest paid, interest income and spread respectively. These are significant at one per cent level. This reflects that the interest paid ratio grew faster than interest earned ratio. A similar trend emerges in the ratio of spread to working fund. The results are shown in the **Figure 5.4.**

5. Burden:

Burden (B) is the excess of manpower (M) and other (O) expenses over non – interest income or other receipts (C). That is B = (M + O – C). In other words, the difference between non – interest expenses and non – interest income is defined as 'burden' for a bank. Non – interest expenses of bank comprise establishment expenses/ other operating expenses and provisions and contingencies. On the other hand, non-interest income of a bank consists of income from sources other than interest earned, i.e., commission, exchange and brokerage, other miscellaneous receipts. It is assumed that interest paid and interest earned is purely the prices of funds hired and lent by bank. A bank incurs man – power and all other expenses to provide related and other services to different customers including depositors and borrowers. In other words, conceptually a borrower pays interest only as the price of funds put at his disposal. Lending by the bank involves many other activities. For example, processing of proposals, payment and collection of cheques, follow – up accounts – all involving cost to the bank. These are services and it is a different matter whether the bank charges for them separately or it provides them free or at a nominal service charge. Considering in this way, all man – power and other expenses, to the extent they are not recovered through service charges, are in the nature of burden. The difference between spread and burden determines the profit (or loss) of a bank. Hence, in order to enhance the profitability, each and every bank must endeavour to reduce its burden to the minimum extent possible by exercising effective control over it. However, it is quite difficult on the part of a bank to control the non – interest expenses. This is so because bank operations are essentially of service nature and so a substantial element of non – interest expenses for banks are for personnel, owning and maintenance of buildings, computer and equipments, etc. These costs are relatively fixed because it is necessary to maintain the capacity to handle some part of peak activity workloads.

A close perusal of the **Table 5.12** and **Figure 5.5** show the trend in the burden ratio of SGB during 2005 – 14. The burden was Rs. 982.32 lakhs in 2005 vis – à – vis Rs. 3,897.11 lakhs in 2014. In the meantime, the fluctuations are significant. The decline in the yearly addition was 7.57 per cent and 14.12 per cent during 2007 and 2012 serially. Whereas, the increment was in the order of 3.21 – 56.49 per cent in the remaining period. It can be observed that growth in the recent past is relatively higher than that of initial period. The ratio of burden to volume of business has declined from 1.39 per cent in 2005 as against the lowest at 0.67 per cent in 2014. In the meantime, there are variations in it. This reflects that the other incomes ratio declined faster than operating expenses ratio. The man – power expenses and other expenses ratios have declined on account of increase in the volume of business. The other incomes ratio also declined slowly. Hence burden ratio has receded. This was due to the fact that other incomes ratio had decreased marginally while man-power and other expenses ratios increased considerably.

The ratio of burden to working fund is computed by subtracting the ratio of non – interest income to working fund from the ratio of non – interest expenses to working fund. Or it can also be calculated by dividing burden by working fund and multiplied by100 to arrive at percentage terms. There is a declining trend with fluctuations in the ratio of burden to working fund. It was 1.74 per cent in 2005 vis – à – vis 1.02 per cent in 2014. In between these two years, there are considerable variations. The year 2013 registered the lowest at 0.92 per cent whereas the highest rose up to 2.40 per cent in 2006. It infers that the rise in burden is slower than that of the increase in working fund. It can be said that the SGB was able to exercise control over its burden in the recent past as compared to earlier one. On an average, per year, operating expenses and non – interest income stood Rs. 3,071.80 lakhs, and Rs. 714.63 lakhs respectively during the period. The C.V. in non – interest income is 69.79 per cent, which reveals higher variability and less consistency. It is 43.56 per cent in the case of burden, which shows less variability and more consistency. The CAGR in non – interest income was 24.82 per cent, 16.73 per cent in operating expenses and 14.78 per cent in burden. These are significant at one per cent level. This may enhance its profitability.

Table 5.12: Burden Ratio of the SGB during 2005 - 14

(Rs. lakhs)

| Year | Operating expenses | Non – interest income | Burden | % of change | Ratio of burden to | |
					Volume of business (%)	Working fund (%)
2005	1,142.36	160.04	982.32	0	1.39	1.74
2006	1,699.54	162.29	1,537.25	56.49	1.94	2.40
2007	1,684.03	263.12	1,420.91	-7.57	1.11	1.46
2008	2,127.74	458.05	1,669.69	17.51	1.03	1.66
2009	2,298.24	569.22	1,729.02	3.55	0.83	1.36
2010	3,001.49	562.58	2,438.91	41.06	0.93	1.51
2011	4,595.12	990.09	3,605.03	47.81	1.09	1.68
2012	4,150.31	1,054.31	3,096.00	-14.12	0.76	1.15
2013	4,652.80	1,457.35	3,195.45	3.21	0.66	0.92
2014	5,366.39	1,469.28	3,897.11	21.96	0.67	1.02
Average	3,071.80	714.63	2,357.17			
S.D.	1,500.92	498.78	1,026.87			
C.V. (%)	48.86	69.79	43.56			
CAGR (%)	16.73	24.82	14.78			
't' cal	6.47**	4.53**	7.26**			

Note: S.D. : Standard deviation
       C.V : Coefficient of variation
       CAGR: Compound annual growth rate
       **   : Indicates significant at 1 per cent level
Source: As in Table 5.1.

6. Profitability performance:

Profit is indispensable for economic viability of every organization irrespective of its nature of business. Therefore, it is essential for an organisation to earn a reasonable amount of profit for its survival and growth. From the view point of measurement of success, profit is used as a barometer of measuring the degree of efficiency, progressiveness and stability of an undertaking. Sometimes, it is also considered as the acid test of ability and competence in business planning and programming. Profitability plays a significant role while evaluating the performance an organisation by acting as a common denominator of effectiveness of different operations of the bank.

Profitability is a relative measure of operational efficiency of a bank. It is a ratio of earnings to funds used in the bank. It is a measure of resource use efficiency of investment. Thus, profitability is a ratio of profit to working funds used for earning such profit. Usually, working fund refers to total fund employed in a bank. Alternatively, it represents the balance sheet total excluding contras being bills for collection, acceptances and endorsements on behalf of customers. In relation to banks, profitability refers to accounting profit or operating profit. Accounting profit is the difference between spread and burden. Accounting profit may also be defined as the difference between operating earnings and operating expenses. Operating earnings is the sum of earnings from assets i.e., interest and discounts received and earnings from miscellaneous services or other services. On the other hand, operating expenses are the sum of interest cost and other costs.

The profitability performance of the SGB during 2005 – 14 is furnished in the **Table 5.13** and exhibited in **Figure 5.6**. During the entire period of study, the spread ratio was higher than that of burden ratio. Hence, there is a profitability performance. The profitability performance ratio was 1.22 per cent in 2005 as against 1.67 per cent in 2014. There are marked fluctuations in the intervening period. It was less than one per cent in two years while 1.07-1.72 per cent in the remaining period. In none of the years, profitability performance was negative. The mean spread, burden and profitability performance ratio stood 2.33 per cent, 1.04 per cent and 1.28 per cent serially during the period. The consistency is higher in burden ratio (37.29 per cent) followed by profitability ratio (23.25 per cent) and spread ratio (11.05 per cent). The CAGR in spread and burden ratios is negative at 1.09 per cent and 17.04 per cent serially. The profitability ratio has registered the positive growth at 3.19 per cent. These are significant at one

Table 5.13: Profitability Performance of the SGB during 2005 - 14

(%)

Year	Spread ratio	Burden ratio	Profitability ratio (2-3)
(1)	(2)	(3)	(4)
2005	2.61	1.39	1.22
2006	2.75	1.95	0.80
2007	2.18	1.11	1.07
2008	2.34	1.03	1.31
2009	1.79	0.83	0.96
2010	2.18	0.93	1.25
2011	2.34	1.09	1.25
2012	2.34	0.76	1.58
2013	2.38	0.66	1.72
2014	2.34	0.67	1.67
Average	2.33	1.04	1.28
S.D.	0.26	0.39	0.30
C.V. (%)	11.05	37.29	23.35
CAGR (%)	-1.09	-7.04	3.19
't' cal	16.50**	11.00**	8.51**

Note: S.D. : Standard deviation
       C.V. : Coefficient of variation
       CAGR : Compound annual growth rate
       ** : Indicates significant at 1 per cent level
Source : As in Table 5.9 and 5.10.

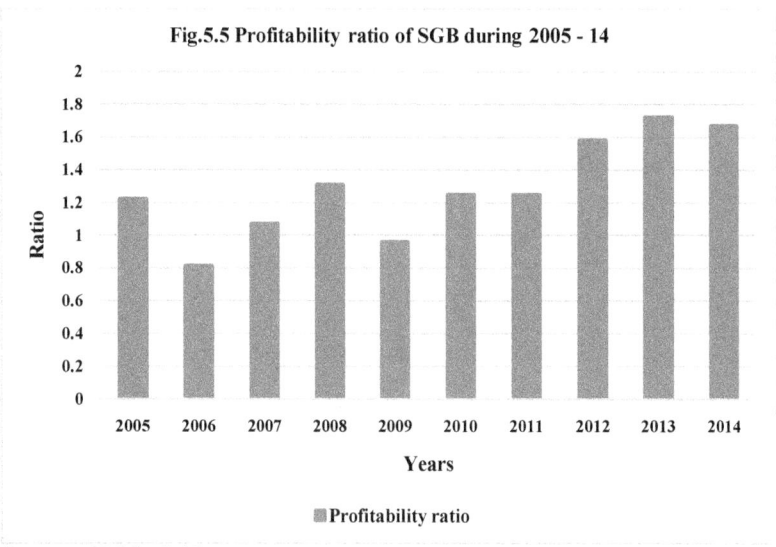

Fig.5.5 Profitability ratio of SGB during 2005 - 14

Source: Table 5.13

per cent level. It may be summed up that there was a growing trend in the profitability percentage in the recent past as compared to that of middle of the period. It was relatively more in the last 3 years. However, it was not commensurate with the size of the bank. Therefore, it calls for an enhancement in the volume of business with a better control over expenses so as to further strengthen its economic viability in the years to come and achieve the avowed objectives of rural development, particularly assist the weakest of weak in rural India.

The financial ratios of the SGB for the period 2005 - 2014 are shown in the **Table 5.14.** It can be observed from the Table that the financial return has declined from 10.03 per cent in 2005 to 10.47 per cent in 2014. While financial cost has increased from 5.81 per cent to 6.93 per cent in the aforesaid period. As a result, the financial margin has declined from 4.22 per cent in 2005 to 3.54 per cent in 2014. This is due to the fact that the financial return has declined faster than financial cost. The operating margin has formed 2.52 per cent in 2014 as against 2.61 per cent in 2005. The miscellaneous income stood at 0.37 per cent in 2005, which moved up and down to reach 0.38 per cent in 2014. The operating profit was 1.98 per cent in 2005 as against1.25 per cent in 2014. It may be concluded they have these declined in 2014 over 2005. Financial ratios indicate the fluctuating trend in the efficiency of bank during the period under study.

There is a dire need to raise the margin on loan business from the view point of future growth of the bank. This is to retain the existing low rates at which the weaker sections are lent. Further, the small net margin ratio is the indicative of the bank that in some of the years, the SGB is just over the break - even point. If it earns a little higher margin on loan business, it can

Table 5.14: Financial Ratios of the SGB for the period 2005 - 14

(Percentage)

Year	2005	2006	2007	2008	2009	2010	2011	2012	2013	2014
Financial return	10.03	9.59	8.97	9.00	9.42	10.11	10.66	10.10	9.87	10.47
Financial cost	5.81	5.16	4.78	5.19	6.37	6.61	6.86	6.57	6.56	6.93
Financial Margin	4.22	4.43	4.19	3.81	3.05	3.50	3.80	3.53	3.31	3.54
Operating margin	2.61	3.47	2.61	1.81	1.80	1.85	2.14	2.38	2.39	2.52
Misc. income	0.37	0.33	0.43	0.40	0.43	0.44	0.46	0.39	0.42	0.38
Operating profit	1.98	1.29	1.99	2.40	1.68	2.03	1.92	1.41	1.38	1.25

Source: As in Table 5.1.

comfortably build up reserves and surplus in the years to come. A new dimension to profit analysis and financial ratios is given by margin on loan business.

7. Margin on loan business:

Interest on lending constitutes a major source of income for the SGB as any bank, which was observed in the previous analysis. A group of five related ratios are employed to examine the adequacy/ inadequacy of margin on loan business to meet the establishment charges. Gross income to outstanding loans ratio (G) is ascertained by dividing gross income by outstanding loans and expressed in percentage terms. The ratio of interest paid to outstanding loans (I) is computed by dividing interest paid by outstanding loans in percentage terms. The difference between G and I ratios is known as gross margin ratio (N). The ratio of establishment expenses to outstanding loans (E) is calculated by dividing establishment expenses by outstanding loans and shown in percentage terms. The excess of E over N is referred to as net - margin ratio (N_1).

Of the income earned on loaning operations, obligations on deposits and borrowings are to be met. Surplus, if any, after meeting interest is used for meeting establishment charges. If any residual is still left over, it would be termed as return on loan business that gives net - profit. Following this line of thinking, the aforesaid ratios are calculated and presented in the **Table 5.15** and exhibited in **Figure 5.7**. The percentage of gross income to outstanding loans ratio has gradually declined from 12.80 per cent in 2005 to 13.23 per cent in 2013. In the following year, it came down to 12.73 per cent. The percentage of interest paid to outstanding advances has gone up from 7.15 to 8.13 in the former and latter respectively. In the intermediate period, there are to and fro changes. The year 2013 registered the highest at 8.43 per cent while the least at 4.67 per cent during 2007. Like these two ratios, the gross margin ratio showed a declining trend. It was 5.65 per cent during 2005 as compared to 4.60 per cent during 2014. It submerged steadily from 2005 to reach the lowest at 3.87 per cent in 2009. The establishment expenses to outstanding loans ratio was 3.21 per cent in 2005 and exhibited a downward trend with relative ups and downs to register 1.54 per cent in 2014. Thus, there is a mixed trend in this ratio throughout the period. The net margin ratio was 2.44 per cent in 2005 as against 3.07 per cent in 2014. In the meantime, there are to and fro changes. The year 2006

Table 5.15: Margin on Loans Business in the SGB during 2005 - 14

(%)

Year	Gross income to outstanding loans ratio (G)	Interest paid to outstanding loans ratio (I)	Gross margin ratio (N) (G-I)	Establishment expenses to outstanding loans ratio (E)	Net margin ratio (N₁) (N-E)
2005	12.80	7.15	5.65	3.21	2.44
2006	11.54	6.01	5.53	4.03	1.50
2007	9.31	4.67	4.64	2.57	2.07
2008	11.81	6.75	5.06	2.54	2.52
2009	11.29	7.42	3.87	1.94	1.93
2010	12.21	7.66	4.55	1.99	2.56
2011	12.39	7.41	4.97	2.54	2.43
2012	12.80	8.02	4.78	1.77	3.02
2013	13.23	8.43	4.80	1.59	3.21
2014	12.73	8.13	4.60	1.54	3.07
Average	12.01	7.17	4.85	2.37	2.48
S.D.	1.13	1.12	0.51	0.78	0.54
C.V. (%)	9.41	15.68	10.49	33.09	21.78
CAGR (%)	-0.05	1.29	-2.04	-7.08	2.32
't' cal	30.43**	22.58**	28.41**	11.76**	15.00**

Note: **S.D.** : Standard deviation
     C.V. : Coefficient of variation
     CAGR : Compound annual growth rate
     ** : Indicates significant at 1 per cent level
Source : As in Table 5.1 and 5.4.

180

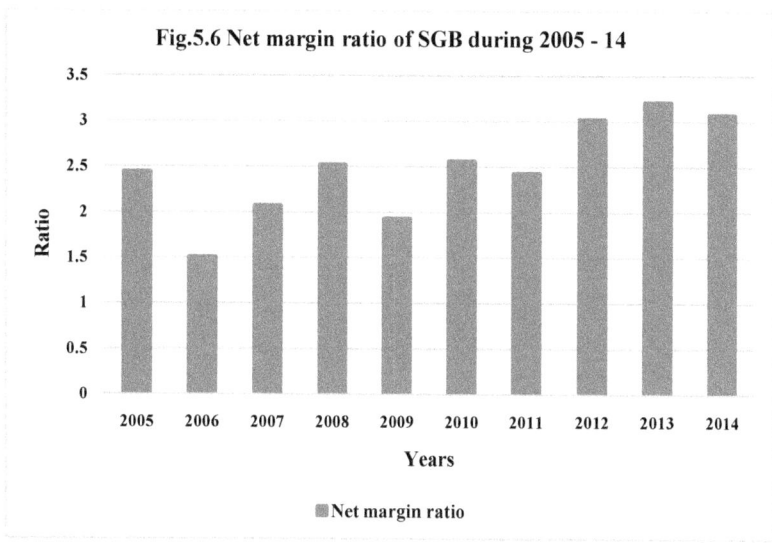

Fig.5.6 Net margin ratio of SGB during 2005 - 14

Source: Table 5.15.

reported the lowest at 1.50 per cent while highest at 3.21 per cent in 2013. This is low in 2006 due to the fact than the N has declined while E rose. Whereas in 2013, the latter has decreased faster than the former. Finally, it may be said that the N_1 is favourable in the recent period relative to initial one. There is obvious need to raise N_1 in the years to come so as to strengthen the SGB. On an average, per year, gross income to outstanding loans, interest paid to outstanding loans, gross margin, establishment expenses to outstanding loans and net margin ratio stood 12.01 per cent, 7.17 per cent, 4.85 per cent, 2.37 per cent and 2.48 per cent sequentially during the period. CV in establishment expenses to outstanding loans ratio is 33.09 per cent indicating more variability and less consistency when compared to rest of the ratios. It is 9.41 per cent in gross income to outstanding loans ratio, which shows less variability and more consistency. The establishment expenses to outstanding loans, gross margin and gross income to outstanding loans ratios have reported a negative growth at 7.08 per cent, 2.04 per cent and 0.05 per cent respectively. Whereas interest paid to outstanding loans and net margin ratios during the study period have recorded a positive

181

growth of 1.29 per cent. They are significant at one per cent level. It can build strong reserves and surplus by increasing the existing small gap between income earned and expenditure incurred. It can go a long way.

CHAPTER – VI
NON-PERFORMING ASSETS

The performance of any institution depends on various factors including the use of assets. All advances do not yield income due to several factors. While the advances which yield income fall under the category of performing advances, those advances which do not yield income to the bank are non – performing assets (NPAs). The concept of NPAs has found its way into the banking arena as a part of financial sector reforms. Since then, it occupied the central stage drawing the attention of policy makers and bankers. Till early 1990s, there used to be non availability of correct health of banking assets because legal provision provides shelter to banks that there was no obligation to disclose bad and doubtful debts. However, there were certain indications which spelt out the fact that the health of banking assets deteriorated over a period of time.

The balance sheet of a bank has to reflect its actual financial health. A proper system of recognition of income, classification of assets and provisioning for bad debts on prudential basis is necessary. Most of the banks in the world follow international accounting standards while preparing the balance sheet, which reflects financial health. The Narasimham Committee examined the issues and recommended that a policy of income recognition should be objective and based on recovery rather than any subjective consideration. Likewise, assets are to be classified on the basis of objective criteria which would ensure a uniform and consistent application of norms. The Committee recommended that provisions should be made on the basis of classification of assets.

The severity of the incidence of the NPAs in Indian banks, noted in the early 1990s, had caused a severe hue and cry in various quarters. In fact, the problem started much earlier, which became evident from continued recapitalisation of many banks since mid-1980s. Whatever be the root cause, malfunctioning of banks increased by the end of the 1980s. This led to the setting up of the Narasimham Committee which, in fact, identified NPAs as one of the possible causes/effects of malfunctioning. In order to quantify the NPAs problem, Narasimham Committee made it mandatory on the part of the banks to publish annually the magnitude of the NPAs. NPAs are those categories of assets (advances, bills discounted, overdraft, cash credits etc.) for which any amount remains due for a period of 180 days. Following the recommendations, banks started publishing NPAs data in their annual reports, which were astonishingly high. The RBI reports of NPAs stated that reduction in should be treated as a 'national priority'. Hence an attempt is made in this chapter to study the NPAs in the Saptagiri Grameena Bank (SGB).

1. Concept:

NPA is a new name given to old disease called bad and doubtful debts. The success of a banker lies in keeping bad debts to the bare minimum as they cannot be avoided completely. NPAs is a credit facility or an advance as on the date of balance sheet, in respect of which interest as remained unpaid for a period of quarters during a year. NPA is an asset which did not directly contribute to profitability of a bank. NPAs were essentially loans and advances, interest on which was doubtful to realise. Examples of NPAs are excess of holding as balances, mounting overdue and sticky loans, bad and doubtful debts and deteriorating productivity of employees. In other words, NPAs are those loans given by a bank or financial institution where the borrower defaults or delays repayment of interest or principal. An asset which ceases to generate income for the bank is called as NPAs.

Currently NPAs is defined as an advance where interest and / or installment of principal remains overdue for a period of more than 90 days in respect of a term loan; the account remains out of order for a period of more than 90 days in respect of an overdraft/cash credit; bill remains overdue for a period of more than 90 days in the case of bills purchased and discounted; interest and/or installment of principal remain(s) overdue for two harvest seasons for short - term and one harvest season for long - term crop loans in the case of an advance granted for agricultural purpose; and any amount to be received remains overdue for a period of more than 90 days in respect of other accounts.

2. Assets:

The assets of the SGB are classified into two broad groups such as performing and non - performing as shown in the **Table 6.1** and exhibited in **Figure 6.1**. The performing assets were Rs. 34,721.78 lakhs in 2005 and

Table 6.1: Assets of SGB during 2005 - 14

(Rs. lakhs)

Year	Performing	NPAs	Total	% of col (3) to col (4)
(1)	(2)	(3)	(4)	(5)
2005	34,721.78	834.89	35,556.67	2.35
2006	51,681.47	1,157.43	52,838.90	2.19
2007	64,462.10	1,138.12	65,600.22	1.73
2008	82,089.92	1,565.94	83,655.86	1.87
2009	110,095.61	1,297.88	111,389.93	1.17
2010	137,158.05	1,303.79	138,461.84	0.94
2011	173,700.31	1,774.52	175,474.83	1.01
2012	219,501.92	1,854.39	221,356.31	0.84
2013	267,973.98	2,663.28	270,637.26	0.98
2014	320,325.18	6,013.10	327,165.40	1.84
Average	146,171.03	1,960.33	148,213.72	
S.D.	97,077.02	1,512.08	98,508.88	
C.V. (%)	66.41	77.13	66.46	
CAGR (%)	24.88	21.83	24.85	
't' cal	4.762**	4.100**	4.758**	

Note: S.D. : Standard deviation

C.V. : Coefficient of variation

CAGR: Compound annual growth rate

** : Indicates significant at 1 per cent level

Source : Relevant issues of the SGB, Annual Report, Chittoor.

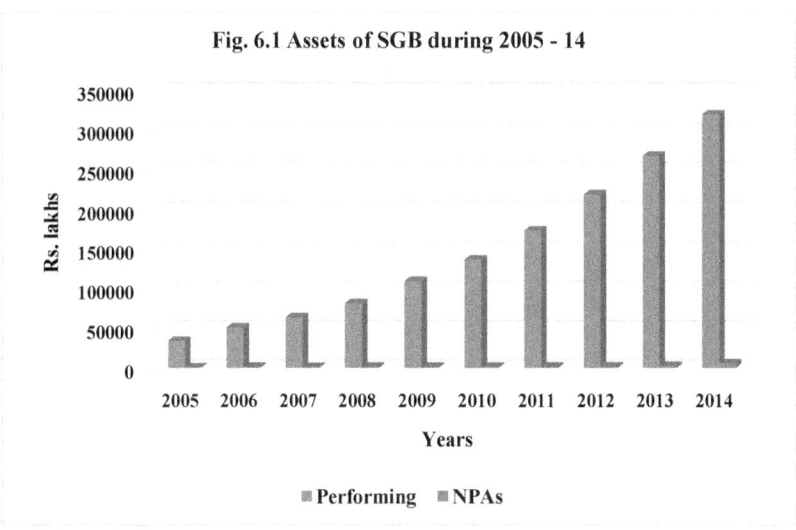

Fig. 6.1 Assets of SGB during 2005 - 14

Source: Table 6.1.

gradually raised to Rs. 320,325.18 lakhs in 2014. There is no decline in any one of the years. On the other hand, NPAs were Rs. 834.89 lakhs in 2005 as against Rs. 6,013.10 lakhs in 2014. During the period, the ups and downs were significant. These were more than Rs. 1000 lakhs in nine out of ten years. In the remaining one year, it was lowest at Rs. 834.89 lakhs in 2005. The proportion of NPAs in the total assets was the highest at 2.35 per cent in 2005. It declined gradually to reach 0.98 per cent in 2013. In the following year, rose again to reach 1.84 per cent in 2014. It was the least at 0.84 per cent during 2012. On an average, per year, performing and non - performing and total assets stood Rs. 146,171.03 lakhs, Rs. 1,960.33 lakhs and Rs. 148,213.72 lakhs during the period sequentially. Coefficient of variation in NPAs is the highest (77.13 per cent) followed by total assets (66.46 per cent). Inconsistency in performing is 66.41 per cent. The growth rate is 24.88 per cent, 24.85 per cent and 21.83 per cent in performing, total assets and non - performing respectively. The calculated value of 't' is more than the corresponding critical value at one per cent level. Hence, it is significant at one per cent level. It may be concluded that there is a steady increase in performing assets while there is a growing trend with fluctuations in NPAs. Further, the proportion of NPAs in the total assets has witnessed a decline with to and fro changes during the period understudy. This may be due to the enforcement of Securitisation and Reconstruction of Financial Assets and Enforcement of Security Interest Act, 2002 (SARFAESIA) and the efforts put in by the SGB during the period.

3. Proportion of NPAs:

The trend in the growth of gross NPAs of the SGB during 2005 - 14 is furnished in the **Table 6.2** and depicted in **Figure 6.2.** It can be observed from the Table that there are volatile changes in the annual progress. It declined in five years. The decline was in the order of 1.67 – 17.12 per cent. The decrease in NPAs indicates that the fresh accretion to NPAs is less than the recoveries that were effected. In other words, the decrease in the level of NPAs shows that the provision made in the year and the recoveries made are much more than the fresh accretions. The rate of addition in the remaining period was in the range of 0.46 – 125.78 per cent. The percentage of NPAs to outstanding advances has continuously declined from 2.35 in 2005 to 0.98 in 2013. In the following year, it rose to 1.84 per cent. With relative ups and downs, it reached to 1.84 per cent in 2014. On an average, per year, NPAs and total outstanding advances stood Rs. 1,960.33 lakhs, Rs. 147,144.11 lakhs serially during the period. The degree of variation was least in total outstanding advances (67.76 per cent) followed by NPAs (77.13 per cent). The CAGR in total outstanding advances was 24.85 per cent and in NPAs 21.83 per cent which are significant at one per cent level. It may be summed up that there is a growing trend with to and fro changes in the amount of NPAs. The yearly fluctuations are noticeable. These include increases and declines in certain years over the period of study. The share of NPAs to

Table 6.2: Growth of Gross NPAs in SGB during 2005 - 14

(Rs. lakhs)

Year	Amount	% of change	Total outstanding advances	% of NPAs to outstanding advances
2005	834.89	0	35,556.67	2.35
2006	1,157.43	38.63	42,142.82	2.75
2007	1,138.12	-1.67	65,600.22	1.73
2008	1,565.94	37.59	83,655.86	1.87
2009	1,297.88	-17.12	111,389.93	1.17
2010	1,303.79	0.46	138,461.84	0.94
2011	1,774.52	36.10	175,474.83	1.01
2012	1,854.39	4.50	221,356.31	0.84
2013	2,663.28	43.62	270,637.26	0.98
2014	6,013.10	125.78	327,165.40	1.84
Average	1,960.33		147,144.11	
S.D.	1,512.08		99,710.27	
C.V. (%)	77.13		67.76	
CAGR (%)	21.83		24.85	
't' cal	4.10**		4.67**	

Note: S.D.   : Standard deviation
    C.V.   : Coefficient of variation
    CAGR: Compound annual growth rate
    **   : Indicates significant at 1 per cent level
Source: As in Table 6.1.

189

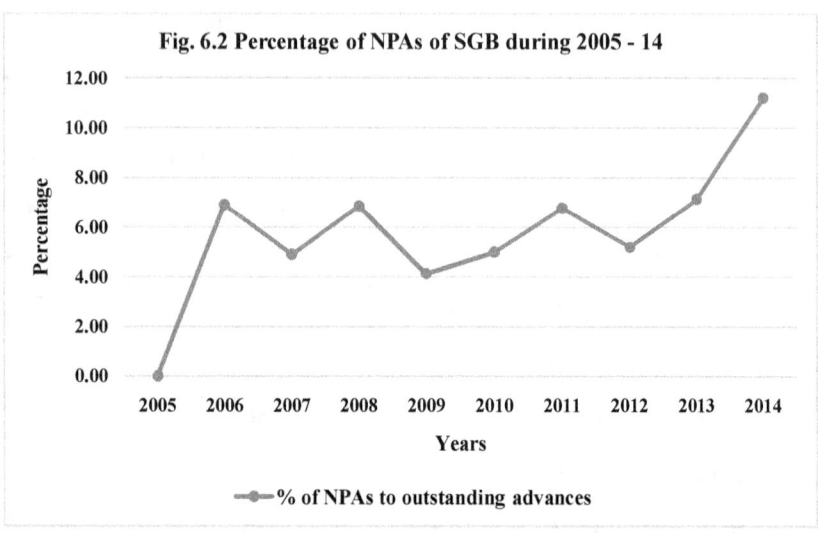

Fig. 6.2 Percentage of NPAs of SGB during 2005 - 14

Source: Table 6.2

outstanding advances has declined with fluctuations in the period under reference. This is a welcome trend for the bank as well as the nation.

4. Classification of NPAs:

The target of banks is to shift more assets to standard category so as to make more profits and improve their financial position. The NPAs of the SGB were classified into three classes such as sub - standard assets, doubtful assets and loss assets. Of these, sub - standard assets were at Rs. 362.02 lakhs in 2005 as compared to Rs. 4,307.58 lakhs in 2014 (**see Table 6.3**). This shows that the SGB never crossed the international benchmark. In the meantime, there are to and fro changes. In percentage terms, these have formed 43.36 per cent in 2005 while 71.64 per cent in 2014. Thus, there are volatile changes in sub - standard assets in absolute as well as relative terms. The doubtful assets were Rs. 472.87lakhs in 2005 vis - à - vis Rs. 1,695.96 lakhs in 2014. The ups and downs in it were remarkable. Its share in the total assets varied between 19.90 per cent and 56.64 per cent. It shows the

Table 6.3: Classification of NPAs in SGB during 2005 - 14

(Rs.lakhs)

Year	Sub - standard	Doubtful	Loss	Total
2005	362.02 (43.36)	472.87 (56.64)	-	834.89 (100)
2006	376.54 (32.53)	497.87 (43.02)	283.02 (24.45)	1,157.43 (100)
2007	549.67 (48.30)	226.51 (19.90)	361.94 (31.80)	1,138.12 (100)
2008	823.98 (52.62)	709.92 (45.34)	32.04 (2.04)	1,565.94 (100)
2009	663.43 (51.12)	631.15 (48.63)	3.30 (0.25)	1,297.88 (100)
2010	675.64 (51.82)	607.62 (46.60)	20.53 (1.58)	1,303.79 (100)
2011	1,087.55 (61.29)	676.63 (38.13)	10.34 (0.58)	1,774.52 (100)
2012	946.75 (51.05)	894.06 (48.21)	13.58 (0.74)	1,854.39 (100)
2013	1,544.92 (58.01)	1,100.39 (41.32)	17.97 (0.67)	2,663.28 (100)
2014	4,307.58 (71.64)	1,695.96 (28.20)	9.56 (0.16)	6,013.10 (100)
Average	1,133.81 (52.17)	751.30 (41.60)	75.23 (6.23)	1,960.33 (100)
S.D.	1,169.83	407.45	131.94	1,512.08
C.V. (%)	103.18	54.23	175.39	77.13
CAGR (%)	28.10	13.62	-28.74	21.83
't' cal	3.07**	5.83**	1.81*	4.10**

Note: Figures in brackets indicate the percentage to total
       S.D. : Standard deviation
       C.V. : Coefficient of variation
      CAGR : Compound annual growth rate
       ** : Indicates significant at 1 per cent level
       * : Indicates significant at 5 per cent level
Source: As in Table 6.1.

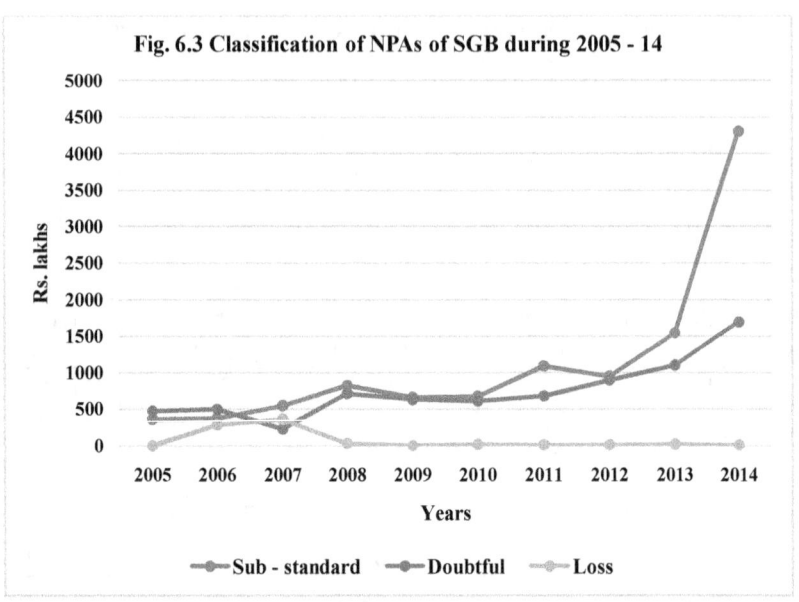

Fig. 6.3 Classification of NPAs of SGB during 2005 - 14

Source: Table 6.3.

variations in the amount of doubtful debts. The loss assets were absent in 2005. These emerged in the rest of the period and the loss assets were Rs. 283.02 lakhs in 2006 whereas Rs. 9.56 lakhs in 2014. In relative terms, these have varied between 0.16 per cent and 31.80 per cent in the period. In the meantime, there are to and fro changes. In percentage terms, these have formed 28.50 per cent assets. These are depicted in **Figure 6.3** for clarity. It may be said that the sub - standard assets have increased as against doubtful debts. This is favourable to the bank. The loss assets were less in the middle of the period. But their presence with decreasing trend in the recent 5 years is a good one for the bank. There has been a marked improvement in the asset profile of the SGB. It is held that the recoveries are due mainly from sub – standard and doubtful categories and not from the loss category. On an average, per year, sub - standard assets, doubtful assets, loss assets and NPAs stood at Rs. 1,133.81 lakhs, Rs. 751.30 lakhs, Rs. 75.23 lakhs and

Rs.1,960.33 lakhs respectively during the period. The degree of variation was least in doubtful assets (54.23 per cent) followed by sub - standard assets (103.18 per cent) while highest in loss assets (175.39 per cent). The overall variation in total NPAs is 77.13 per cent. The growth is negative (28.75 per cent) in loss asset. It is positive at 28.10 per cent, 21.83 per cent and 13.62 per cent in sub - standard assets, total NPAs and doubtful assets respectively during the study period. The CAGR is significant in the loans to sub - standard assets, total NPAs and doubtful assets at one per cent level whilst at 5 per cent level in loss assets. Then it can be rightly said that the core component is hard to recover.

5. Recovery of NPAs:

The recovery of NPAs in the SGB for the period 2005-14 is given in the **Table 6.4** and exhibited in **Figure 6.4.** The amount recovered from NPAs was Rs. 366.12 lakhs in 2005 as against Rs. 451.76 lakhs in 2014. In the meantime, there are ups   and downs. The year 2009 reported the highest at Rs. 931.49 lakhs while the lowest at Rs.358.09 lakhs in 2006. The proportion of recovery to NPAs was 43.85 per cent in 2005. It has undergone to and fro changes over the period and finally stood at 7.51 per cent at the end of 2014. The percentage of recovery was maximum at 71.77 during 2009 while the minimum at 7.51 in 2014. It may be concluded that the amount collected from NPAs was higher in 2014 when compared to 2005. On an average, per year, NPAs and amount recovered from NPAs stood Rs. 1,960.33 lakhs and Rs. 557.59 lakhs serially during the period. The degree of variation was highest in NPAs (77.13 per cent) followed by amount recovered from NPAs (35.03 per cent). The CAGR in NPAs was 21.83 per

Table 6.4: Recovery of NPAs in SGB for the period 2005 – 14

(Rs. lakhs)

Year (1)	NPAs (2)	Amount recovered (3)	% of col (3) to col (2) (4)
2005	834.89	366.12	43.85
2006	1,157.43	358.09	30.94
2007	1,138.12	464.20	40.79
2008	1,565.94	396.58	25.33
2009	1,297.88	931.49	71.77
2010	1,303.79	669.74	51.37
2011	1,774.52	472.47	26.63
2012	1,854.39	736.27	39.70
2013	2,663.28	729.14	27.38
2014	6,013.10	451.76	7.51
Average	1,960.33	557.59	36.53
S.D.	1,512.08	195.30	17.40
C.V. (%)	77.13	35.03	47.63
CAGR (%)	21.83	2.12	-16.17
't' cal	4.10**	9.03**	6.64**

Note: S.D.   : Standard deviation
      C.V.   : Coefficient of variation
      CAGR: Compound annual growth rate
      **   : Indicates significant at 1 per cent level
      Source: As in Table 6.1.

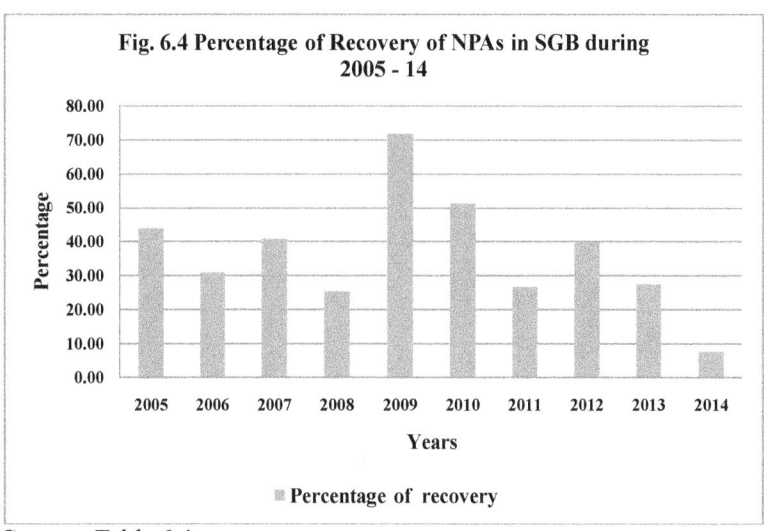

Fig. 6.4 Percentage of Recovery of NPAs in SGB during 2005 - 14

Source: Table 6.4.

cent and in the amount recovered from NPAs 2.12 per cent. These are significant at one per cent level.

6. Provision to NPAs:

The year - wise provision made towards NPAs in the SGB is provided in the **Table 6.5** and exhibited in **Figure 6.5.** The addition to NPAs was Rs. 420.57 lakhs in 2005 when compared to Rs. 1,609.10 lakhs in 2013. In the meantime, the amount of provision varied considerably. For example, it was highest at Rs. 1,690.47 lakhs during 2010 and no provision during 2014. The provisions created varied due to the variation in the opening NPAs, collection during the year, write off and up gradation of NPAs. The share of provision to NPAs was in the range of 50.37 – 129.66 per cent. On an average, per year, NPAs and provision to NPAs stood Rs. 1,960.33 lakhs and Rs. 1,002.79 lakhs serially during the period. The C.V. in NPAs is 77.13 per cent indicating more variability and less consistency. It is 51.84 per cent in the provision to NPAs which shows less variability and more consistency.

The CAGR in NPAs was 21.83 per cent and provision to NPAs 14.36 per cent. They are significant at one per cent level. As per the norms stipulated,

Table 6.5: Year - wise Accretion to NPAs in SGB during 2005 - 14

(Rs. lakhs)

Year	NPAs	Provision	% of col (3) to col (2)
(1)	(2)	(3)	(4)
2005	834.89	420.57	50.37
2006	1,157.43	949.64	82.05
2007	1,138.12	790.12	69.42
2008	1,565.94	927.84	59.25
2009	1,297.88	1,075.60	82.87
2010	1,303.79	1,690.47	129.66
2011	1,774.52	1,217.17	68.59
2012	1,854.39	1,367.39	73.74
2013	2,663.28	1,609.10	60.42
2014	6,013.10	-	0
Average	1,960.33	1,002.79	67.42
S.D.	1,512.08	519.81	32.18
C.V. (%)	77.13	51.84	47.70
CAGR (%)	21.83	14.36	1.83
't' cal	4.10**	6.10**	6.63**

Note: S.D.   : Standard deviation
     C.V.   : Coefficient of variation.
     CAGR : Compound annual growth rate
     **   : Indicates significant at 1 per cent level
Source: As in Table 6.1.

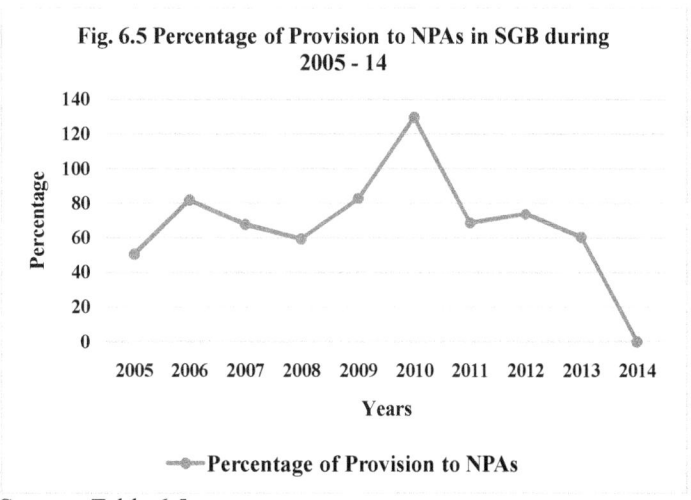

Fig. 6.5 Percentage of Provision to NPAs in SGB during 2005 - 14

Source: Table 6.5.

the SGB created provision for NPAs, which is dependent on several factors as already referred to. It may be said that there are variations in the provision created for NPAs in absolute and relative terms during the period. However, there is almost a declining trend in percentage terms.

7. High value NPAs:

The high value NPAs borrowers, the amount outstanding and per - capita is furnished in the **Table 6.6.** The high value here means the borrowers whose NPA due is one lakh rupees or more. The number of NPAs accounts has risen from 45 in 2005 to 462 in 2014. The amount outstanding was Rs. 99.23 lakhs and Rs. 972.54 lakhs in former and latter respectively. The per capita outstanding amount was more than two lakhs during 2005-08 and 2013-14. On an average, per year, number of NPAs accounts, amount outstanding and per capita stood 144.10, Rs. 290.10 lakhs and Rs. 2.00 lakhs sequentially during the period. The C.V. in amount outstanding is the highest at (94.54 per cent) followed by number of NPA accounts (94.54 per cent).

The inconsistency in per capita is 7.38 per cent. The CAGR in number of NPAs accounts was 26.22 per cent whereas in amount outstanding, it was

Table 6.6: Particulars of High - Value NPAs of SGB during 2005 - 14

Year	No. of accounts	Amount outstanding (Rs. lakhs)	Per capita (Rs. lakhs)
2005	45	99.23	2.21
2006	49	99.28	2.03
2007	54	110.01	2.04
2008	49	105.14	2.15
2009	123	221.05	1.80
2010	83	153.83	1.85
2011	80	142.05	1.78
2012	242	479.10	1.98
2013	254	517.70	2.04
2014	462	972.54	2.11
Average	144.10	290.10	2.00
S.D.	136.23	286.28	0.15
C.V. (%)	94.54	98.68	7.38
CAGR (%)	26.22	25.64	-0.49
't' cal	3.34**	3.20**	68.84**

Note: S.D. : Standard deviation **C.V.** : Coefficient of variation.
CAGR: Compound annual growth rate ** : Indicates significant at 1 per cent level
Source: As in Table 6.1.

25.64 per cent. These are significant at one per cent level. It may be said that there is a progress in the high value NPA accounts despite regulation and concerted efforts of the bank. Probably these borrowers may be wilful defaulters. They do not repay the dues to the bank on time because of malintention.

8. Upgradation of NPAs:

The details of upgradation of outstanding advances as NPAs and written off NPAs during 2005 – 2014 is provided in the **Table 6.7.** The amount of outstanding advances upgraded as NPAs has declined from Rs. 89 lakhs in 2005 to Rs. 63.40 lakhs in 2014. In the meantime, there are fluctuations. The year 2011 reported the highest at Rs. 130.27 lakhs and 2006, the lowest at Rs. 4.42 lakhs. And there is no upgradation during 2009 and 2010.The amount written off from NPAs was Rs. 40.06 lakhs in 2005 as compared to Rs. 0.35 lakhs in 2014. On an average, per year, upgradation of outstanding advances and written off NPAs stood Rs. 42.25 lakhs and Rs. 17.47 lakhs serially during the period. The C.V. in written off NPAs is the highest at 115.44 per cent followed by upgradation of outstanding advances (100.98 per cent). There is a negative growth in the upgradation of outstanding advances (3.33 per cent) and written off NPAs (37.75 per cent) during the study period. The CAGR was significant at one per cent level and at 5 per cent level in the former and latter respectively. Thus, the SGB has additionally upgraded NPAs out of outstanding advances and simultaneously had written off some of the amount from NPAs. This is so because the past

Table 6.7: Details of Write Offs and Upgradation of NPAs in SGB

during 2005 - 14

(Rs. lakhs)

Year	Upgradation	Written off
2005	89.00	40.06
2006	4.42	32.17
2007	13.50	59.11
2008	30.65	6.65
2009	0.00	0.00
2010	0.00	0.00
2011	130.27	14.07
2012	42.80	17.77
2013	48.46	4.52
2014	63.40	0.35
Average	42.25	17.47
S.D.	42.66	20.17
C.V. (%)	100.98	115.44
CAGR (%)	-3.33	-37.75
't' cal	3.14**	2.75*

Note: S.D. : Standard deviation

C.V. : Coefficient of variation

CAGR: Compound annual growth rate

** : Indicates significant at 1 per cent level

* : Indicates significant at 5 per cent level

Source: As in Table 6.1.

due has elapsed and the SGB thought that some of NPAs could not be recovered in the future also. Hence they are upgraded and written off.

9. Capital adequacy:

It is necessary for a bank to have sufficient capital to absorb operational losses without infringing upon the depositors' interest. Therefore, a provision has been made in the law to stipulate certain absolute minimum capital requirement for a bank depending upon the operational

Table 6.8: Details of CRAR in SGB during 2005 – 14

(Percentage)

Year	CRAR	% of change
2005	0	0
2006	0	0
2007	11.20	0
2008	11.50	2.68
2009	10.82	-5.91
2010	10.14	-6.28
2011	10.05	-0.89
2012	10.15	1.00
2013	10.23	0.79
2014	9.75	-4.69

Source: As in Table 6.1.

area of the bank and not according to volume of business. The statutory requirement for a minimum ratio of capital to risk weighted assets ratio (CRAR) of a bank improved during the period. The improvement in CRAR reflects the higher rate of growth in capital was made possible because of the surge in profits of the banking system as a whole and mobilisation of equity capital from the market by a number of banks. In the SGB, CRAR was 11.20 per cent in 2007, which declined to 9.75 per cent in 2014. Thus, the CRAR of the SGB is in excess of the stipulated 9 per cent. Perhaps, in view of the impending organisation of the new capital accord, the SGB held capital well above the stipulated level.

10. Perceptions of managers:

The perceptions of 25 managers and the causes for NPAs are presented in the **Table 6.9.** Of the 25 managers, 56 per cent blamed the elaborate and time - consuming legal system as the main cause for NPAs in the SGB. They were of the opinion that it is due to the implementation of SARFAESIA. The recovery has drastically changed. They were of the opinion that the Act will not only help in the recovery of past NPAs but also would act as a preventive method in the minds of the borrower. Previously, the borrower knew that in case of default, the banker has limited options as the judicial process is slow and unique. If a suit for recovery is filed, it would easily be prolonged for a long period. The Act has empowered the banks to seize the security without the intervention of the court or even take over the management of the institute. Out of 25 managers, 52 per cent expressed that there is a frequent change in government policy. This has resulted in not paying the dues hoping that the government would waive the principal amount or interest. Forty eight per cent of managers felt that lack of proper post follow - up action resulted in failure to take action against wilful defaulters. They feel that a strong follow - up foots mental pressure on borrower to return the past debt on priority vis - à - vis private debt. This follow - up, if backed by strong legal measures to recover the money, would persuade the borrower to try his best to return the money.

The seeds of NPAs are the wrong decision of the bank as well as the act of borrowers. If the project selected is technically non - feasible and economically unviable or the borrower is skill - wise incompetent, obviously, the account becomes non - performing. This was reported by 24 per cent of managers. The answer, to this question that naturally arises as to why the aforesaid events occur, like the pressure put forth by government agencies i.e., directed and target lending. This problem gets multiplied with the local politicians and caste groups putting pressure on the bank, which

Table 6.9 Perceptions of Managers on the Causes for NPAs in SGB.

Name of cause	Number of	%
Elaborate and time consuming legal system.	25	56
Frequent change of government policy.	25	52
Lack of proper follow up and failure to take up punitive action against wilful defaulters.	25	48
Mismanagement and diversion of funds.	25	44
Socio - political pressures and directed lending.	25	40
Delay in obtaining financial statement from borrowers.	25	36
Time and cost over runs.	25	28
Faculty pre - sanction appraisal and wrong selection of borrowers/activities.	25	24
Inadequate and untimely disbursement of credit.	25	20
Lack of motivation of staff.	25	16
Natural calamities.	25	12
Power shortage.	25	12

Source: Field survey.

leads to NPAs. Even, a properly selected activity though economically viable, would suffer from non - availability of adequate and timely credit. Twenty per cent of the managers ascribed to it. If credit is inadequate, the borrower has to either compromise with the quality of inputs and services or restrict the scope of operations. Under either of the circumstances, the account becomes NPA.

Once the bank takes proper care at the pre - sanctioning stage and there are no external factors causing failure of production and/or fall in the expected income generation, the role of the borrower becomes crucial. Forty four per cent of respondents have indicated mismanagement and/or misutilisation of funds as an important factor contributing to incidence of NPAs. Nevertheless, if the monitoring and post follow up of the bank is strong, it can immediately sight the diversion and mismanagement of funds. Time overruns and cost in the implementation of the activity due to various factors may have a cumulative effect on the health of account. This may be a significant cause of NPAs. This was stated by 28 per cent of respondent managers. The fall in income generation, whether on account of external causes like natural calamities or power shortage or due to internal factors like mismanagement and diversion of credit or cumulative effect of various factors together, constrains the ability of the borrower to repay the loan with the result NPAs raise.

Wilful default, another important factor identified by the respondent managers is mainly on account of laxity on the part of the bank in terms of appraisal, supervision, and follow - up. The bank is either not in a position to identify a wilful defaulter or take punitive action on account of its own and/or the style of functioning of legal system and/or non - cooperation of government. Wilful default can also arise on account of typical mentality of people in the area, which destroys the will and initiative to repay. Such a mentality is further nurtured by interference of self - centered politicians. One of the reasons responsible for NPAs has also been the lack of proper appraisal. Though most bankers opine that proposals are appraised with respect to the activity, industry, geographical area, etc. and the details of promoters; directors/guarantors are checked with the RBI circulated caution list, the growing NPAs do not support this opinion. The fact is that most of the banks do not have proper appraisal teams and usually resort to appraisal by other institutions/banks, who themselves have done a cut - paste job, thereby leading to half - baked appraisals, devoid of any similarity to ground realities. The SGB introduced a centralised cell for appraisal for proposals above a certain value, which are processed by experienced and qualified officers.

The respondent managers are also of the view that in some cases, irrespective of value of the account, impractical and unrealistic sanction stipulation results in creation of NPAs. They are of the opinion that cash budgeting will be more appropriate and relevant to the present banking environment than the conventional balance sheet system. This is due to the fact that it is of the utmost important to the bank to ascertain whether the borrowing companies have cash with them to service the loan rather than knowing the financial position as on a particular date which could be moulded to suit to their interest. Taking the issue of submission of financial statements further and discussing it with borrowers, they were also of the opinion that the submission of financials was a mere formality, as these were not properly analysed because of lack of specialised staff. It was expressed by 36 per cent of respondents. The various factors discussed above were relevant in the context of the SGB.

CHAPTER – VII

SUMMARY AND SUGGESTIONS

This chapter presents the summary of findings of the present enquiry and incorporates suggestions to increase financial profitability of the Saptagiri Grameena Bank (SGB) and contain and reduce the magnitude of the non - performing assets (NPAs). Besides, hints for further research in future on topic of research are incorporated.

1. Summary:

This section deals with the summary of findings arrived at in the earlier chapters.

1.1.RRBs in India:

During the planning era, a number of rural development programmes were designed and implemented to improve the well being of rural India. All the programmes considered institutional credit one of the strategic and vital inputs for the successful implementation of rural development programmes since non - institutional agencies would not provide productive credit adequately and timely. The government has set up several institutions for the supply of credit to the rural clientele. Firstly, cooperatives were nurtured as primary institutions for rural credit. Subsequently, commercial banks were established inter alia to provide rural credit with emphasis on the opening of rural branches. Both the cooperatives and commercial banks would not fully meet the demand for rural credit.

In the light of the experiences and on the recommendations of Narasimham Committee, regional rural banks (RRBs) came on the rural credit scene to form the third component of multi - agency credit system during 1975. RRBs have opened branches far and wide in the country. There were 57 RRBs at the end of 2014. The number of branches stood at 19,082 spread over 642 districts in the country in the aforesaid period. The branches are located in 27 states. Twenty two banks have sponsored all RRBs in the country. These banks have mobilised deposits worth Rs.2,39,504 crores and outstanding advances were Rs. 1,59,660 crores and registered a credit deposit ratio (CDR) of 66.66 per cent at the end of 2014. The share of recovery of advances to demand was 81.90 per cent. All the banks put together earned a profit of Rs. 283,300 crores. State – wise and sponsor - wise there are variations in the amount of profit / loss earned by RRBs. The accumulated losses were Rs. 90,300 lakhs. The NPAs were Rs. 280,434.65 lakhs in 2005 as against Rs. 702,504.00 lakhs in 2014. The proportion of NPAs to outstanding advances was 8.53 per cent in the former as against 4.40 per cent in the latter. There is an improvement in the earning capacity of RRBs and thereby the NPAs declined. This testifies the fact that RRBs are on the path of success. In the course of time, they may attain the objectives for which they were brought into existence.

1.2. Research design and methodology:

A well developed banking system is considered the pre - requisite for economic development of any country. RRBs were assigned a vital role to play in the realm of rural poverty eradication. Hence, it became imperative to have a critical evaluation of working of such institutions. In the light of this, the present study has been undertaken by the researcher. No doubt there are many studies at the macro and micro levels concerning RRBs at national, state, regional and bank specific. These studies touched upon branch expansion, deposit mobilisation, credit deployment, recovery performance, etc. The existing studies on specific RRBs have just touched up on operational results. There is no specific study either at the aggregate or at the bank level on financial performance and viability. Thus, there is an imminent need to wipe out this serious deficiency in the research based studies on RRBs. In the literature, the earlier studies have revealed the need for undertaking case studies on RRBs and to have a better evaluation taking into consideration their backdrop of working in different agro climatic and environmental conditions. Further, as the banks are restructured, some of the findings of earlier studies may not hold good for the present. There is no specific research based study on the financial profitability of the SGB as far as the knowledge and information of the researcher is concerned. Therefore, there is an urgent need to undertake an evaluative study on the SGB concerning the void referred to.

The objective of the present enquiry is to analyse the financial performance of the SGB in terms of trend, magnitude and progress in the earning capacity and impact of variables on the financial profitability. Besides, an attempt is made to evaluate the NPAs. Secondary information is the main source of data. Further, the perceptions of managers on the NPAs are elicited. The data is processed, classified, tabulated, analysed and interpreted with the help of appropriate tools like percentages, ratios, number of times, standard deviation, coefficient of variation and compound annual growth rate (CAGR). Wherever possible and feasible, appropriate graphs are drawn to illuminate the facts and figures. The period of study is confined to ten years i.e., 2005 - 14. The study suffers from certain limitations. For example, it carries all the limitations inherent with the secondary data. The qualitative aspects of profitability were ignored. Only quantitative financial data was considered for the purpose of analysis. The statistical devises used for the analysis have their own limitations. The thesis is organised into seven chapters.

1.3. Profile of the Saptagiri Grameena Bank:

The SGB formerly known as Sri Venkateswara Grameena Bank (SVGB) was established at Chittoor during 1981. It was sponsored by the Indian Bank, the lead bank of Chittoor district. The Kanaka Durga Grameena Bank (KDGB) was merged with the SVGB to form the SGB on 1st July 2006. The operational area of the SGB is spread over Chittoor and Krishna districts of Andhra Pradesh. The bank was established with the avowed objective of uplifting the rural public. The bank performs several functions like mobilisation of deposits, credit deployment by covering weaker sections of society and schemes. The management is vested in the Board of Directors. The Chairman, Board of Directors, general manager, senior managers, branch managers, field officers, clerical staff and subordinates are in its organisational fold. There are 393 officers, 236 office assistants and 47 office attendants totaling to 676 at the end of 2014.

There are 163 branches spread over its operational area. Of these, 111 are rural, 40 semi - urban and the rest urban. The share capital was Rs. 200 lakhs. The share capital deposit Rs.1,577.05 lakhs and reserves and surplus were Rs. 24,571.32 lakhs during 2014. The total owned funds of the bank were Rs. 2,775.51 lakhs in 2005 and progressively reached to stand at Rs. 26,348.37 lakhs during 2014. The SGB borrowed funds from the sponsored bank and the NABARD. The total borrowings were Rs. 9,470.64 lakhs in 2005 as compared to Rs. 110,131.95 lakhs in 2014. Out of the total borrowings, more than 70 per cent was from the sponsored bank. Of the total funds, owned funds were in the range of 14.85 – 22.85 per cent during the period. The bank has parked funds in different avenues of investment. Out of all the sources of investment, government securities constituted more than 75 per cent. The average working funds of the SGB were Rs. 56,576.80 lakhs in 2005 as compared to Rs. 383,837.00 lakhs during 2014.

1.4. Deposit mobilisation and loan operations:

The SGB has introduced several types of deposit schemes keeping in view the poorer sections in its operational area. The aggregate number of deposit accounts which stood at 3,34,000 lakhs in 2005 has progressively increased to 12,56,518 lakhs by the end of 2014. The annual increment was in the range of 4.61 – 54.03 per cent. The growth in 2007 was remarkable due to amalgamation of the KDGB with the SVGB. The deposits mobilised have increased from Rs. 35,295.80 lakhs in 2005 to Rs. 252,363.50 lakhs in 2014. The average deposits per branch were Rs. 470.61 lakhs in 2005 as compared to Rs. 3,555.39 lakhs in 2014. The amount of deposit per employee has increased progressively from Rs. 85.46 lakhs to Rs. 857.29 lakhs during the aforesaid period. The per capita deposits constituted Rs.10,567.60 in 2005 while Rs.20,084.35 in 2014. There is a spectacular increase in aggregate deposits and accounts and also per branch, per employee and per capita. Among deposits, savings deposits, in terms of accounts, ranked first. The term deposits ranked second in accounts while occupied first place in amount. The bank could not fulfil the targets in deposit mobilisation in 4 out of 10 years. In other words, the performance of the bank in the matter of attainment of deposits is unsatisfactory.

The bank disbursed Rs. 27,650.38 lakhs in 2005 and it has progressively increased year after year to reach Rs. 215,628.33 lakhs during 2014. The share of priority sector in the total disbursement was 78.37 per cent in 2005 as against 83.36 per cent in 2014 and the rest is accounted for non - priority sector. In the case of priority sector, short - term agricultural loans (STAL) accounted for a major share ranging between 78.97 per cent and 57.70 per cent during the study period. The proportion of small scale industries (SSI) was least. Out of different categories of borrowers, weaker sections occupied a first place with a share ranging between 71.22 – 87.37 per cent followed by women (13.79 – 24.25 per cent), Scheduled Castes (SCs)/ Scheduled Tribes (STs) (3.62 – 11.53 per cent) and minorities (0.10 – 2.21 per cent). In the disbursement of credit, accomplishments far exceeded budgeted targets except 2009 and 2014.

The outstanding advances have gone up gradually from Rs. 35,556.67 lakhs to Rs. 327,165.40 lakhs during 2005– 14. Similarly, the amount per branch and per employee has increased from Rs. 474.06 lakhs and Rs. 68.64 lakhs in 2005 to Rs. 3,555.39 lakhs and Rs. 857.29 lakhs in 2014

sequentially. Like disbursement, the priority sector dominates the non -
priority sector in outstanding advances. Similar is the case with the coverage
of small farmers (SFs), marginal farmers (MFs), agricultural labourers (Als),
SCs/STs/minorities. The business per branch has continuously risen from Rs.
474.06 lakhs to Rs. 3,555.39 lakhs during 2005-14. An identical trend can be
found with regard to business per employee. This had gone up from Rs.
68.64 lakhs to Rs. 857.29 lakhs in the same period. The credit- deposit ratio
(CDR) was more than 100 per cent during 2005 – 14, which reflects that the
deposits mobilised locally were fully deployed in the operational area of the
bank. The percentage of recovery to demand has increased from 86.61 in
2005 to 87.42 in 2014. In other words, the proportion of overdues to demand
has declined. In the case of farm-sector, the proportion of collection to
demand was 85.97 per cent in 2005 as compared to 84.85 per cent in 2014.
In respect of non-farm sector, the recovery performance was 90.10 per cent
in 2005 as against 91.88 per cent in 2014. When both the sectors are
considered together, the recovery efficiency was higher in the farm-sector in
four years while a contrary picture emerges in the remaining six years.

1.5. Financial Performance:

The income of the SGB includes interest and non-interest. The total
income of the bank has progressively increased from Rs. 4,549.79 lakhs in
2005 to Rs. 41,642.90 lakhs in 2014. Of the total income of the bank, interest
income was more than 95 per cent and the rest, non-interest income. In the
case of interest income, interest / discount on advances and bills was in the
range of 75.25-89.00 per cent. Income on investments occupied second place
while interest on balances with banks third. The ratio of interest earned to
working fund declined from 7.76 per cent in 2005 to 10.47 per cent in 2014.

It signifies that, in the initial period, the bank has earned the least interest as a percentage of working fund whereas it turned the highest in the recent past. It means that the initial period proved to be the less efficient in utilising working funds at the command of the bank. Similarly, interest earned to volume of business was 6.20 per cent in 2005 while 6.23 per cent in 2014. It infers that lending operations of the bank have declined during the period.

The bank earned commission, exchange and brokerage to a tune of Rs. 102.92 lakhs in 2005 as compared to Rs. 196.47 lakhs in 2014. Out of the total non – interest income, their proportion was in the range of 13.37 – 64.31 per cent and the rest is miscellaneous income. The non-interest income to volume of business was less than 0.30 per cent. The ratio of non-interest income to working fund was less than one per cent. It declined due to the fact that the working fund has grown faster than that of non – interest income. This is unwelcome from the point of profitability of the bank.

The aggregate expenditure of the SGB had gradually increased from Rs. 4,383.98 lakhs in 2005 to Rs. 34,242.58 lakhs in 2014. The components of total expenditure such as interest paid, operating expenses, provisions and contingencies and provisions for investments have also grown in the period as a sequel to increase in resources and expansion of business. The proportion of interest paid to total expenditure was more than 55 per cent during the period. The operating expenses and provisions and contingencies and provisions for investments follow it in the order. Of the interest expended, interest paid on deposits was Rs. 2,102.09 lakhs in 2005 vis - à - vis Rs. 18,219.15 lakhs in 2014. In percentage terms, it formed 82.67 per cent and 68.53 per cent in the former and latter respectively and the rest is accounted for the interest paid on borrowings. The ratio of interest paid has declined with fluctuations. The ratio of interest expended has submerged from 4.49 per cent to 6.93 per cent during the period. The increase was due to the fact that the working fund has decreased faster than interest expenditure. A similar trend emerges in the interest paid to volume of business. It infers that there may be a disproportionate progress in interest payments and volume of business. The trend in these two ratios is unfavorable from the view point of profitability. Of the total non – interest expenditure, expenses towards employees constituted 67.90 – 85.81 per cent during the period. The remaining proportion is accounted for other establishment expenses.

The ratio of manpower expenses to volume of business and ratio of other establishment expenses to volume of business have declined. It shows that the turnout of employees has improved when compared to expenses incurred on them. An identical trend exists in the ratio of other expenses to volume of business. The ratio of non-interest expenses to working fund has also declined from 2.02 per cent to 1.40 per cent during the period. It shows that the increase in working fund is higher than that of corresponding increase in non-interest expenses. It implies that there is no better control over non-interest expenditure in relation to working fund. All these ratios are favourable from the view point of the bank in the recent past as compared to earlier period. Of the other operating expenses, others came first (33.80 per cent) followed by depreciation and repairs (28.25 per cent), rent, taxes and lighting (22.53 per cent), postage, telephone and telegram (4.71 per cent), printing and stationary (4.21 per cent), fee (3.05 per cent), insurance (2.88 per cent) and advertisement and publicity (0.58 per cent) during 2014.

The gross-profit was Rs. 165.81 lakhs in 2005 while it was Rs. 7,400.32 lakhs in 2014. The amount of net – profit fluctuated between Rs. 347.93 lakhs and Rs. 5,894.98 lakhs. The ratio of net - profit to total assets has declined during the period. It infers that there is no corresponding movement between net – profit and total assets of the bank. A similar trend can be observed in the ratio of net - profit to working fund / total income and total deposits. The efficiency of the bank has declined over the period. This is so because profit as a percentage of working fund has declined in the recent past relative to initial period. The decline in the share of net – profit to total income may be attributed to adoption of prudential norms by the SGB. The declining trend in the ratio of net - profit to total deposits implies that the SGB had utilised its deposits more efficiently. Therefore, it generated higher profits in the beginning as compared to recent period of the study. The interest coverage ratio showed an upward trend with to and fro changes. It reveals that the interest charges have increased at a galloping pace without a corresponding increase in the net – profit.

The spread in the SGB has steadily increased from Rs. 1,846.93 lakhs to Rs. 13,587.43 lakhs during the period under study. The ratio of spread to working fund reveals that the SGB in the recent period of study was able to earn more income by way of spread at a higher rate as compared to that of initial period. The ratio of spread to volume of business also declined reflecting the fact that the interest paid ratio grew faster than the interest earned ratio. The burden was Rs. 982.32 lakhs in 2005 vis - à - vis Rs. 3,897.11 lakhs in 2014. The ratios of burden to volume of business / working fund have declined. The former indicates that the operating expenses ratio has declined faster than other incomes ratio. The manpower and the other expenses ratios have declined on account of increase in the volume of business. In this context, it may be remembered that the other income ratio has declined slowly. Hence, burden ratio has receded. This was due to the fact that other incomes ratio had decreased marginally while manpower and other expenses ratios have increased considerably. The ratio of burden to working fund reflects that the rise in burden is lower than that of the increase in working fund. Therefore, we may conclude that the SGB exercised better control over burden in the recent past as against the earlier period of the study period. This might have led resulted in the enhancement of profitability of the bank.

The SGB has attained profitability performance in the period since spread ratio was higher than that of burden ratio. The profitability performance ratio in 2005 was more than that of 2014. There are wide fluctuations in the profitability performance. For example, there was a growing trend in the beginning, declining trend in the middle and again increasing trend in the closing period of the study. However, it may not be commensurate with the size of the bank. Therefore, it calls for an enhancement in the volume of business with a better control over expenses so as to further strengthen its economic viability in the years to come and achieve the avowed objectives of rural development, particularly assisting the weakest of weak. The percentage of gross income to outstanding loans ratio (G) has gradually gone up from 12.80 per cent in 2005 to 13.23 per cent in 2013 and declined to 12.73 per cent in 2014. The percentage of interest paid to outstanding advances ratio (I) has declined during the aforesaid period. As a result, the gross margin ratio (N) has also declined. The establishment expense to outstanding loans ratio (E) has also exhibited a downward trend. The net – margin ratio (N_1) was 2.44 per cent in 2005 as against 3.07 per cent in 2014. It is more favourable in the recent period of the study rather than in the initial period. Thus, there is an obvious need to raise net margin ratio so as to build strong reserves and surplus in future.

1.6. Non – Performing assets:

The non – performing assets (NPAs) in the SGB was Rs. 834.89 lakhs in 2005 as against Rs. 6,013.10 lakhs in 2014. The proportion of NPAs in the total assets was in the range of 0.94 – 2.35 per cent during the same period. The share of the NPAs in the total outstanding advances was 2.35 per cent in 2005 as compared to 1.84 per cent in 2014. The proportion of NPAs in the total assets as well as in outstanding advances has declined remarkably due to implementation of Securitisation and Reconstruction of Financial Assets and Enforcement of Security Interest Act, 2002 (SARFAESIA). Of the NPAs, substandard assets were in the order of 32.53 – 71.64 per cent during the period under reference. The doubtful assets formed 19.90 – 56.64 per cent in the same period. The loss assets exist in nine out of 10 years. There is a marked change in the profile of the NPAs. For example, the amount of loss assets has declined while sub - standard and doubtful assets improved during 2005 - 14. The amount recovered from the NPAs was Rs. 366.12 lakhs in 2005 and it has gone up to reach Rs. 451.76 lakhs in 2014 with to and fro changes. The proportion of recovery to NPAs was 43.85 per cent in 2005 and stood at 7.51 per cent in 2014 with relative ups and downs. The addition to NPAs was Rs. 420.57 lakhs in 2005 vis - à - vis Rs. 1,609.10 lakhs in 2013 and no provision was made during 2014. The share of provision to NPAs was in the range of 50.37 – 129.66 per cent. The year 2010 reported the highest provision of 129.66 per cent. The provision of NPAs is dependent on the guidelines prescribed. The high value NPAs accounts were 45 with an outstanding advance of Rs. 99.23 lakhs in 2005. The per capita outstanding amount works out to Rs. 2.21 lakhs. By 2014, the outstanding amount rose to Rs. 972.54 lakhs spread over 462 NPA accounts. The per capita advances have declined in 2014 over 2005 which is a welcome trend. The amount of outstanding advances upgraded as the NPAs has declined from Rs.89 lakhs in 2005 to Rs.63.40 lakhs in 2014. The amount written off from the NPAs also showed a similar trend. It was Rs. 40.06 lakhs in 2005 as compared to Rs. 0.35 lakhs in 2014. The ratio of capital to risk weighted assets ratio (CRAR) was 11.20 per cent in 2007 and 9.75 per cent in 2014. These are in excess of minimum statutory requirement of 9 per cent. Thus, the capital held was above the stipulated level and there is a sufficient capital to absorb operational losses, if any, without infringing upon the interest of depositors. The respondent managers of the SGB expressed different causes for the NPAs. In the order of priority, they include elaborate and time – consuming legal system; frequent change of government policy; lack of proper follow – up ; mismanagement and diversion of funds by borrowers; socio – political pressures; and directed and targeted lending.

2. Suggestions:

In light of the findings of the present investigation, the following suggestions are made to enhance the economic viability and financial performance of the SGB. It is evident that there are certain issues in the functioning of the bank. These factors to a certain extent may become detrimental to earn profit and profitability thereon. This indeed, could affect the financial profitability of the bank. Earnest implementation of the following suggestions will enable the SGB to improve its operational efficiency and prompt earnings, apart from rendering a better service to the rural poor and achieve its avowed objectives.

2.1. Share capital:

Since the quantum of cost free funds is meagre, local people may be allowed to participate in the share capital of the SGB.

2.2. Refinance:

Till now, the refinance policy followed by the National Bank for Agriculture and Rural Development (NABARD) has been liberal so as to ensure that credit needs are met by the SGB and no fund constraint comes in this way. However, over a period of time, it is expected that the SGB should improve its resource mobilisation and excessive dependence on refinance should be reduced gradually. The NABARD and sponsor bank should reduce the interest on the funds made available to the SGB.

2.3. Sponsor bank:

Apart from the present marginal contribution, the sponsor bank should aid and assist the SGB in its operational matters, particularly the following: (i) in the matter of appraisal of bankable schemes and project loaning and proper end use of credit; (ii) in the development of a proper system of control over branches and in adopting sound procedures right from the beginning; (iii) assume responsibility in providing staff for internal audit; (iv) undertake periodical inspections; and (v) the share of sponsor bank in the refinance be brought down simultaneously to enhance the involvement of the SGB.

2.4. Branch expansion:

As a first step in the direction of perspective plan, the SGB should be empowered to identify centres for its future expansion. It would, in fact, be desirable that the SGB should itself chalk out a programme of expanding its branch network by first identifying the centres and then earmarking them for opening of branches in a phased manner over a definite span of time. The list of centres thus identified could be submitted to the NABARD with a time horizon of about 3 to 5 years for extending banking facilities. The government of AP may be requested to provide necessary infrastructure to the identified centres before the branch is opened. A coordinated programme involving the SGB, the NABARD and the Government as a nodal agency and instrument of promoting welfare should be evolved. The SGB should strive to attain a balanced regional development in locating branches and transacting business. Mere numerical expansion of branches and fulfilment of physical targets should not be the only aim of the SGB. The SGB should review the profitability of each of its branches and choose those branches which are chronic loss - making and cannot be made to run on viable lines. Further, loss - making branches which have potential to turnaround should be put on a well defined programme and their performance be closely watched.

2.5. Working hours:

The working hours during busy and slack seasons may be altered so as to be suitable and convenient to the rural clientele. The SGB may prescribe late evening and early morning business hours. Then only the SGB branches may become perfect substitutes to money - lenders.

2.6. Personnel:

Only personnel who are specially trained and attuned to the rural culture should be posted to different positions in the bank. Reasonable promotional opportunities have to be provided to the staff in their career path. The promotional avenues at present are limited in the SGB. Hence, some posts in the officer cadre of the sponsor bank may be made available to the SGB officers with requisite experience and qualification. The staff has to be deputed to programmes of rural orientation, apart from their regular familiarisation with practices of banking and maintenance of accounts. All activities connected with recruitment, training and promotion of the staff may be centralised at the State level through the setting up of a separate institute for the purpose for all RRBs in AP. The researcher is of the opinion that the staff, especially those at the middle level management, has not accepted the management of NPAs as an essential and integral function. On account of this, higher authorities have imposed the collection of dues on them. Thus the emphasis on discipline both at the end of borrower as well as bank will be beneficial for both.

2.7. Deposit mix:

The SGB should initiate steps to improve low cost deposits so that average amount of interest payable on various types of deposits could be reduced. Interest is not payable on the amount lying in current accounts and low rate of interest is payable on saving deposits when compared to fixed deposit accounts. Higher proportion of current account or saving account can bring down the average rate of interest payable on deposits. In turn, cost of funds would improve the earnings of bank. The SGB should motivate the rich and well - to - do farmers to keep their deposits with its branches. The employees have to develop a close rapport with villagers and dispel their misunderstanding that the branches of the SGB may not repay the deposits in time because of their small size operations. It may mobilise large amount of deposit. Like credit camps, deposit camps should be organised.

2.8. Credit – mix:

Broadly speaking, bank credit can be categorised into priority and non-priority sectors. For priority sector lending, which generally carry a lower rate of interest, RBI fixes goals for the SGB. In its anxiety not only to achieve the goal but also to surpass the same, the bank organises loan camps to sanction and disburse such loans. Such an approach to priority sector lending without proper appraisal not only reduces the interest income but makes the recovery of such loans difficult and even doubtful. Priority sector is redefined to cover only small/marginal farmers, artisans, tiny and small units, transport, operators, etc. The targets are reduced from the existing percentage of aggregate credit. The SGB in the light of these recommendations and RBI guidelines, should re - examine its funds with regard to Priority sector. It has to deploy its funds so as to have a credit - mix which could provide to improve interest earnings. Liberal sanction of loans; quick disbursements to show active participation in government sponsored programmes; and achieve targets hurriedly have to be discontinued in the interest of the bank. The bank should independently identify the target group. Organisation of credit camps should be discontinued forthwith. Hurried identification and hasty disbursal of credit through spot sanctions are likely to cause more harm than good. Instead of granting loans to each and every small farmer to buy implements of modern design, the SGB should purchase and lend them out to farmers. Crop insurance is to be widely encouraged in order to save borrowers from the risk of natural calamities. There should be inter - agency coordination between the SGB and SC, ST and BC corporations in respect of margin money and subsidy. In order to develop a scientific lending programme, the SGB should conduct surveys of all the villages in its operational area to identify the credit needs of target population. Afterwards, they can formulate bankable schemes taking into consideration forward and backward linkages. For the purpose of proper monitoring of credit, a separate advances division for each district is to be created. The SGB may be allowed to undertake a complete package of banking services in order to increase the volume of business. The business of rural branches of commercial banks should be transferred to the branches of the SGB in a phased manner so as to avoid unhealthy competition. The SGB may be permitted to provide assistance to other target groups subject to a maximum of 40 per cent by fixing suitable ceilings for each individual to attract sizable deposits from them. The SGB should formulate schemes for providing term loans to purchase houses, cars and consumer durables which are quite remunerative. It is high time that the SGB, which has gained sufficient experience and expertise, should now diversify and get into term lending business which may comparatively be more rewarding.

2.9. Effective management of investment Portfolio:

Under the Provisions of law, the SGB has to make investment in approved securities issued by the government and authorised public sector bodies to maintain statutory liquidity ratio (SLR) which is linked to its demand and time liabilities. Substantial funds of the SGB remain tied up in such securities and the average rate of return on these securities vary. It is seen that the existing interest rate on government securities is less than the prime lending rate. Because of negligible difference in interest rate, choice of investment in the government securities is increasingly determined, not by statutory consideration, but by the risk / reward consideration when compared to normal lending. The investment portfolio should be guided by return.

2.10. Proper cash management:

The bank should take all possible steps to reduce the cash holdings in the branches to the bare minimum to meet their daily operational requirements and to remit the idle cash to the currency chests expeditiously so that the same could be accounted for while computing cash reserve ratio and to earn the interest on such cash balances. At the level of the branch, every effort should be made to keep the cash ratio as low as possible.

2.11. Control on establishment expenses:

Periodical review should be undertaken at fixed intervals to correlate operating expenses with the business of a branch to check erosion of profit. Miscellaneous expenditure should also be kept under constant review.

2.12. Avoidance of income leakages:

Banks should check revenue leakages which may be due to under – charging of interest and commissions, etc. by the branches inadvertently or intentionally. A system of expenditure audit on regular basis is to be introduced by entrusting the job preferably to outside agencies. Action should also be taken against erring staff and inspecting officials.

2.13. Refinance to augment lendable funds:

The SGB should avail refinance at concessional rate of interest under various schemes formulated by the IDBI, the SIDBI and the NABARD to augment funds which can be recycled to improve its earnings. However, in case the surplus funds fetch lower return than the refinance rate, it would not be desirable to avail refinance/returns till such time the position changes in favour of availing refinance. Care should be taken to avail refinance within a specified time after disbursement of loans.

2.14. Recovery:

Credit has to be supervised where not only its end use can be watched but borrower can be guided in maximising his output by the adoption of improved techniques of production including bettering of his skills. The repayment schedule should coincide with income generation. To reduce diversion of credit to other than specified purposes, there should be strict vigilance and incessant inspection; adequate number of supervisory staff at the branch level has to be appointed; encouragement of joint loans; sanction of consumption credit along with production credit; timely supply of credit; and scale of finance be fixed rationally. The bank should infuse repayment - ethics among the borrowers. It should see that the borrowers strictly adhere to repayment schedule with the help of social organisations. Some of the ways open to the SGB are constant contacts, frequent persuasion and insistence on the implementation of techno - economic terms and conditions of sanction. To have a close monitoring of sticky and NPA accounts and to exercise close follow - up of individual NPA accounts, a recovery and legal section has to be created at the Head Office of the bank. It should make constant reviews of recovery position of individual branches and advise them to pay special attention to bring down the NPAs. The bank has to make vigorous effort by launching certain special programmes and by implementing area - wise specific measures to ensure hundred per cent recovery. In the case of non - wilful default, since the seeds of NPAs are sown at the time of granting of loan itself, it is necessary that a thorough appraisal of the project at the grass - root level regarding its technical feasibility and financial viability is made. The intentional defaulters should be tackled either by making tie - up arrangements or by constant follow - up and persuasion. Whenever defaults arise due to natural calamities like droughts and circumstances beyond the control of borrowers, these cases are to be considered sympathetically by rescheduling of loans through extension, conversion and rephasement. If the situation comes to worst, it should write - off the loan which was considered absolutely irrecoverable. Incentives are to be introduced for the field level staff so as to make them recover with strong drive and zeal. In the case of crop loans, disbursement should take place before sowing and recovery immediately after harvest. The borrowers are to be informed in advance about the due dates. It is necessary that concerted action is taken on a priority basis by all concerned to remove the causes and reduce NPAs.

2.15. Viability:

While on the one hand, the SGBs image as small mans bank has to be preserved for fulfilling the objectives for which it was established. On the other hand, it is also essential to evolve certain schemes which would give higher rate of return or at least reduce the cost of servicing a loan. Therefore, the SGB may be allowed involve public bodies like village panchayats, housing boards, SC and ST corporations etc. Higher involvement in short - term loans is required. The instruction that the CDR should be progressively brought down to 100 per cent may not be insisted upon as it lends to an overall shrinkage of loans by the SGB. For undertaking projects, both investment credit and adequate short - term credit are to be provided to fructify the scheme. The SGB should endeavour to fulfil all the credit needs of the target group to qualify for a higher rate of interest. The bank may be allowed to earmark a portion of its loans to big farmers whom they can charge a higher rate of interest and thus increase its income. Since expenditure on staff and other establishment activities constitutes a sizable proportion, a proper policy of manpower planning and recruitment of staff has to be adopted so as to keep the staff to the bare minimum required. It is utmost important that the SGB has to keep the staff at such a level that business per employee is maximised.

2.16. Credit monitoring:

The researcher is of the view that credit monitoring and credit approval should be viewed as a complementary function to ensure meaningful integration of feedback from each other. The author is also of the opinion that credit monitoring can be meaningful only if the required credit is made available on time. For efficient credit monitoring, it is necessary to have a separate department headed by a senior official with full support staff, motivated to function with right spirit.

2.17. Legal action:

In the opinion of managers, speedier legal action is the only remedy left for the SGB to book wilful defaulters. Speedy disposal of suits and decrees in favour of the bank will, therefore, improve the recovery rate of the bank particularly in suit filed accounts. Assistance from outside agencies for recovery may be taken as in the case of some foreign countries. The courts should be more pro - active to timely disposal of cases and imposition of costs.

2.18. Others:

The relationship manager has to keep in constant touch with borrowers and report all developments impacting borrowal account. He is also expected to conduct scrutiny and account inspection. In the existing know your client profile system visits to clients are not properly structured as to the needs and nature of relationship. This has to be properly organised to the place of business of clients. The credit rating system is absent at the time of sanction of new borrowal account and renewal of existing credit facility in the SGB. The credit rating system is essentially one point indicator of an individual credit exposure and used to identify, measure and monitor credit of individual proposal. It enables the SGB to track the health of entire credit portfolio. The SGB has to put certain borrowal accounts, which under adverse business or economic conditions exhibit distress signals under watch list. These accounts generally exhibit weaknesses, which are correctable but warrant the closer attention of the bank. The categorisation of such accounts in watch list provides early warning signals enabling relationship managers to anticipate credit deterioration and take necessary preventive steps to avoid their slippage into NPAs. The default in the payment of interest and installment, deterioration in operating activities of the borrower etc. may be identified to assess the emerging problem in the credit exposure at an early stage. Thus the SGB has to introduce a watch dog team to identify the early signals of NPAs among the borrowal accounts. The SGB has to popularise the one time settlement of NPAs by offering concessions/rebate/waiver of certain past dues. Lok Adalat settlements may be encouraged further. The SGB should access the credit information so as to minimise the adverse selection at appraisal stage. All the banks working in the district including the SGB should establish credit information bureau. The SGB should publicise the list of wilful defaulters. The Securities Exchange Board of India (SEBI)/RBI should prevent access to these borrowers to capital market. When the aforesaid measures are implemented as a package and not in isolation, they would result in an improvement in the financial viability of the SGB. If all this is done, there is no reason why the SGB cannot continue as a small mans' bank and yet unburden itself from the NPAs. If these were available from its inception, the profit would have been much more. Then, it would have served the rural poor better than the present. 3 Hints for further research in future: Studies may be conducted in the direction of determining what proportion of profit could be considered as being earned due to non-availability of the benefits of the measures suggested in this study and what part could be attributed to management. In addition to the above, the more important is to create a committed and motivated workforce. The SGB should endeavour to bring about professional approach in the management and their style of functioning by inducting specialist staff to manage certain functions like investment, treasury, appraisal of projects, monitoring and recovery of loans, computerisation and information technology and so on. Further, the bank should also simplify and standardise its systems and procedures relating to branch operations which will not only improve customer service but also result in cost reduction and in turn improve profits. The impact of the SGB credit on beneficiary households in terms of employment creation, income generation and asset formation may be carried out. Further, beneficiaries may be compared with a control group of non -beneficiaries with similar characteristics. Such a comparison is essential so as to assess the real impact of the SGB credit on beneficiaries because changes in employment, income and asset holding are likely to take place even without the credit of SGB. Studies may be undertaken at the level of branch. Hence, it is suggested that research studies at a micro - level may be conducted in future on all these issues. This will enable the researchers to throw a greater light on these and more effective, meaningful and feasible ways and means can be found out to the problems. This will tone up the efficiency of operations of SGB, apart from stepping up its level of profitability.

SELECT BIBLIOGRAPHY

Abdul, N.B. (1981). *"Rural Banks Towards an Efficient Lending Business,"* Capital, 187 (4679), 3- 4.

Abdul Noorbasha., & Jyothi, M., (2001). *"Viability of Regional Rural Banks- A Case Study,"* Yojana, 33, 18- 20.

Abhiman Das. (2002). *"Risk and Productivity Change in Public Sector Banks,"* Economic and Political Weekly, 17 (3), 10- 25.

Agarwal, B., & Kumar, H., (2009). *Regional Rural Banks as Catalyst of Rural Development in India.* In: Agarwal, ed., M, *Regional Rural Banks in India,* New Century Publication, New Delhi.

Agarwal, H.N. (1979). *A Portrait of Nationalised Banks*, New Delhi, Inter-India Publications.

Agarwal, K.P. (1985). *"Regional Rural Banking: Challenges Ahead,"* Economic Times, 1- 2.

Agricultural Finance Corporation. (1981). *A Study of Two RRBs*, Bombay.

Aiyar, S. (1978). *"Future of Rural Banks Seems Assured,"* Times of India, 2-3.

Amandeep. (1993). *Profits and Profitability in Commercial Banks,* New Delhi, Deep and Deep Publications.

Ammannaya, K.K. (1982). *"Profitability and Productivity in Banks,"* Secular Democracy, 20 (24), 15- 18.

Anand S.C., & Jagat Ram., (1989). *Handbook on RRBs*, New Delhi, Vision Books.

Ananda Kumar, V. (1988) *"Performance of RRBs – A Study,"* Kurukshetra, 37 (21), 16-20.

Angadi, V.B., & John Devraj, V., (1983). "*Productivity and Profitability of Banks in India*", 'Economic and Political Weekly,' 18 (48), 160- 61.

Angadi V.B., & John Devraj, V., (1986). *"Policy Constraints and Banks Profitability",* Economic and Political Weekly, 21 (24), 1081- 84.

---------------*"Are NPAs Grossly Misunderstood?"* (1999). Business India, 7 (10), 60-64.

Angol, Malti. (1992). *"Financial Institutions Increase Rural Credit,"* Economics Times.

Asha, P. (1988). *Evaluation of Performance of Commercial Banks- Norms and Techniques,* The Banker, 6 (3), 1- 12.

Baiju, S., & Gabriel Simon Thattil., (2000). *"Performance Banks with Non-Performing Assets: An Analysis of NPAs,"* Yojana, 3 (2), 5- 9.

Balishter, et. al. (1986). *"Performance of Regional Rural Banks, An evaluation of a Rural Bank in Agra District of Uttar Pradesh,"* Yojana, (9), 31- 38.

233

Balishter, et.al. (1990). *"Role of Regional Rural Banks in up- liftment of Weaker Sections- A study in Agra District of Uttar Pradesh,"* Agricultural Situation in India, 45 (5), 345- 49.

Banambar Sahoo. (1999). *"Rating of Banks of NPA Management,"* IBA Bulletin, 7 (3), 29 – 34.

Banerjee, S. (1979). *"Why Rural Banking Has Failed,"* Southern Economist, 18 (21), 31- 32.

Bapna, M.S. (1989), *RRBs in Rajasthan,* Delhi, Himalaya Publishing House.

Bapanna, M.S. (2001). *"Regional Rural Banks in Rajasthan",* Himalaya Publishing House, Mumbai, 32- 35.

Belshaw, H. (1965). *Agricultural Credit in Economically Underdeveloped Countries,* Rome, FAO, 232-38.

Bhagavan Reddy, B., & B. Krishna Reddy., (1988). *"An Evaluation of Sri Venkateswara Grameena Bank,"* Banking Finance, 1 (10), 9-10.

Buat. (1999). *Rural Banking in India,* Bombay, Himalaya Publishing Company, 121- 22.

Chakravarty, Nitya. (1994). *"Credit Policy and Priority Sector Lending,"* Yojana, 13 (7), 12- 18.

Chandra, M. (1992). *"On Increasing Profitability of Public Sector Banks – A Note,"* Pigmy Economic Review, 38 (2), 31- 40.

Chauhan et.al, B.R.S. (1991). *"Income and Savings of Weaker Sections consequent upon Financing by Regional Rural Banks in Etwah District of Uttar Pradesh,"* Agricultural Situation in India, 45 (11), 761- 65.

Chorafas Dimitris, N. (1998). *The New Technology of Financial Management,* Canada, John Wiley & Sons, Inc.

------------, *"Cost of Banking Services,"* (1978). RBI Bulletin, 244- 45.

Das. (1999). *"Profitability of Public Sector Banks: A Decomposition Model,"* Reserve Bank of India Occasional Papers, 20 (1), 55- 73.

Das. (2002). *"Risk and Productivity Change of Public Sector Banks,"* Economic and Political Weekly, 37 (6), 437- 47.

Demirguc-Kunt., Asli., & Harry Huizinga., (1999). *"Determination of Commercial Bank Interest Margins and Profitability: Some International Evidence,"* Word Bank, WPS.

Deshpande, D.D. (1986). *"Bank Profitability Analysis: Need to take into Account Loss of Interest on CRR and Penalties on CRR/SLR,"* Banks Economists Meet, Punjab National Bank, New Delhi, 5 (3), 151- 55.

Devaraj, V.J. (1983). *"Productivity and Profitability of Banks in India,"* Economic and Political Weekly, 18 (48), 20- 25.

Dey, N.B., & Adhikari, K., (2004). *"Performance of Regional Rural Bank in Barak Valley of Assam: An Analytical Study",* Kangleipak Business Review, 3 (1), 120- 25.

Dhabbal, A., & Bhattacharya, K., (1989). *"Poor Recovery of Institutional Loans: An Analysis of its causes"* Indian Journal of Economics, New Delhi, 69 (274), 307- 10.

Dilip Khankhoje., & Milind Sathye., (2008). *"Efficiency of Rural Banks: The Case of India",* International Business Research - CCSE, 1 (2).

Divatia, V.V., & Venkatachalam T.R., (1978). *"Operational Efficiency and Profitability in Public Sector Banks,"* Reserve Bank of India Staff Papers, 3 (1), 1- 16.

Elias, A.H. (1977). *Operational Problems of Rural Banking,* Bombay, Vora and Co.

Elic, A.N. (1967).*Operational Problem of Rural Banking,* Bombay, Vora and Co.

Ganguly, A.K. (1983). *Impact on Banks' Profitability,* The Banker, 1 (3), 5- 7.

Garg, S. (1989). *Indian Banking: Cost and Profitability*, New Delhi, Annual Publications.

Golait, R. (2007). *Current Issues in Agriculture Credit in India: An Assessment*, New Delhi: Reserve Bank of India.

Government of India. (1975). *Report of the Committee on Rural Banks,* New Delhi. (D.O. NO.F. 1-10/75/AC).

Government of India. (1976). *National Commission on Agriculture,* 568- 70 (abridged report).

Government of India. (1976). *The Gazette of India,* New Delhi, Part II, Section 1, 149-50 (extra ordinary).

Government of India. (1978). *Report of the Working Group on Simplification of Application Form and Lending Procedures,* New Delhi, Ministry of Finance.

Government of India. (1986). *Report of the Working Group on RRBs*, New Delhi, Ministry of Finance.

Gupta, M., & Goswami, S., (1986). *"Profitability and Profit Planning in Banks",* BEM, 5 (1), 92- 100.

Gupta, V.K. (2004). *"Whether Defaulters can get Indulgence of DRT's – New Opportunities to Banks for Recovery,"* IBA Bulletin, 13 (2), 37- 38.

Harsha, S.V., & S.P. Singh., (1986). *"Approaches to planning in banks,"* BEM, 6 (3), 32- 35.

Hasan. (1975). *Theory of Profit,* New Delhi, Vikas Publishing House Pvt. Ltd.

Hebber, A.R.K. (1989). *"Grameena Banks - Viability No Criterion,"* The Economic Times, 5I- 52.

Hossain, M. (1984). *"Credit for the Rural Poor," Bangladesh Institute of Development Studies,* Bangladesh, Monograph, (4), 43- 48.

Howard, B., & Upton Miller., (1953). *Introduction to Business Finance,* New York, McGraw Hill Book Company Inc.

Ibrahim, M. (2011). *"Role of Indian RRBs in the Priority Sector Lending- An Analysis,"* International Journal of Management and Technology, 1 (1), 85- 97.

Indian Institute of Banking & Finance. (2004). *Bank Financial Management,* New Delhi, Taxmann publications Pvt. Ltd.

Inu Jain. (1980). *"Rural Credit and Regional Rural Banks"* Khadi Gramodhyog, 28 (3), 3- 5.

Jagadish Prasad., & Sunil Kumar., (1985). *"Regional Rural Banks: A Study"* Kurukshetra, 33 (8), 31- 33.

Jain, M.K. (1989). *Rural Banks and Rural Poor*, Jaipur, Printwell Publishers.

Jha, P.K. (1982). '*Banking and Economic Growth*,' in Subramanya K.N. (ed.) Modern Banking in India, Deep and Deep publications, New Delhi, 54- 55.

Joseph, F., & Sinkey., Jr. (1983). *Commercial Bank Financial Management,* New York, Macmillan Publishing Co., Inc.

Joshi, M.K. (1981). *"A Study on RRBs,"* Financing Agriculture, 24 (4), 20- 25.

Kalkundrikar, A.B. (1990). *RRBs and Economic Development,* Delhi, Daya Publishing House.

Kallu Rao, P., & Shaji Tomas., (1992), *"Performance of Manipur Rural Bank-An Analytical Study"* Journal of Rural Development, 11 (4), 443- 59.

Karkal, G.L. (1982). *"Profit and Profitability in Banking,"* Prajnan, 11 (7), 19- 58.

Karnel, Gopal, (1997). *Perspectives in Indian Banking,* Bombay, Popular Prakashan, 86.

Karulkar, R.P. (1983). *Agricultural Finance in a Backward Region,* Bombay, Himalaya Publishing House.

Kaveri, V.S. (1998). *"Prevention of NPAs – Suggested Strategies,"* National Institute of Bank Management Seminar.

Kaveri, V.S. (1999). *"Loan Default and Profitability of Banks,"* IBA Bulletin, 18-19.

Kaveri, V.S. (2001). *"Loan Default and Profitability of Banks,"* IBA Bulletin, 20-21.

Kiran Chopra. (1987). *"Managing Profits, Profitability and Productivity in Public Sector Banking,"* Jalandhar, ABS Publications.

Krishnan, C. (1990). *"Regional Rural Banks and Rural Development",* Yojana, 33 (24), 32- 34.

Kumar Raj. (1993). *"Growth and Performance of RRBs in Haryana"* New Delhi, Anmol Publications.

Kurup N.P., & Madhu Sarin., (1987). *"Branch Banking and Profitability,"* Bank Economists Meet, Vijaya Bank, Bangalore.

Lakshmi Narayana, V. (1984). *"Regional Rural Banks-Problems and Prospects A Case Study,"* Financing Agriculture, 14 (2), 54- 56.

Mishra, A.N. (1992). *"Analysis of Profitability of Commercial Banks",* Indian Journal of Banking and Finance, 5 (3), 6- 11.

Mohana Rao, L.K. (1980). "*Impact of Programmes on Target Groups-Case Study of Regional Rural Banks*", Indian Journal of Agricultural Economics, New Delhi, 25 (4), 73- 77.

Moin Quazi. (1989). *"Banking and Rural Development",* Financial Express, Mumbai, 6.

Mithani, D.M. (1998). *Money Banking, International Trade and Public Finance,* Mumbai, Himalaya Publishing House.

Mittal. (2007). *Profitability and Productivity in Indian Banks: A Comparative Study,* AIMS, 1 (2), 6-12.

Nakkirani. (1980). *Agricultural Financing & Rural Banking in India,* Coimbatore, Rainbow Publishers.

Narasaiah., & Ramudu, R., (2008). *"Financing of Agriculture by Regional Rural Banks",* Sonali Publications, New Delhi.

Nagi Reddy., & Ratna Kumari., (1986). *"Credit Repayment Performance of Borrowers of Regional Rural Banks: A Case Study",* Southern Economist, 15- 17.

Naidu, L.K., & Naidu, M.C., (1988). *Financing of Rural artisans by Regional Rural Banks-A Case Study of Rayalaseema Grameena Bank in Cuddapah District in Bank Finance For Rural Artisans* (Ed), Ashish Publishing House, 56- 58.

Naidu, L.K. (1988). *"Bank Finance for Rural Artisans,"* Ashish Publishing Housing.

Nigam., & B.M. Lall., (1979). *"Financial Analysis Techniques for Banking Decision,"* Somaiya Publications Pvt. Ltd.

Padmini, E.V.K. (1989). *"Profitability Analysis of Commercial Banks: A Case Study,"* Indian Banking Today & Tomorrow, 3 (2), 10- 14.

Palliian, D.L., & Shirk, S.E., (1964). *"Cost Accounting & Banking Profits Management Control,"* Bankers Magazine, 6 (3), 12- 18.

Panandikar, V.A. (1982). *"Regional Rural Banks",* The Economic Times, 26th, 9- 10.

Panandikar, V.A. (1995). *"Regional Rural Banks"*, The Economic Times, 9- 10.

Panda, J., & Lal, G.S., (1991). *"A Critical Appraisal on the Profitability of Commercial Banks,"* Indian Journal of Banking and Finances, 5 (6), 12- 15.

Parikh, M.G., & others. (1980). *Commercial Banking,* Bombay, Vora & Company Publishers Pvt. Ltd., 173- 74.

Parmar, G.D. et al. (1988). *"Performance of Banaskantha- Mehsana Grameena Bank in Gujarat State,"* Agricultural Banker, 2 (3), 23- 25.

Patel, K.V., & Shete, N.B., (1980). *"RRB's: Performance and Prospects",* Prajnan, 9 (1), 1- 40.

Patel, K.V., & Kaveri, V.S., (1998). *"Non – Performing Advances in Priority Sector – A Study,"* IBA Bulletin, 16- 23.

Patnaik, L.M. (1997). *A Comprehensive Analysis of Profitability in Corporate Sector,* Unpublished Doctoral Thesis, Berhampur University.

Patnaik, Umesh C., (1994). *Reforms in the Banking Sector & the Task Ahead,* SBI Monthly Review, 13 (7).

Patnaik U.C., & Manoj Patnaik., (2005). *Profitability in Public Sector Banks,* New Delhi, Sonali Publications.

Pattern, James. (1983). *Fundamental of Bank Accounting,* Virginia: Reston Publishing Company Inc.

Phadtare, R.R. (1986). *"Profitability of Regional Rural Banks,"* Agricultural Banker, 7 (3), 18- 19.

Prabhakar, M.R. (1985). *"Viability of RRBs – An Analysis,"* Financial Express, 27th.

Prabhakar, M.R. (1996). *"Viability of RRBs,"* Financial Express, 30th.

Prasad, B.V.S. (1985). *"Credit and Rural Bank: A Case Study,"* M.Phil, Dissertation submitted to S, V. University, Tirupathi, 89- 91.

Prasadarao, M.S.V. (1986). *"Banks & Profitability,"* Bank Economists Meet, Punjab National Bank, New Delhi.

--------------*Programme on Management of NPAs & Recovery Strategies,* (2001). NIBM, Pune.

Rakesh Mohan. (2007). *"Reforms, Productivity & Efficiency in Banking: The Indian Experience,"* The Pakistan Development Review, 5 (2), 10- 18.

Ramana Murthy, D.V. (1977). Regional Rural Bank – An Assessment of Performance, Southern Economist, 16 (7), 1-12.

Ramana Murthy, P.V. (1996).Cost & Profitability of Public Sector Banks, New Delhi, Mohit Publications.

Rao., & Someswar., (1998).Economics of Rural Banking, New Delhi, Anmol Publications Pvt. Ltd.

Raut, C. Kishore., & Das, K., Santosh., (1996). *Commercial Banks in India - Profitability, Growth & Development,* New Delhi, Kanishka Publishers Distributors.

Ravindranath, K.V. (1978). "Profitability of Public Sector Banks in India, An Econometric Analysis, Prajnan, 11 (3), 6- 13.

RBI. (1971). *Report of the Study Group on Banking Cost,* Banking Commission, Government of India, Bombay, 164- 65.

RBI. (1975). *Report of the Expert Group on Simplification of Forms & Procedures to be adopted by RRB's,* Bombay.

RBI. (1976). *Report of the Working Group on Simplification of Operational & Accounting Procedures,* Bombay.

RBI. (1978). *Report of the Working Group on Multi- Agency Approach in Agricultural Finance,* Bombay, 2- 3.

RBI. (1978). *Report on Review Committee on RRBs,* Bombay.

RBI. (1981). *Liability of RRBs: A Study,* Bombay, Rural Planning & Credit Cell.

RBI. (1981). *Report of the Committee on Control Over Branches of RRB's,* Bombay.

RBI. (1981). *Report of the Committee to Review Arrangements for Institutional Credit for Agricultural & Rural Development,* Bombay, 117- 49.

RBI. (1981). *Viability of RRBs: A Study,* Bombay, Rural Planning & Credit Cell.

RBI. (1988). *Rural Credit Planning Cell,* Mumbai, 67- 69.

RBI. (1990). *A Review of Agricultural Credit System in India,* Bombay, 139- 40.

RBI. (1990). *Report of the Agricultural Credit Review Committee* (A Review of the Agricultural Credit System in India), New Delhi, 43- 44.

RBI. (1992). *Report of the Working Group on Regional Rural Banks* (Kelkar Committee), New Delhi, 24- 26.

Reddy, B. R., Sakunthala, B., & Reddy, S. V., (1998). *"Growth and Performance of Regional Rural Banks in India,"* The Indian Journal of Commerce, 31 (2), 71- 76.

Reddy G. R., & Suresh Kumar, D.V.. (1982) *"Regional Rural Banks and Weaker Sections Uplift Rural"*, Land Bank Journal, New Delhi, 20 (3), 73- 75

Reed, E.W. (1964). *The Commercial Bank Management*, A Harper International Student reprint, 1- 2.

Rehman, A. (1986). *"Impact of Grameena Bank Intervention on the Rural power Structure",* Bangladesh Institute of Development Studies, 6 (61), 76- 79.

Rehman, A. (1987). *"Alleviation of Rural Poverty: Replicability of Grameen Bank Model,"* Economic and Political Weekly, 7, 29- 34.

Ramakrishnan, K.R. (1988). *"Problems and Prospects of Regional Rural Banks"* The Banker, (43), 34- 36.

Rao, P.S.M. (1988). *"Inherent Weaknesses of Regional Rural Banks",* The Hindu, Supplement, p.1.

Report on Productivity. (1978). *Efficiency & Profitability on Banking,* Bombay.

Robert, C.V. (1981). *"Rural Financial Markets: Performance Implications of Low Delinquency Rates,"* American Journal of Agricultural Economics, 63 (1), 539-42.

Sadare, A.M. (1992), *"Profitability in Banks"*, Pigmy Economic Review, 37 (9), 20- 25.

Sahana Gosh. (1988). *"Losses no Justification for Removal"*, Business Standard, Mumbai, (54), 5- 6.

Sambasiva Rao, S. (2002). *"A Printer for NPA Management,"* IBA Bulletin, 7 (2), 23-26.

Saraswathy Athmanathan & R. Venkatakrishnam., (2001). *Management of Non-Performing Assets,* Hyderabad, State Bank of Staff College.

Satyanarayana, S., & Rafthunnisa, S. (2000). *"Financing of Indian Agriculture: Some Issues"*, The Indian Journal of Commerce, 53 (3), 48- 53.

Satyamurty, B., (1994). "A Study on Interests Spread Management in Commercial Banks in India," NIBM, Working paper.

Saveeta Bhatia, (1999). *"Factors Determining Profitability of Public Sector Banks in India: An Application of Multiple Regression Model,"* Prajanan, 27 (6), 12- 17.

Sethymadhan, R., & Stella Colaco., (1985). *"Nationalised Banks: Factors Affecting Profitability,"* Economic Times, 5 (1), 12- 13.

Shete, N.B., & Karkal, G. L. (1989), *"Regional Rural Banks: Problems & Perspectives of Rural Credit",* Prajnan, 18(2), 131- 34.

Shete, N.B. (1990). *"Regional Rural Banks- An Analysis,"* National Bank News Review, 6 (7), 32- 44.

Shivpuje, C. R., & Kaveri, V. S., (1997). *Management of Non-Performance Advance,* Sultan Chand & Sons.

Singh P.K., & Upadhya, K.M., (1984). *"A Study of loan recovery of Regional Rural Banks in Bihar",* Finacing Agriculture, 16 (2), 20-26.

Singh, R. P. (1988). *"Disbursement, Overdues & Factors Affecting Repayment Capacity of Barrowers,"* Indian Journal of Agricultural Economics, 43 (3), 37- 39.

Singh, S. (1987). *"Profitability of Commercial Banks in India,"* Punjab National Bank Monthly Review, 11 (11), 20- 25.

Singh, S. (1982). *Profitability & Profit Planning in Banks,* The Banker, 5 (3), 25- 28.

Sood, R.K. (1998). *"Non-Performing Assets (NPAs) in Public Sector Banks: An Analysis of Causes & Solutions Thereof,"* IBA Bulletin, 6- 13.

--------- *"Some Aspects & Issues Relating to NPAs in Commercial Banks,"* (1999). RBI Bulletin.

Soudamani Nagar. (1979). *Regional Rural Banks: Rajasthan Experience,* Eastern Economist, 72 (24), 81- 83.

Subhas, K.B. (1988). *"Credit Worthiness of Purpose: A Study of RRBs,"* Kurukshetra, 37 (7), 13- 15.

Sudhakar, V.K. (1998). *"Managing NPA Menace in Banks,"* IBA Bulletin, 27- 30.

Sudhakar, V.K. (1998). *"Policies & Perspectives of NPA Reduction in Banks,"* IBA Bulletin, 6 (7), 8- 16.

Sunil, K., (1982). *"Regional Rural Banks: An Evaluation of Performance,"* Southern Economist, 21 (6), 37- 38.

Suresh Ch., & Garg., (1989). *"Indian Banking Cost & Profitability,"* New Delhi, Anmol publications.

Swaminathan., Ramachandran, V.K., & Madhura., (2002), *"Rural Banking & Landless Labour Households, Institutional Reform & Rural Credit Markets in India,"* Journal of Agrarian Change, 2 (4), 502- 44.

Syed Ibrahim. (2010). *"Performance Evaluation of Regional Rural Banks in India",* International Business Research-CCSE, 3 (4).

Toor, N.S. (1993). *"Banking Business Mix & Profitability; Recent Trends in Nationalised Banks",* Punjab National Bank Monthly Review, 15 (2), 10- 25.

UNO. (1954). *Rural Progress through Cooperatives,* Washington DC, 6- 7.

Van Pische, J.D., et al. (1983). *Rural Financial Markets in Developing Countries,* London, Johns Hopkins University Press.

Varde V.S., & Singh, S.P., (1982). *"Profitability Performance of RRB's",* Prajnan, 11 (4), 47- 56.

Varde, V.S., & Sampath P. Singh., (1982). *"Profitability: The Inter-Bank Comparisons,"* Prajnan, 10 (2), 60- 65.

Varde Vasha Singh, S., & Sampat, P., (1995). *"Profitability & Performance of Regional Rural Banks"* Prajnan, 11 (4), 97- 98.

Varghese, S.K. (1983). *"Profit and Profitability of Indian Commercial Banks in 1970's,"* Economic and Political Weekly, 7 (2), 145 - 57.

Varsha S. Vardhe., & Singh, S.P., (1980). *"Towards an Analytical Framework for Profit Management in Banks,"* Prajnan, 16 (3), 1069-70.

Varsha S. Vardhe., and Singh, S.P., (1986). *"Approaches to planning in banks,"* BEM, 6 (3), 32- 33.

Varsha S., Varde., & Sampat P., Singh., *Profitability of Commercial Banks,* National Institute of Bank Management.

Velayudhan, T.K. (1990). *"Regional Rural Banks and Rural Credit-Some Issues,"* Economic and Political Weekly, 20 (38), 157- 59.

Venugopal. D., & Somaskanden, V., (1986). *"Profitability of Nationalised Banks",* BEM, 5 (3), 101- 11.

Verma, M.L. (1988). *"Rural Banking in India,"* Jaipur, Rajendra Printers, 191- 92.

Vipin Shah. (1987). *Cost & Efficiency in Banking,* New Delhi, Prentice Hall.

Wadhva, C.D. (1980). *Rural Banks for Rural Development*, Macmillan.